D0942550

Alfred McCoy lives in Sydney and lectures in Southeast Asian history at the University of New South Wales. He has spent four of the past twelve years on Negros Island in the central Philippines, first doing research for his Yale doctoral dissertation on the island's history and later on field trips to study mechanization of its sugar plantations. He has published a number of academic articles on the social history of Negros and writes for Australian newspapers on Philippine politics.

His earlier works include *The Politics of Heroin in Southeast Asia* (1972), the book the CIA tried to suppress, and *Drug Traffic: Narcotics and Organized Crime in Australia* (1980). He has edited *Southeast Asia Under Japanese Occupation* (1980) and, with Edilberto de Jesus, *Philippine Social History: Global Trade and Local Transformations* (1982).

Penguin Books
Priests on Trial

Priests on Trial

Alfred W. McCoy

Penguin Books

Penguin Books Australia Ltd,
487 Maroondah Highway, PO Box 257
Ringwood, Victoria, 3134, Australia
Penguin Books Ltd,
Harmondsworth, Middlesex, England
Penguin Books,
40 West 23rd Street, New York, NY 10010, USA
Penguin Books Canada Ltd,
2801 John Street, Markham, Ontario, Canada
Penguin Books (NZ) Ltd,
Private Bag, Takapanu, Auckland 9, New Zealand

First published by Penguin Books Australia, 1984
Reprinted, with corrections, 1984

Copyright © Alfred W. McCoy, 1984

Typeset in Palatino by Leader Composition Melbourne

Made and printed in Australia by
The Dominion Press - Hedges & Bell, Victoria

CIP

McCoy, Alfred W.
Priests on Trial

Bibliography.
Includes index.
ISBN 0 14 007038 6.

1. Catholic Church – Developing countries.
2. Christianity and justice – Developing countries.
3. Christianity and politics.
4. Clergy – Developing countries – Political activity.
5. Developing countries – Social conditions.
6. Gore, Brian.
7. Catholic Church – Missions.
8. Missionaries – Philippines – Biography.
9. O'Brien, Niall.

261.8

For the sugar workers of Negros,
        the stevedores of Iloilo City,
                and the peasants of Panay.
Who took me into their homes,
        taught me their language,
                and told me their stories.

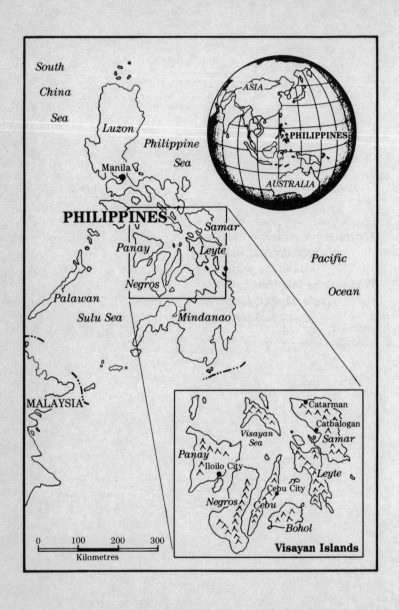

CONTENTS

PREFACE

In March 1984, an Australian trade unionist dropped by my university in Sydney with a letter he had carried from Negros Island in the central Philippines. It bore the heading 'Cell Seven, Bacolod Provincial Jail' and was signed by Fr Niall O'Brien, an Irish missionary I had met two years before on a visit to his mountain mission in southern Negros. As every Irish and Australian television viewer knows, Fr O'Brien and his fellow Columban Fr Brian Gore were in prison on trumped up charges of murdering their local Filipino mayor.

'It's quite some time since you and Bishop Fortich sat on my balcony in Tabugon discussing the history of Negros', began Fr O'Brien. 'You remember my round house? For a long time we have wanted to write to you. We feel you are one of the few who could do something to reveal the Benedicto factor in this multiple murder equation. The case is a lot more interesting than it appears. I mean the death of the mayor could be quite a complicated affair not just involving the NPA [guerillas]. Getting to the bottom of it is important. We presume you have difficulties coming this way. But if you do, don't miss coming to us. All of the lads here, especially Mickey [Martin] and Brian [Gore] send their greetings'.

As soon as classes closed in June, I flew north to Negros for another round of academic research into the island's sugar industry and perhaps, time and interest permitting, an article on the trial of the 'Negros Nine' for a Sydney newspaper. As a graduate student in the early 1970s, I had spent three years on Negros learning the local language and doing research for my doctoral dissertation on the island's history. This was my fourth trip back and I did not think this island still held any secrets for me. I was, as it turned out, wrong.

From that first night back on Negros when I talked myself past the prison guards and into Cell Seven, I became swept up in the case and its remarkable drama. Never before had I seen this island as I would see it then. In the past I had come as an historian, a detached social scientist seeking data and avoiding emotion. As a white, Western scholar, I was slotted into a comfortable social role that ensured a respectful deference and afforded a certain distance from the agony of the island's pervasive poverty. As the guest of planters and mill managers, I enjoyed my first trips to Negros.

Watching the trial of the Negros Nine was a concentrated exposure to the demoralized elements of a dying society – a blatantly biased judge, bribed peasant witnesses, and a brutal military all conspiring to frame priests whose only crime was a commitment to social justice. The trial forced me out of the past to deal with the unpleasant face of present day Negros. To discover the reasons for the military's involvement in the frame-up, for example, I spent a day leafing through Church files on Constabulary torture of civilians – dozens, maybe hundreds of large, glossy colour photographs of corpses mangled with the marks of soldiers taking pleasure in their work. After two weeks observing this plantation society closely, as if through the microscope of the Bacolod City courtroom, I knew that I could not put the present so comfortably behind me any longer.

I also began to sense another dimension to this case. It seemed as if nothing else I had read about dramatized so well the invisible forces of social change at work in the modern Third World. The trial of the Negros Nine was not a simple matter of legal fact, but a bitter struggle between social forces – powerful sugar planters allied with a heavy-handed dictatorship against a coalition of peasants, workers and progressive priests. The meaning of Third World poverty, liberation theology and military dictatorship were so clear when set off against the social extremes of Negros. This trial on one tropical island exemplified the tensions of change throughout the Third World.

When I first arrived, the priests urged me to write a book on their case and the social turmoil that had provoked it. I demurred, saying that I was not sure I could write such a book.

By the time I left the island two weeks later I had started a newspaper article and when that was done I knew that there was much more to say.

There are a number of people in Negros who gave their time to explain the case to me. The accused, Brian Gore and Niall O'Brien, spent days in Cell Seven going over the details of the case, and their Superior, Fr Michael Martin, took a day off from his hectic schedule in the middle of the trial to explain its background. Another Columban, Fr John Brannigan, gave me a memorable introduction to Philippine liberation theology nearly ten years ago when we met at the Jaro Seminary in Iloilo City. Bishop Fortich was, as usual, frank and forthright in discussing the problems of his diocese and his priests were particularly helpful in assembling the several thousand documents that provide the basis of much of this text. The workers of Central La Carlota and Hacienda Esperanza have been patient over the years in answering my questions and sharing their thoughts with me about their lives.

In Manila, Dr Rey Ileto of the University of the Philippines has taught me, in his writings and conversations, a great deal about Filipino Christianity and many of his ideas are reflected in almost every chapter. In conversations at the Philippine National Archives in 1981, Ruby Paredes of the University of Michigan explained contemporary Filipino nationalism and the country's latest revolution, insights essential to my transition from scholar of the Philippine past to observer of its present.

In Australia Dr Brian Fegan of Macquarie University's Anthropology Department has given me considerable insight into aspects of Philippine rural society. Adele Horin has been a sympathetic editor for several parts of chapter one which originally appeared, in another form, in the *National Times*. Her colleague Marian Wilkinson has encouraged these ventures into journalism. Penguin Australia's publisher, Brian Johns, accepted this unwritten manuscript from a stranger over the phone, and his editor, John Curtain, has been supportive throughout. The secretaries in the School of History at the University of NSW, Sue Jones and Tina Patterson, not only typed the manuscript quickly, they also corrected my stylistic lapses with notes in the memory of our word processor. Finally, colleagues Mike Pearson and Jim Levy together with our students in History 51.536, *The Creation of the Third World*, have helped me think through some of these problems over the past two years.

Alfred W. McCoy
Kensington, New South Wales
September, 1984.

Chapter One
The Church on Trial

At dusk on 10 March 1982 a red Ford pick-up truck was moving fast through the foothills of Kabankalan on Negros Island in the central Philippines. It passed through the bamboo-stilt houses of Bayhaw village and was climbing the last ridge that separated it from the safety of the open canefields below. At the wheel was Mayor Pablo Sola, recently released on bail for the torture-murder of seven peasants from a nearby village. Riding in the back were two heavily armed police and the manager of Sola's sugarcane plantation. As the truck crested the ridge and passed under the boughs of a camonsil tree, fifteen communist guerillas opened up with a blaze of M-16 and M-2 carbine fire from the high grass above the road. Several seconds and 100 rounds later, the truck crashed to a halt, most of its occupants dead instantaneously from multiple wounds. After a *coup de grace* into the skulls of any who showed signs of life, the guerillas retreated southwest into the mountains where the New People's Army (NPA) has won a vast liberated zone.

Several days later the guerilla command issued a press release which began: 'In a successful ambush, Red fighters of the New People's Army (NPA) killed Pablo Sola, despotic mayor of Kabankalan and one of Negros Occidental's biggest landlords... By getting rid of Sola, the NPA scored a victory in the anti-fascist and anti-feudal struggle that it is launching'. The 28 March issue (volume 4, number 2) of *Paghimakas* (Struggle), the NPA's local newspaper, denounced Sola for 'landgrabbing' of 1,900 hectares and involvement in the torture-murder of at least eleven peasants. The special six-page issue had graphic, step-by-step illustrations of the ambush, an eye witness account of the operation and an eleven-stanza folk ballad detailing Sola's role in the brutal torture of seven peasants.

The local Philippine Constabulary units soon gathered conclusive evidence of NPA responsibility for the killing. Only five days after the ambush, Constabulary provincial commander, Colonel Deinla, issued a press release which 'attributed' the killing to the NPA, a statement confirmed a few months later when Task Force Kanlaon captured two guerillas in a firefight in a nearby town. In an interview with the *Visayan Daily Star* published on 21 July, the Task Force commander Colonel Hidalgo stated that the two communists had 'admitted participating in the ambuscade of Kabankalan mayor Pablo Sola'.

Clearly, the murder of Mayor Sola was just one more bit of violence in the revolution which has been sweeping much of the central and southern Philippines over the decade past. But these days in the Philippines almost nothing is as simple as it seems. On 25 February 1983, Captain Galileo Mendoza, an officer in the same Task Force Kanlaon that had captured the NPA guerillas responsible for killing Mayor Sola, formally charged an improbable group of Catholic conspirators with the mayor's murder – six Filipino layworkers, a Filipino parish priest, Irish missionary Fr Niall O'Brien, and Australian missionary Fr Brian Gore.

A few days later, the Constabulary showed its hand when it filed deportation proceedings against Fr Gore before the Immigration Commission in Manila. Since deportation requires a far lower standard of evidence than conviction, the Constabulary evidently hoped to short-circuit a long legal battle by deporting Fr Gore on unsubstantiated allegations of murder. After only two days of hearings, however, Constabulary investigators so embarrassed the government by presenting a pathetic case that Philippine President Ferdinand Marcos called the Commissioner of Immigration to Malacañang Palace. When hearings resumed next morning, the Commissioner dismissed the deportation case within three minutes and returned Fr Gore to the custody of the courts. The unexpected collapse of the deportation hearings left the Constabulary with an unconvincing court case based entirely on hired witnesses telling contradictory, often impossible tales.

The prosecution's charge was nothing if not bold, and its

witnesses wove a tale as intricate as it was incredible. After meeting three times to plan the murder over a two week period, the priests allegedly set out at midnight on 10 March 1982 in the distinctive blue parish truck – Fr Gore at the wheel, Fr O'Brien at his side, and thirteen Catholic layworkers armed with M-16s and carbines in the back. Driving from Fr Gore's parish in the hills through the town centre of Kabankalan to Fr O'Brien's parish further south, they picked up Fr O'Brien's cook, alleged commander of the 'blocking force'. Arriving at the ambush site about 5.00 a.m., the two priests left a 'strike force' commanded by Fr Dangan, a Filipino priest armed with an M-16, at the camonsil tree and dropped off the 'blocking force' at a mango tree 100 metres down the road. They then drove off towards town, leaving Fr Dangan's 'strike force' to murder the mayor in a blaze of gunfire some twelve hours later. Other charges filed against Fr Gore allege that he also planned to lead his Christian guerillas in a rebellion to overthrow the municipal goverment of Kabankalan.

Delayed by the prosecution's unexpected need to fabricate a coherent case, the trial of the 'Negros Nine' dragged on with long delays for over sixteen months. Denied a fair and speedy trial for its priests, the Philippine Catholic Church mobilized protests, politics and diplomacy in their defence. In a nation that has been at least 85 percent Catholic for nearly 400 years, the Church could command sufficient moral and material resources to battle even a dictatorial state. In the Catholic Philippines, the arrest of a priest is a political act. Not surprisingly, political expediency overwhelmed legal nicety at every significant point in these proceedings.

The day warrants were served on 6 May 1983, Archbishop Jaime Sin of Manila interceded immediately with President Marcos to win the priests the privilege of house arrest. With the support of the Archbishop, Negros Bishop Antonio Fortich mobilized the full resources of his diocese to exonerate the priests. Over the next eight months, Church lawyers waged a frustrating battle for bail that exposed the blatant bias of the court. After seventeen hearings for bail in July and August 1983, Judge Emilio Legaspi, a political appointee with no prior judicial experience, went on an indefinite holiday without handing down a decision – leaving the layworkers in jail and the priests in legal limbo. The trial did not resume until February 1984 when Australian Foreign Minister Bill Hayden flew to Manila and met personally with President Marcos to complain of the unreasonable delays. There were faint diplomatic hints that millions of dollars in Australian aid, desperately needed by a failing Philippine economy, would be withheld until the Gore case was resolved.

When the court hearings suddenly quickened their pace only days later, they took on the electric air of a political show trial. Before an audience of Australian television cameras, foreign diplomats, Irish priests and Negros peasants, the Bacolod City courtroom became a stage for high political drama. Beneath sheets of peeling paint and whirling ceiling fans, protagonists played roles that seem almost scripted – a strutting, pot-bellied prosecutor who slandered clergy with innuendos of sexual impropriety; a transparently biased judge who allowed the prosecutor to trample the rules of court procedure; activist defence lawyers whose withering cross-examination demolished every prosecution witness; and a gallery of peasant and religious supporters who burst into applause at every point for the defence. At times the court atmosphere became tense with conflict and I found myself applauding hard, as if cheering for the Light in a losing match against the Dark.

Moved by the prosecution and imprisonment of men so obviously innocent, a global protest movement reached from Negros to Australia, Ireland and America. The streets outside the Negros court were frequently filled with demonstrations, the largest in April when 25,000 peasants marched for up to five days from remote mountain villages to rally in the broad plaza before the Cathedral. In Ireland, Catholics were outraged at Fr O'Brien's persecution and mounted massive protests that eventually forced President Ronald Reagan to intercede. Concerned that demonstrations might mar his state visit to Ireland, Reagan instructed his UN ambassador to raise the matter personally with President Marcos on an official visit to Manila. Under intense diplomatic pressure from Australia and America, two of his closest allies, Marcos finally intervened in June 1984. Within weeks, the priests were released on a face-saving legal technicality. After a brief emotional return to the mountain parishes of southern Negros they had served for over a decade, Gore and O'Brien left the Philippines – perhaps never to return.

Ironically, the intense international media coverage of the courtroom proceedings over sixteen months has raised some question about the priests' innocence. By simply reporting – in 90 seconds or 500 words – prosecution allegations and defence rebuttal, without critical commentary, the media has lent an evident credibility to charges which are in fact, a total fabrication. Most citizens of First World democracies assume that the state does not go to the expense of a trial unless it has at least some strong evidence against the accused. Before leaving Sydney to cover the trial, I spoke with several Australian Catholic priests who asked me quite seriously if Fr Gore might somehow have been involved in the mayor's murder.

Even a cursory examination of the prosecution's case exposes signs of a crude manufacture. Although Philippine Constabulary investigators collected ninety-one steel casings from the ambush site, the prosecution failed to produce any forensic evidence linking the priests to the mayor's murder. The same investigators claimed an absolute ignorance of the confessions from communist guerillas captured by their own military unit. Since there was no physical evidence against the priests, the prosecution's case rested entirely on allegations by supposed eye witnesses. Two alleged participants in the Catholic conspiracy failed to identify Gore and O'Brien in open court. In every case, the witnesses were on the military payroll and gave testimony that was riven with obvious lies, contradictions or simple errors of fact. This trial then had very little to do with legal questions of guilt or innocence.

Despite months of intensive media coverage of the daily legal rituals, the essential question remains unanswered. If these priests were not guilty, or even seriously suspected of being so, why were they on trial? Gore and O'Brien were victims of the growing conflict between Church and State in the Philippines. For over a decade, they worked to shatter the subservience of peasants on Negros Island, the poorest of Third World poor. Their mobilization of the poor sugar workers through democratic Christian communities threatened the social control of the planter elite in southern Negros. Their exposés of the Constabulary's torture and murder of their parishioners embarrassed the military. Their religious order angered the island's most powerful politician, Marcos ally and 'sugar czar' Roberto Benedicto, by publishing a strong attack on his management of the island's sugar industry. The growing opposition of their Church to the regime's corruption and abuse has embittered President Marcos. In revenge, local planters, sugar czar Benedicto, the Constabulary and Marcos combined to frame these priests on charges of murder.

In Negros, as in the Philippines and much of the Third World, the old order is dying in the midst of social upheaval. Like other priests in Asia, Africa and Latin America, these three were caught in a conflict between revolution and dictatorship, Church and State. The case of the Negros Nine was but a tremor sparked by the grinding tectonic plates of social change.

Such broad historical forces are invisible and usually remain beyond the grasp of even the most careful observer. The trial of the Negros Nine captured the attention of media audiences across the globe because it suddenly made the invisible seem quite visible. The trial at times took on the character of a crude historical pageant with the principals personifying social forces – Constabulary investigators playing the fist of *repression*, the Negros Nine the face of *oppression*, and peasant demonstrators the chorus of *liberation*. Like no other incident of recent memory, the trial of the Negros Nine dramatized the tumult of change in the Third World.

With extremes of wealth and poverty unequalled anywhere in Southeast Asia, the island of Negros seems almost a caricature of a Third World society. From the time its virgin forests were felled and the large pagan tribes slaughtered over a century ago to clear the land for cultivation, the island's society has been shaped by the demands of a single product – sugar. An ugly colonial crop, sugar has a long history of labour exploitation on tropical islands across the globe. Whether in Cuba,

Jamaica, Java, Fiji or Negros, cane sugar has enriched the planters and enslaved their workers. With plantations of 50 to 500 hectares, the 'sugar barons' of Negros today sport late model Mercedes and treat themselves regularly to lavish world tours. For ten hours of cutting cane under a tropical sun, their workers subsist on wages of a dollar a day. A century of sugar production on Negros has left a squalid legacy of a million poor sinking deeper into a miasma of unemployment, malnutrition and disease. Never prosperous, Negros has nonetheless suffered a marked decline in living standards in the decade past.

Although the Negros sugar workers are the poorest of Philippine poor, other islands have suffered a similar degradation. After declaration of martial law in 1972, President Marcos ruled the country with a combination of corruption and incompetence which has brought the Philippines to the brink of economic disaster. While similar Southeast Asian nations are maintaining growth rates of five and six percent through the 1980s, the Philippines will suffer a negative growth of minus one or two percent for the rest of the decade. With over 55 percent of its 53 million population under the age of nineteen, the Philippines has a critical need for economic expansion simply to maintain its present low standard of living. Economic contraction in the midst of such explosive population growth is a sure formula for social disaster. Instead of promoting labour growth as the International Labour Organization recommended, the Marcos regime has used a massive inflow of foreign capital to finance introduction of labour-saving machinery which has eliminated many jobs in both town and country. After twenty years of the Marcos regime, the Philippines exhibits all the classic characteristics of an impoverished Third World nation.

The mass of Philippine poor is thus doubly oppressed. Economic collapse is crippling whole industries while new technology eliminates jobs in the farms and factories still operating. Massive capital investment in many industries has both rationalized production and reduced employment. Since the declaration of martial law in 1972, the Philippines has accumulated a foreign debt of $28 billion, some $2.6 billion of that to the World Bank. Aside from the several billion skimmed off and deposited abroad by the Marcos family and its cronies, this foreign loan capital has financed both the modernization of existing firms and new, large-scale development projects. On the large southern island of Mindanao, extensive banana, palm oil and pineapple plantations have forced Christian and tribal small holders off the land into poorly paid wage labour. In many islands, Christian and tribal settlers are being dispossessed by large timber corporations, dam construction or simple landgrabbing. The sailcraft fishermen who inhabit the strand about the archipelago's thousands of islands have recently found their catch dwindling in the face of competition from sonar-guided trawler fleets that drain the seas with their drag nets. Manila's legions of petty entrepreneurs – jeepney drivers and market vendors – are losing out to competition from palatial, airconditioned shopping malls and government-financed bus companies. The great numbers of landless rural workers in the sugar and rice industries are finding tractors and mechanical implements reducing their work. On Negros Island, for example, Australian farm implements are revolutionizing sugar cultivation and will soon eliminate some 90 percent of plantation labour with grim social consequences.

As the job market shrinks, the country's postwar population explosion has spawned a vast reserve of unskilled labourers who are just now flooding into the work force. In the past five years unemployment has doubled nationwide to 15 percent and reached 26 percent in Manila, figures that probably conceal the true extent of the problem. After the assassination of ex-Senator Benigno Aquino at Manila Airport in August 1983, Filipino and foreign businessmen panicked and began liquidating their investments. As billions in capital surged outward on the telex cables, factories in greater Manila began shutting down and the city's unemployment rate shot past 30 percent and is still climbing.

Although imposed in 1972 with the stated aim of uplifting the masses, President Ferdinand Marcos' decade of dictatorship has seen a dramatic decline in living standards from a base that was already dangerously low. It has been a downward slide from poverty towards misery. Economic indicators show a 30 percent decline in real wages between 1972 and 1978. In 1978 the Minister of Industry claimed that the Philippines had the cheapest real labour costs in Asia – US 49 cents an hour, compared to 95 cents in Singapore and $1.41 in Hong Kong. The slide continues today. In 1982 there was a 16 percent increase in consumer prices and little wage increases for most workers. In the panic following the Aquino assassination in 1983, inflation shot upward and is expected to reach 50 percent per annum by the end of 1984. Wages, by contrast, have remained relatively constant since unions have little bargaining power when there is one unemployed worker for every two jobs.

Such statistics cannot even begin to describe the real meaning of poverty in an impoverished nation. It is not a simple matter of just feeling hungry. Most of the poor can still fill their stomachs with a diet of banana, rice and fish sauce. But such nutrition cannot resist the heat and disease of the tropics. The statistics on infant disease and mortality can only be described as appalling. Several years ago I asked a physician to give my infant son a TB test. He replied with an amused smile. 'When 95 percent of the children here have primary complex TB, who needs a test? It's a waste of money'. A pediatrician working in a mining town in southern Negros told me that over 90 percent of the children in her area were infested with intestinal worms up to 20 centimetres long and the thickness of a fat earthworm. The first time she dewormed the village children the average number of worms per child was 60 and the top notcher was 251. Several children's stomachs bulged with knots of worms and surgery was required to remove them.

While most developed nations have an infant mortality rate below 25 per 1,000 live births, the Philippines has an average of 65. In poor areas like Samar Island the rate is 80 and in Manila's Tondo slum district the infant death rate reaches 130 per 1,000. Every time I took the hour-long drive down the Negros coastal highway to the sugar plantation where I was doing research, I inevitably passed at least one or two funeral processions with tiny silver coffins. Government surveys show that the percentage of underweight pre-school children increased from 69 percent in 1965, the year Marcos was first elected President, to

78 percent in 1980. During the same period, the rate of third degree malnutrition among infants – that is, hunger so severe it produces either death or permanent brain damage – doubled from 3 to 6 percent.

Those who survive to adulthood do not escape health problems. One factory physician told me that 75 percent of the 1,200 workers under his care had some degree of TB infection. Indeed, the World Health Organization has surveys showing that the Philippines has the highest TB rate in its Western Pacific Region. 'Most of my patients,' said one rural doctor from Central Luzon, 'carry TB in their lungs, amoebae in their intestines and inadequate nutrition in their stomachs – a situation that makes them exceptionally vulnerable to infectious diseases such as influenza, cholera and hepatitis'. The First Lady and Governor of Metro-Manila, Madame Imelda Marcos, who styles herself the Eva Peron of the Philippines, has responded to the TB epidemic by moving to close the city's Quezon Institute, a free TB clinic with a long history of treating the poor. Observers point out that the Institute occupies one of the largest blocks of prime real estate still left in the heart of Manila. In its place, and on a much smaller block of land, she has built the lavish new Lung Center of the Philippines, a hospital that devotes much of its resources to treating tobacco-induced lung cancer, a disease of the affluent.

Although the Philippines was a relatively prosperous Third World country when Marcos was first elected president in 1965, thirteen years later the Asian Development Bank reported that its daily food consumption had declined to the lowest level in Asia. Add to that yet another statistic: between 1973 and 1977 malnutrition climbed from seventh place to third as a cause of death in the Philippines.

Such statistics bring in their train the inevitable horror stories. One rural welfare worker showed me his files on a documented case of cannibalism in Leyte Island. A poor fisherman, forced to abandon the seas by the trawler fleets and unable to find farm work, eventually went mad and butchered his seven-year-old daughter for food. I will omit the details. There are other such stories about.

After a decade of such unrelenting pressures, the country's workers and peasants now feel a very strong sense of injustice. When Marcos declared martial law a decade ago, most were inclined to believe his promises of a revolution from above for the common man. Marcos promised land reform, social justice, the destruction of an old and corrupted oligarchy, and a new society. More than a decade later, people have seen injustice from an abusive military, the creation of a rapacious new oligarchy of presidential cronies, massive land alienation and a society more tawdry than the one it replaced. Perhaps, more importantly, the constant erosion in working conditions and living standards has pushed most into a grinding poverty that offends their fundamental sense of dignity. Listening to this outpouring of anger from workers over the past four years, I am reminded of the inscription by the writer Nick Joaquin at the base of a massive bronze water buffalo that stands in Manila's Luneta Park. I quote from memory. 'Like the Filipino *tao* [peasant], the *carabao* [water buffalo] is patient and long-suffering, but when finally aroused rampages in an uncontrollable rage'.

I had a chance to witness this anger in 1982 during a month-long strike at the La Carlota sugar mill in Negros Island. Although their working conditions were generous by comparison with those in the fields and the export processing zones, nearly the entire 1,200 man work force supported the strike with an unprecedented militance. Over the past thirty years most sugar industry unions have operated with a corruption and opportunism that alienated workers and reduced their strikes to two or three day rituals. Led by the National Federation of Sugar Workers, a union founded by radical Catholic priests in the early 1970s, the La Carlota strike surprised both mill management and the military with its resilience. Instead of collapsing within a week as management had expected, the picketing continued night and day for three months before being broken by the pressures of a dwindling strike fund and an escalating military presence. Although strike funds were exhausted, most workers refused to return to the mill until hunger left them no alternative. A year later, there were still 100 to 200 militants who prefer penury to capitulation.

Through conversations with several of these die-hards I gained the impression that their anger was over something more than just hours and wages. They were bitter about the government, the military who broke the strike and the misery of their lives.

I had been visiting these sugar plantations to do research since 1973, but it was only then that I began to notice a change in workers' attitudes. Once described as docile and dependent upon the plantation's patronage, workers in Negros and other islands were becoming militant and sometimes violent. Listening to the strikers' stories, I began to think that I was witnessing one of those sea changes in popular consciousness that precedes every major political upheaval, every revolution.

Although longer than most, the La Carlota strike is by no means exceptional. To attract export processing industries, the Marcos government successfully banned strikes and held down wages until 1975. Between 1975 and 1979 there were 400 strikes led by a radical underground labour movement. In defiance of the government's own trade union confederation, these wildcat unions coalesced into the 'May 1st Movement' on May Day 1980, a million member confederation with undefined ties to the underground Communist Party.

The most dramatic evidence of this growing mass anger is the sudden growth of the New People's Army in the past five years. Founded in 1968 by student leaders from the University of the Philippines in Manila, the Communist Party of the Philippines broke definitively with the old Moscow-line party and organized the New People's Army (NPA) to wage Maoist-style guerilla warfare. The new Party spent its early years mixed in bitter internecine warfare with the old Party that involved a number of assassinations in Manila and mutual betrayals to the Philippine Army's intelligence service. Once martial law was declared in 1972, the new Party's student membership fled to the hills and joined the NPA. Its early attempt at guerilla warfare was rather like a children's crusade. Raised in the cities and indulged by their middle class parents, most NPA guerillas stumbled hopelessly about the mountains falling victim to disease, insects, peasant informers or military ambush. Betrayals were common in these early years. In the mid 1970s, for example, the NPA's ambitious expansion program in the Bikol region of southern Luzon collapsed when the zone's number two commander bartered the names of his followers to the Philippine Army for amnesty and money. After observing NPA operations in the mountains of the central Philippines for three years, I left the country in 1976 convinced that these innocents were incapable of anything more substantial than getting themselves killed.

When I came back to Negros six years later the change was remarkable. Supported by embittered workers and peasants, the local NPA organization had grown from a nucleus of incompetent and idealistic students into an effective guerilla unit of 100 to 200 troops that controlled a sprawling liberated zone in the southern part of the island near Fr O'Brien's parish.

As the NPA strength in the area grew, the local Philippine Army command sent in regular and irregular forces to suppress the revolt. Army task forces swept the plateau repeatedly – raping women, torturing civilians, executing suspected NPA supporters, stealing pigs and demanding bribes. For several years in the late 1970s, the army, as it has across the archipelago, unleashed a death squad under the command of a notorious army sergeant, a real killer. In the end his reign of rapine became an embarrassment and he was gunned down, many suspect by the army itself. Since the NPA faded away as the army approached, neither tactic caused the guerillas any serious difficulties. Quite the contrary. Military excesses strengthened civilian support for the NPA.

By the late 1970s, the NPA guerillas had spread northward into Fr O'Brien's parish at Tabugon on the fringe of the island's rugged Tablas Plateau. As his parishioners came to him with evidence that the military was savagely torturing innocents, he felt compelled to complain. Once his parishioners led him to a spot in a recently vacated military camp where he dug up several decaying corpses. As the military campaign of rape, torture, and murder intensified, so did the strength of Fr O'Brien's protests. Like Fr Gore and other priests to the poor throughout the Philippines, O'Brien was caught between revolution and repression. His trial and deportation were, at least in part, the work of a vengeful military.

It is in the remote areas like southern Negros where the NPA has built its mass base over the past five years. The Marcos government has filled Manila and the secondary cities with a dense network of spies and informers that regularly deliver NPA cadres for lavish rewards. The lowland plains have terrain and road networks appropriate for the Philippine Army's conventional search-and-destroy operations. As the NPA moved into the mountains in the 1970s, they found tribal and Christian small farmers who welcomed their arms as a counterweight to the military. Many frontier farmers face eviction at army gunpoint to make way for dams, plantations or simple landgrabbers. Beginning with 60 soldiers and 35 arms in 1969, the NPA has grown into a guerilla force of 12,000 troops. It conducts guerilla operations across the archipelago and can claim liberated zones in a number of remote areas – the mountains of northern Luzon, the Bikol Peninsula in southern Luzon, Samar Island, southern Negros, Panay Island and Mindanao in the far south.

The island of Mindanao, the archipelago's second largest, will probably be the site of the first major NPA victories. Exploiting a situation similar to southern Negros, the NPA has built up an extensive mass base and strong guerilla forces in the Christian areas of the island's eastern half. Throughout 1983-84, NPA offensives have punished the army's Southern Command, and the regime was forced to transfer forces from other islands to Mindanao. In March 1983 First Lady Imelda Marcos dramatized the threat when she hosted a heavily publicized farewell for Marine detachments as they were airlifted from Manila Airport. By the late 1970s the Muslim separatist revolt in western Mindanao had faded, and these new Army troops were being massed against NPA guerillas in Christian areas at the centre and east of the island.

The Army's mobilization has failed to blunt the NPA's growth from village militia into main-force units capable of meeting Constabulary companies in a conventional firefight. As a show of its strength in mid-1984, a NPA unit of 250 armed men captured a 5,000 hectare plantation in eastern Mindanao, owned by Marcos' crony and probable successor Eduardo Cojuangco. The guerillas systematically destroyed all his machinery and standing crops before withdrawing. Since the land had been taken at gunpoint from several hundred peasant and tribal farming families, the operation swelled the NPA's local prestige. Drawing upon counter-insurgency tactics used by the US Army in Vietnam, the Philippine Army has begun concentrating the peasants of central Mindanao into strategic hamlets, a tactic that has failed to impede NPA operations. Indeed, guerilla warfare in Mindanao has now reached a level that seems comparable to South Vietnam in the early 1960s.

By any standard, the NPA growth is impressive. But the guerillas are still years away from their final march on Manila. In an archipelago like the Philippines a long march becomes a long swim. As long as Marcos holds the loyalty of his 150,000 troops, he can maintain strategic control over the sea lanes and contain the NPA on remote islands. Cut off from Manila by a natural sea barrier, the NPA cannot concentrate its scattered forces for an assault on Manila, a final offensive like Mao's drive for Shanghai in 1949 or the Vietnamese Army's push for Saigon in 1975. Given the current balance of forces in the archipelago, the NPA can only take power if the Marcos regime self-destructs. And even if the regime does collapse, the Communist Party will still have to form a broader coalition with elements of the old Manila oligarchy, the urban middle class and the military before the guerillas can march into downtown Manila. Even the most optimistic of NPA partisans speak in terms of a ten-year road to revolution.

Its supporters point out that the NPA is already something of a coalition. Founded by the best and the brightest from the University of the Philippines, the NPA has attracted a number of star recruits over the past decade – an international beauty queen, a top graduate of the Philippine Military Academy, a brace of Catholic priests, several university professors and the deputy director of the Development Academy of the Philippines, the regime's own think tank. The latter recruit, Horacio Morales, announced his defection at a banquet honouring him as one of the nation's Ten Outstanding Men of the Year. The Light-a-Fire Movement, which set off bombs in Manila hotels in 1980, was led by the Dean of the Asian Institute of Management, the country's prestige business school. The most convincing testimony to the old elite's disaffection came in September 1982 when the army, offering Marcos a present for the tenth anniversary of martial law, executed the NPA's overall commander, Edgar Jopson, in a Mindanao ambush. His alma mater, the elite, Jesuit-run Ateneo University, announced a memorial service – and then cancelled it under pressure from the army. After a storm of protest from its affluent alumni, the university was forced to hold the service. Among the 200 mourners for this communist guerilla were company directors, lawyers, and senior civil servants. One management consultant told me he attended to pay tribute to a 'great Filipino patriot'.

Such an alliance between urban oligarchs and jungle guerillas at first struck me as improbable. At a glance, Manila's high society shimmers with a sophistication bordering on the degenerate. Anyone who is anybody has a mansion in a guarded subdivision with lavish furnishings, a staff of four to twelve liveried servants, a collection of original oils, a garage crowded with a Mercedes and lesser vehicles, and a case of heirloom jewelry. The men take their MBAs at Harvard and Wharton and the women do their shopping in Hong Kong and San Francisco. I recall one evening at a dinner dance at the elite Club Filipino. The dance floor was crowded with dozens of matrons, aged fifty to seventy, cavorting with their twenty-year-old male 'dancing instructors' while their husbands looked on. Some instructors are favoured, as the fashion has it, with a new car or a world tour.

Despite the dazzle, the men tend towards a passionate nationalism and the women a Catholic moralism. Marcos offends on both counts. The business community bitterly resents his partiality towards cronies and multi-nationals which has made it difficult to do business under the decade of martial law. The economic collapse, which began in 1981 and worsened after the Aquino assassination, has denied businessmen both credit and markets, forcing many into bankruptcy and exile. After the Aquino killing, businessmen large and small began to liquidate their holdings and export all their savings.

The massive capital flight may yet have serious political consequences. Over the short term, negative investment erodes both employment and the Marcos regime's credibility. Over the long term, it may hasten a revolution of the left. Once centuries of capital accumulation evaporate into the electronic blips of outgoing bank-to-bank telex transfers and the bourgeoisie follow their assets in a fleet of jumbo jets, there is no longer any capitalism left to struggle against revolution. The telex and the wide-bodied jet may ultimately render the guillotine techno-logically redundant as an instrument of social change.

For the moralists among Manila's matriarchs, the city seems a Sodom standing as testimony to the regime's corruption. Catholic social workers estimate that there are 200,000 prosti-tutes serving a foreign and domestic clientele in Manila, 16,000 for the US Navy at Subic Bay, 10,000 for the US Air Force at Clark Field, and lesser populations for tourists in the provincial centres. Manila's bar and brothel strip occupies a solid square mile of neon honky-tonk at the city's very centre. Its every aspect offends – greying Australians hand-in-hand with teen-aged Filipinas, busloads of Japanese crowding the clubs, European pederasts with eight-and ten-year-old boys. The regime has promoted tourism as a main source of foreign exchange and protests by the matrons of the Catholic Women's League have been ignored. The 1983 Manila International Film Festival, which Imelda financed with two weeks of city-wide soft porn screenings, attracted the same criticism.

Such moral questions have been another source of conflict between Church and State. Wary of confronting Marcos directly on such a sensitive issue, Manila Archbishop Jaime Sin used the appearance of a bare-breasted Filipina in the German edition of *Playboy* to appear at a protest rally sponsored by the Catholic Women's League. Some observers charged the Church with hypocrisy – protesting a *Playboy* photograph while ignoring the solid square mile of industrial-scale prostitution only a block from the rally site. Such criticism misses a more important point. As they hinted at that rally, upper class Catholics are becoming deeply concerned for their city's moral tone. Morality aside, the city's incredible pollution, intolerable congestion, growing vio-lence, and festering squalor have made life in the capital painful for everyone, rich and poor.

Under a vindictive dictatorship, private conversation with Filipino friends is perhaps the most reliable barometer of changing political attitudes. In my research trips over the past three years, I have made it a point to set aside time for long chats with elite Filipinos well placed to discuss their nation's future. One of my most revealing encounters was with a greying matriarch, a descendant of one of the country's oldest and richest families. They controlled a bank, had married into the best families of the old oligarchy, and held extensive properties about Manila. We dined at her mansion in the Wack-Wack Sub-division, an exclusive area surrounded by high walls and patrolled by a motorcycle squad of guards armed with shotguns. As the servants brought course after course, she launched into the usual litany of criticisms of the regime – Marcos was corrupt, Imelda had wasted the national patrimony, and the economy was in a steep plunge. As we moved to sweets and aperitif, she moved on to the subject of the NPA. 'This may seem rather odd for a seventy-year-old lady, but I am convinced that armed struggle is the only salvation for our nation'. Were there others of the old oligarchy who thought the same way? 'Recently, some have. If Marcos stays in power they may lose everything, but with the NPA they might salvage something'.

A friend employed as a management consultant to several banks concurred. 'Almost everyone has gotten their money out of the country already. So they have nothing to lose if the NPA takes power. Five years ago it was only a few big investors moving money out. Now anyone, big or small, with a spare peso is converting to dollars and depositing outside'. The problem was the Communist Party itself. 'Their current line relies on the peasants and workers, and offers no opening to the old elite'.

Over coffee in a downtown hotel, a professor at the University of the Philippines active in the National Democratic Front, the Communist Party's mass organization, argued that the Party was making a mistake. 'There is a debate now in the Party over our long term political strategy. Right now the line is to fight the two enemies – US imperialism and the bourgeoisie. Frankly, I think it's stupid. Until the US becomes neutral as it was in Cuba, the NPA can never win. The US just cannot afford to lose their bases here and they will do anything to keep them. And until the NPA forms an alliance with the Manila bourgeoisie, as the Sandinistas did in Nicaragua, they will have to spend another ten years in the jungle. The country just can't stand this kind of plunder much longer. Once we get power, we are going to need all the capital we can get to repair the damage done to the land and the economy, to prevent this country from winding up a basket case like Ethiopia'.

The Philippines has already suffered two failed revolutions during the past century. Their fate was, in the end, determined by conflict between the Manila oligarchs and the mass of peasants and workers. During the Philippine national revolution of 1896, the Manila elite dallied with the new republic before deciding that independence in the imperial age was an impossibility. They eventually sided with the American colonial regime that crushed the infant republic in 1900, a decision which, unjustly perhaps, earned them the stigma of traitors among later generations. A half century later, the old Communist Party launched the Huk peasant revolt against the newly independent Republic. Threatened by the Party's promise of land reform, the oligarchs sided with the government and the CIA against the peasants. By 1954 the Huk revolt was crushed and the old Party left in disarray. If history and circumstance are any guide, the fate of the NPA's revolution may ultimately revolve about the same dynamic. Convinced that the old oligarchy is tainted by the original sin of their grandfathers' turn-of-the-century treason, the NPA has so far made only a minimal effort to broaden its coalition.

In the meantime, the Marcos regime is indeed rotting from within. After twenty years in power, Marcos cronies have become corrupt beyond imagination, the bureaucracy has ossified, and an entourage of sycophants isolates the regime from the news of its decline. At the close of his constitutional term as president in 1972, Marcos declared martial law with the promise of a revolution from above – destruction of the old oligarchs, social reform and massive economic development. In its early years the regime had some promise. Marcos declared a massive land reform to endow the nation's poor tenant farmers.

He closed Congress, bastion of the provincial warlords, and wiped out several vast financial empires in the name of social reform.

Shorn of its promise, the regime clings to a power that is failing with the health of its leader. Shuffling from room to room in his grand Spanish palace in the heart of Manila, Marcos, the ageing dictator, wastes away visibly from an obscure systemic disease. In the past three years he has seemed to age thirty, his once fit physique withering and his once brilliant intellect lapsing into occasional senility. Although the disease incapacitates him for weeks at a time, he clings to power desperately because he and his entourage have known nothing else for twenty years. The crowds of demonstrators that have filled the streets almost daily since the assassination in 1983 of his chief rival Benigno Aquino are young, nearly all under forty, who can no longer really recall a Philippines without Marcos as its president. Only his death can release them from his dictatorship.

When Marcos came to power in 1965 as a legally elected president, the Philippines had some prospects for future prosperity. There was relatively full employment, economic growth was low but steady, and there was an upper class of entrepreneurs who knew how to manage the economy. Under his two terms as president, the economy faltered slightly and democracy took a bit of battering, but the system had survived. Faced with the end of second term in 1972 and constitutionally barred from seeking a third, Marcos ended Philippine democracy with a declaration of martial law in September of that year.

Over the next decade, Marcos moved to build a political dynasty by a radical restructuring of Philippine society. Understanding that economic assets are the seeds of political power, Marcos destroyed the old oligarchy that had opposed him before martial law. In its place he created a new oligarchy of cronies and relatives who, unfortunately for the Philippine economy, lacked the skills of the old oligarchs. Using the state's licensing powers, Marcos banned all media owned by rival oligarchs and transferred their assets, without compensation, to his allies. Congress was closed and all parties were outlawed except his amorphous 'New Society Movement'. Strikes became illegal and only unions friendly to the regime were allowed registration. All local administration was reorganized to bring police and officials under more direct central control. Most importantly, the military was increased four-fold and moved out of the barracks to defend the regime against communist guerillas and urban demonstrators.

Once society had been restructured to eliminate any possible source of opposition, Marcos moved carefully to erect a facade of political normalization. After promulgation of a new authoritarian constitution, Marcos ordered elections for an interim parliament in 1978 and local officials in 1980. Although he now controlled all media, finance and patronage necessary to win a national election, Marcos made doubly sure of his control with article six of the constitution which allows him to ignore parliament and rule by decree whenever he might wish. So armed, Marcos formally ended martial law by running for president in 1981 and inaugurating himself at a ceremony graced by US Vice-President George Bush who toasted the dictator as a 'lover of democracy'.

Martial law has remained in all but name. The regime exposed its continuing lust for absolute power with the assassination of ex-Senator Benigno Aquino, Marcos' chief rival, at Manila Airport in August 1983. Returning from America to assume leadership of the opposition after a decade in prison and exile, Aquino was executed as he stepped off the aircraft – probably by Air Force security men responsible to General Fabian Ver, Chief of Staff of the Philippine Army and Marcos' closest confidante. Despite its massive power, the regime is incapable of tolerating any threat to its rule.

The murder of Aquino appears, in retrospect, something of a tactical error. Moved by his martyrdom, the Filipino nation reacted in a rage that snapped a decade of subserviance to dictatorship. In the May 1984 parliamentary elections, anti-Marcos parties overcame enormous odds – government control of media, massive funding for the regime's KBL party, and systematic electoral fraud – to win a third of the seats. Although Marcos is now faced with his first non-revolutionary opposition in over a decade, the minority parties do not pose a real threat to his rule. Backed by the military and his extraordinary powers, Marcos will endure until death.

In his progress from populist reformer to corrupted autocrat, Marcos has followed the pattern of most Third World dictators. Indeed, Marcos is the very model of a modern Third World dictator. After twenty years in power, he has outlasted Thai generals, African lieutenants and Latin America colonels. In Asia his political longevity is equalled only by General Ne Win of Burma and General Suharto of Indonesia. All these authoritarian regimes began by seizing power with a rhetoric of reform. Unrestrained by any opposition, most eventually slide into a downward spiral of corruption, economic decline and brutality. As popular support evaporates, arms and torture maintain the regime until it either consumes itself in violence or paralyzes in police-state paranoia.

In the Third World of the 1980s, dictatorship has become the norm and democracy an exception. Despite its nominal principles, the United States has played a key role in the rise of these authoritarian regimes. After the rapid liquidation of European empires in the decades following World War II, these former colonies, now the newly independent nations of the Third World, experimented briefly with democracy. America had pressed its European allies to liberate their colonies after the war. But in the 1950s, its commitment to liberal principles was modified by a militant anti-communism that allowed a qualified acceptance of dictatorship. Under President Kennedy in the 1960s, however, there was a short-lived attempt at supporting democracy in the Third World – the Alliance for Progress in Latin America, withdrawal of support for the Diem dictatorship in South Vietnam, and the overtures to neutralist India. In comparison with what followed, the 1960s seem a brief flowering of economic and electoral democracy in the Third World.

The democratic experiment was short, and by the late 1960s a uniquely brutal form of authoritarianism was emerging in the Third World. Battered by its defeat in Vietnam, America wavered in its support of democracy. The Nixon administration supported authoritarian allies and subverted the democratically elected Allende government in Chile. President Carter, by contrast, distanced himself from the dictators by his advocacy of human rights. Through all administrations, however, the US military aid program to the Third World continued to tilt the political balance in favour of authoritarian rule. With the advent of the Reagan administration in 1980, rhetoric has finally caught up with reality. In Asia and Latin America, the United States has committed itself to the defence of dictatorship and seems satisfied with the faintest of nods to democratic reform.

There was a certain logic to President Reagan's embrace of the dictators. In the wake of the OPEC oil boycotts, the world economy experienced some major adjustments in the 1970s that changed America's relations with the Third World. As oil prices shot upward through the 1970s, the Arab producers were awash in billions of dollars their economies could not readily absorb. They deposited much of the windfall in European and American banks, spending some on high technology weapons but letting most accumulate interest. Since banking profits are the difference between interest paid to depositors and interest earned from borrowers, the American banks needed new customers to absorb this massive capital.

The new borrowers were, of course, the non-oil producing nations of the Third World. While the billions circulated easily from First World to OPEC and back again, the Third World states found their economies ravaged by the escalating costs of oil imports. Not only was gasoline needed to fuel transport, but the new high-yielding varieties of rice and wheat, now common in much of the Third World, required oil-based fertilizers and pesticides to feed swelling populations. In the Philippines, for example, oil costs increased from 10 percent of all import expenditures in 1970 ($119 million) to nearly 30 percent in 1980 ($2,250 million). In the midst of this crisis, the Third World offered the American banks exceptionally high interest for desperately needed capital. Short term loans simply provided cash to meet the high cost of oil imports. But the longer term credits would hopefully establish new export industries that would eventually earn the Third World nations enough foreign exchange to meet the oil bill on their own. As American banks competed vigorously to extend massive credits, the Philippine foreign debt shot from only $2 billion in 1970 to $28 billion fifteen years later, an awesome burden for a poor island nation.

The oil shocks of the 1970s destabilized many fragile Third World societies. High inflation, massive haemorrhaging of foreign exchange, and the eventual costs of debt servicing pressed already strained economies. As the loans slowed by the end of the decade and interest payments came due, the Third World poor did not seem inclined to make sacrifices to meet their nation's foreign obligations. Repayment requires a range of almost punitive economies – heavy taxes, low wages to keep exports competitive, and a reduction of social services. No elected government can survive such unpopular measures. Only a dictatorship could maintain discipline in the midst of crisis and force the sacrifices required to meet loan repayments. The United States was thus doubly determined to support the autocrats. Military rule is a safeguard against any popular inclination towards a leftist government at a time of extreme economic hardship. Most importantly, reliable allies are more likely to avoid any default in loan repayments – a move that could spark a chain reaction among other Third World debtors and threaten the stability of the First World's banking system.

The loans themselves are a major source of instability in the Third World. As the billions poured in throughout the 1970s, ruling circles found it temptingly easy to skim off 10 or 20 percent. The American banks cooperated in this corruption by deducting kick-backs at source and telexing the funds to private numbered accounts in Switzerland, the Bahamas or the Cayman Islands. The comparative ease of such foreign graft eventually encouraged loan applications formed to secure an instant private fortune, not needed development capital. The new corruption percolated through Third World states, inducing an unprecedented reign of greed. Once the loans started falling due, repayments were difficult, in part, because systematic corruption had crippled the efficiency of the new enterprises.

The Philippines has suffered more than most Third World nations under this new global economy. Although its corruption follows the same dismal pattern of most tropical dictatorships, certain Philippine peculiarities make it particularly corrosive. While other nations now have severe repayment problems, the Philippines is one of the few borrowers actually on the brink of economic collapse. Much of the malaise seems to stem from the ambitions of the Marcos family. Shaped by a particularly violent system of provincial politics, Marcos and his wife Imelda are driven by a lust for wealth and power that seems almost pathological. Their extravagance and greed have, more than any other single factor, crippled the economy.

Disdainful Manila aristocrats explain the first couple's avarice and ambition by pointing to their middling provincial origins. Child of a poor provincial attorney from Leyte Island in the south, Imelda Marcos grew up in poverty and worked as a housemaid for a relative who had been elected to the postwar Congress. Born into a household of country school teachers in the Ilocos, a region long notorious for its factional violence, Marcos learned the craft of politics in his father's bitter prewar Congressional campaigns. He first came to national prominence in 1939 when, at the age of twenty-two, he was convicted of murdering the man who had defeated his father for Congress. While in prison, Marcos gained first place in the national bar examinations and argued his own appeal before the Supreme Court to win exoneration, achievements that marked him for future success. He was further hardened as a survivor of the Bataan death march and as guerilla officer against the Japanese in World War II. Marcos' character was thus shaped in the crucible of provincial politics under American colonial rule.

During their half century of colonialism, the Americans gradually turned over all political offices to the Filipinos but retained control over a para-military Constabulary to restrain the rise of provincial autocrats. After independence in 1946, provincial leaders began to deliver large blocs of votes to national politicians in exchange for a de facto local autonomy. By the early 1960s, these local warlords had neutralized the power of the national government and ruled their provinces with private armies.

The most notorious of the warlords was Congressman Floro

Crisologo of Ilocos Sur, a poor tobacco-growing province north of Manila and adjacent to Marcos' home province Ilocos Norte. First elected to Congress after World War II, Crisologo had, by the early 1960s, a virtual stranglehold over his province that can only be compared to the power of a feudal baron. With a standing army of 125 men and reserves of 300, all armed with M-16s and M-2 carbines, Crisologo delivered his province's votes as a bloc to favored national candidates, notably his close ally Ferdinand Marcos. The congressman protected himself with an elite squad of killers who terrorized or assassinated political rivals. When one village dared to dally with the opposition, Crisologo troopers burned it to the ground, killing an elderly woman, and decreed it a capital crime to offer food or shelter to the survivors. Congressman Crisologo's wife became the provincial governor, his son commanded the family's private army, and cronies filled most municipal offices.

In this poor province, tobacco was the only money and the Crisologos controlled the industry. Peasant growers got their credit from the Crisologo bank and cured their leaves in the Crisologo drying shed, the only one allowed in the province. The most obvious sign of Crisologo power was the 'tobacco blockade' on the national highway that runs through the province's narrow coastal plain south to Manila. During the late 1960s, Crisologo troopers guarded a highway roadblock and collected an illegal 'tax' of US $500 on every truckload of tobacco leaving the province. Protests to the government in Manila were ignored. It was generally believed that President Marcos and his security chief General Fabian Ver, a native of Ilocos Sur and a Crisologo relative, were partners in the blockade.

Soon after a public break with President Marcos on the eve of martial law, Congressman Crisologo was a victim of a precision-planned assassination. A devout Catholic, the congressman was kneeling in prayer at Sunday Mass in the grandeur of Ilocos Sur's eighteenth-century baroque cathedral. The usual armed bodyguards watched the main gates outside. Two killers stepped out of a confessional booth and emptied a .45 automatic into the bowed skull before slipping away through the sacristy.

Local politicians claim that the two killers were felons convicted of capital crimes and soon died in prison happy in the knowledge that their families were fixed for life.

President Marcos' declaration of martial law in 1972 destroyed the provincial warlords. Philippine Army detachments disarmed the private armies, and special Army intelligence teams moved across the country killing the provincial gunmen personally loyal to the warlords. With a monopoly on military and political power, Marcos stripped offending provincial politicans of their offices and assets.

While these moves were applauded, Marcos' more subtle, long-term campaign against the established oligarchy, the 'Manila 400', has aroused bitter criticism. Like the provincial warlords he destroyed, Marcos has used his monopoly on power and arms to impoverish his enemies and enrich his allies. Through his cronies, Marcos acquired hidden assets of incalculable value in every major sector of the economy – agriculture, media, transport, banking, power, mining, manufacturing, logging, and tourism. Mrs Marcos has been less venturesome, investing her assets, often through her 'blue ladies', in hotels, real estate, retail trade, jewels and cash. They have also acquired great independent assets, making the first couple among the world's richest. Simultaneously, Marcos has centralized control over the country's major industries and entrusted each to a relative or reliable crony, thus ensuring a sound economic base for the perpetuation of his regime.

Five years after the declaration of martial law, it became apparent that Marcos had created a new oligarchy of relatives, in-laws, cronies and allies. As $28 billion in foreign loans poured into Manila's banks, only those deemed 'reliable' had access to credit. While the old elite stagnated with assets of declining value, the new oligarchs scaled the financial heights. With a call from Malacañang Palace, an inconsequential crony could gain access to, let's say, a $60 million loan for a sugar mill. Since the Japanese contractors pay a minimum 10 percent kickback on their machinery, new sugar mills began popping up in unpromising locations in the late 1970s as world sugar prices plummeted to an unprofitable level. Many have since gone bankrupt. The object of the exercise was, after all, a 10 percent kickback, not a 10 percent profit.

Much of the $28 billion in foreign loans has gone to massive construction projects – irrigation, dams, hospitals, government office buildings, highways and great monuments like the Manila Film Center or the Folk Arts Theatre. An architect friend told me a story about the kickbacks in these projects. At an ordinary business luncheon in early 1983, several key men in the construction industry decided, just for fun, to work out the percentage of project cost that went to kickbacks. Even they were surprised. The process starts at the top when a senior official demands that a 20 percent kickback be padded into the contract. As the inflated bid works its way down the system from general contractor, to sub-contractor, to supplier – each adding a modest 10 percent for himself – the total for kickbacks grows to as high as 80 percent of overall contract cost.

The asset stripping operations against the old oligarchs combined a slick military professionalism with a cutting edge of provincial vendetta. In the months before martial law, Marcos' leading antagonists were the Lopez brothers – Fernando, Marcos' own vice-president, and Eugenio, the country's wealthiest and most skilful entrepreneur. Masters of political manipulation, they were believed responsible for a jeepney transport strike, radical student demonstrations and media attacks all aimed at Marcos in the early 1970s. A year after martial law, there was an explosion, believed set by Philippine Army agents, in a generating plant of the Manila Electrical Company, bright jewel in the Lopez corporate crown. The next day front page articles in the government controlled press accused anti-Marcos 'exiles', an obvious reference to Eugenio Lopez, of detonating the plant to sabotage Marcos' 'New Society'.

Within days, the government quietly confiscated the Manila Electric Company, worth some $200 million, and awarded it to a Marcos-controlled foundation. Imelda Marcos' brother seized the Lopez newspaper presses, and the close Marcos crony, sugar baron Roberto Benedicto, occupied their television station. No compensation was paid. The operation's officer for media manipulation, censorship chief Primitivo Mijares, later broke with the regime over some spoils and fled to America where he published an expose of the regime's corruption, *The Conjugal Dictatorship*, with the help of the Lopez family. He later disappeared and is believed dead.

As the regime began to amass an enormity of wealth and power, it split into what Mijares called a 'conjugal dictatorship' or what Manila gossips style a 'His and Hers government'. At the outset of martial law in 1972, 'his' sphere was dominant and Marcos left his imprint on almost all major policy – land reform, military modernization, infrastructure development, and energy conservation. A brilliant lawyer and man of some vision, Marcos won many local and international supporters in the early, reformist years of martial law.

'Her' sphere was initially limited to first lady-like busy-work in art and culture. Surrounded by a claque of sycophantic society matrons, called the 'blue ladies', and endowed with an energy as infinite as her vanity, Imelda threw herself headlong into a range of vast construction projects. Graduate of a mediocre provincial college, Imelda lacked the judgment to temper her guile and energy. Many of her projects were simply silly. In 1974 she decided to throw up a 10,000 seat auditorium the size of the Sydney Entertainment Centre in just seventy days. For months, every bit of cement and construction steel was commandeered for the project, wreaking havoc in the complex construction schedules for docks, highways and irrigation projects. After a vast outlay of time and treasure, her Folk Arts Theatre then was host to the Miss Universe Pageant. In 1981 she spent $100 million to host a film festival at a time when the national economy was teetering on the brink of disaster. To meet her demands for fast construction on the main film palace, engineers accelerated the work, cutting corners, and the roof collapsed killing an unknown number of workers. Like slaves of some ancient Oriental potentate, the surviving workers were ordered to continue working for days midst the stench of the corpses of their fellows rotting beneath the rubble. In between these two grand constructions, there has been a steady succession of such costly 'prestige' projects – The Heart Center, The Philippine Center in New York, several luxury hotels, the

Philippine International Convention Center, the University of Life. Most recently, she spent an estimated $10 to $20 million on her daughter's wedding, a live television spectacle of an ostentation that angered impoverished Filipinos.

As Marcos succumbed to a debilitating systemic disease sometime in the late 1970s, Imelda began to accumulate real power. Starting as minister of a made-up ministry, Human Settlements, she moved on to become mayor of a made-up city, Metro Manila. When Marcos re-established a parliamentary style democracy in 1981, she orchestrated a popular campaign for her selection as prime minister and was outraged when the World Bank's man in Manila, economic technocrat Cesar Virata, was appointed. As revenge, her blue ladies circulated in society salons spreading scandalous details of Virata's alleged liaison with a Filipina in Washington, DC. As Marcos' declining health forced periodic respites from politics, Imelda used the opportunity to widen her power base. She formed the KKK co-operative movement and won it a substantial share of the budget to build a mass patronage machine. More importantly, she secured a place for her eldest daughter and herself on the fifteen person executive committee that was, for a time, designated to pick Marcos' successor in the event of his death. Although she lacked her husband's personal ties to senior military commanders, she had aligned herself with a key figure – General Fabian Ver, armed forces Chief of Staff and head of the Presidential Security Command, a praetorian guard personally loyal to the first family.

Twelve years younger than Marcos and in good health, Imelda seemed well placed to succeed her husband until August 1983 when Senator Aquino returned to Manila. His assassination has dimmed her prospects. The crowds of demonstrators suspected her complicity in the killing and repudiated her candidates in the May 1984 elections. To placate the crowds, Marcos was forced to make some administrative changes that lessen Imelda's direct control over the selection of his successor. As the economy collapsed, the World Bank demanded the abolition of her patronage apparatus, the KKK co-operatives and the Ministry of Human Settlements, before it would extend new loans to bail out the regime. Despite these reverses, she remains a powerful figure who retains great influence over the economy and government.

In its drive for absolute power, the Marcos regime has allowed only one group any significant economic and political power – an entourage of powerful allies known collectively as 'the cronies'. As the foreign loans flooded in during the 1970s, Marcos allowed a large circle of supporters access to credit and business opportunities – siblings, in-laws, cousins, old friends and allies. Both corrupt and incompetent, most were incapable of managing their new resources.

Reeling from body blows of first family extravagance and crony corruption, the economy stumbled towards collapse. The crisis began in January 1981 when a Chinese textile magnate named Dewey Dee fled the country taking an estimated $100 million in stolen funds. Other leading financial figures followed, leaving heaps of bad financial paper that cost Philippine banks $600 to $950 million. The Governor of the Philippine Central Bank later resigned quietly when it was discovered that his office had been accepting 'commissions' from borrowers for approving their loans.

Once the panic set in, the whole fragile edifice of crony capitalism began to collapse. Most of the two dozen luxury hotels built at a cost of $200 million to house a World Bank conference in 1976 went into receivership. Several of the new financial empires were taken over by government banks on very generous terms, and Marcos had to authorize a government bail-out package of several hundred million dollars to avert a total collapse.

In the shake-out only two cronies survived as major powers – 'coconut king' Eduardo Cojuangco and 'sugar czar' Roberto Benedicto. Their backgrounds and operations are nearly identical. Descended from wealthy sugar families, both have capitalized on their close friendships with Marcos to plunder key primary industries. Beginning from their positions at the head of national marketing boards for each crop, they then took control of both processing and finance. With their licit and illicit profits, they purchased political power only surpassed by the first family – key positions in the ruling KBL party and control over their home provinces as Marcos' local plenipotentiary. While Marcos is ailing and Imelda's influence is waning, the power of these cronies has increased steadily.

Of the two, Cojuangco is the more determined. Heir to a vast sugar plantation in Tarlac Province just north of Manila, Cojuangco's early provincial political career was a by-product of a family feud for control over lands and bank shares. For several years he fought bitterly with his cousins – Senator Aquino's wife, Mrs Corazon Cojuangco Aquino, and her brother Jose. Pitted against his cousins, he naturally allied himself with Marcos in the 1960s. He became godfather to one of the Marcos daughters and developed a close personal relationship with the first family.

In 1975 Cojuangco persuaded the president to concede him control over the nation's coconut industry. If the humble coconut does not seem the stuff of great power, then it must be recalled that the Philippines is the Saudi Arabia of coconut oil. It supplies 85 percent of world coconut exports, and coconut oil comprises 8 percent of the global trade in vegetable oils. Grown on 432,000 farms across the archipelago, usually by poor tenant families, coconuts are the country's major export and the main livelihood for some 15 of the 53 million Filipinos.

Cojuangco's coconut scheme aimed at integrating these thousands of farms into a single milling and marketing agency that would give the Philippines real leverage in the global vegetable oil market. This process of vertical integration began in 1974 when President Marcos decreed that farmers would pay an onerous P100 levy on every 100 kilos of coconut. A year later Cojuangco formed the United Coconut Planters Bank and the government ordered that coconut levy collections be deposited there interest-free for the 'development' of the industry. Farmers could then borrow back their own money at 10 percent interest. By 1982 total levy collections reached $900 million, a considerable capital by any standard and one that has never been audited.

With this financial backing, Cojuangco bought up the private coconut mills to form United Coconut Mills, or Unicom, the first step in his bid to dominate the world market. In the end, the effort to corner the US coconut oil market and dictate prices to the First World collapsed in a $10 million loss. Buyers simply switched to other vegetable oils and the US Justice Department retaliated by hitting Cojuangco with an anti-trust suit. But the attempt left him in control of a key industry and rich bank. As the 'coco-levy' deposits climbed beyond US$1,000 million, Cojuangco has used the capital to build a vast political and economic empire. Now among the very richest of Filipinos, Cojuangco has acquired a $25 million horse racing operation in Australia, a controlling interest in the Philippines' premier corporation San Miguel, and a chain of vast sugar and coconut plantations aross the archipelago.

Cojuangco's power cannot be underestimated. In 1981 cabinet minister Emmanuel Pelaez, a former vice-president, launched stinging attacks on the coconut levy from the floor of parliament, denouncing it as exploitation of poor farmers and demanding an audit. Rumors of massive graft in the billion-dollar fund began circulating in Manila. Reportedly urged on by the World Bank, Prime Minister Virata intervened and finally persuaded President Marcos to suspend the levy. Several weeks later when the prime minister was abroad, Cojuangco convinced Marcos to over-rule the cabinet and restore the levy. Some months later after the controversy had died down, Pelaez was gunned down near his home by unknown assailants.

About the same time he gave Conjuangco coconuts, Marcos assigned sugar to his close friend Roberto Benedicto. The son of a leading Negros planter family, Benedicto had studied law at the University of the Philippines in the 1930s where he became Marcos' classmate, fraternity brother and confidante. Although Marcos made him president of the Philippine National Bank after his first election in 1965, Benedicto did not gain real power until martial law. In the mid 1970s, Marcos appointed Benedicto chairman of the Philippine Sugar Commission (Philsucom), a new agency with centralized control over all sugar milling and marketing.

Paralleling his public rise, Benedicto's private fortune grew into one of the country's largest – ownership of several sugar mills and control over two national banks, Traders Royal and Republic Planters, the latter with 1980 assets of $480 million. With the revival of electoral politics in 1978, he quickly translated his money into political power, dictating most provincial and local appointments on Negros Island. Never before had one man achieved so much economic and political power in Negros. When the Columbans published a pamphlet attacking Benedicto's sugar policies in 1982, he could avenge himself by keeping two of their priests under arrest for nearly two years on false charges.

Pressed by an abusive military and a corrupt state, Filipinos have turned to the Church for a refuge and an advocate. It is a reaction very much in keeping with the country's historical traditions. Whether Catholic, Protestant or partly pagan, all Filipinos share an intensely religious culture. Over the past two centuries, Filipino peasants have read the gospels as political testament and launched frequent revolts to bring the Kingdom of Christ to the Philippines.

In the Philippines there is then an intimate interaction between religion and politics. The modern Philippine nationalist movement began in 1872 when the Spanish colonial state executed three Filipino priests on false charges of plotting a mutiny by native garrisons. The Philippine Revolution of 1896 was similarly inspired by the execution of the nationalist leader Dr Jose Rizal. Convicted of subversion against Spain, Rizal was executed by firing squad before a crowd of thousands. He met his death with the calm of an actor playing Christ in the passion plays staged each Easter on the town plazas of the Philippines. Although the revolution was ultimately crushed by the US colonialism that ruled the country until 1946, Rizal remains a national hero to every Filipino schoolchild and a living saint for the hundreds of folk-Christian cults that worship him as a native Christ. And in this third time of crisis the nation has another martyr to inspire its rising – ex-Senator Benigno Aquino.

The months of street demonstrations which followed the Aquino assassination in August 1983 had the fervour of a religious revival. Shocked at the murder of the man who seemed their one hope for non-violent change, the Filipino middle and upper classes were, in a moment, transformed from political passivity into an angered militance. For five months following the killing, businessmen and clerical workers staged mass demonstrations under the curtain-glass towers of Makati, the city's financial centre. Significantly, they were joined by leftist unions and radical student groups. Although Aquino was a typical Filipino power broker with a private army, an entourage of courtesans and CIA contacts before martial law in 1972, his seven years of solitary imprisonment and ultimate assassination transformed him into a national martyr. After a decade of enforced quiescence, the streets of Manila erupted into daily demonstrations uniting rich and poor. Sensing the surge of popular anger, the Marcos regime was forced to yield control over the streets to the opposition.

Although the protests were political, their inspiration was in part religious. Reflecting the country's deep Catholic heritage, Filipinos saw Senator Aquino's death as something of a Biblical parable. After suffering a decade in the wilderness of prison and exile that transformed him from sinner into saint, Aquino returned to redeem his homeland. With the calm of a Christian martyr, he proclaimed his willingness to die before the television cameras on his flight from America to Manila. Struck down by the soldiers of the oppressive ruler at the very moment of his return, he is said to have reached outward in a dying gesture to embrace the ground of his beloved mother country. So punished for their sin of passivity by the loss of their redeemer, Filipinos must do penance by protest. These demonstrations are not simple rallies, they are a collective catharsis, an act of national resurrection.

Indeed, much of the demonstrations' rhetoric and ritual seems religious in its inspiration. Banners display religious themes. Leaders speak of using the streets for 'conscientization', a religious term. And the crowd's cadences are often those of a Sunday mass. In mid-1984, for example, a group of women demonstrators gathered before Rustan's Department Store in

Makati, owned by Imelda Marcos, to chant a litany:
> *Celebrant*: Oh Imelda, Queen of Theft
> *Response*: Spare us thy greed
> *Celebrant*: Oh Imelda, Queen of Theft
> *Response*: Leave this land.

While the opposition uses Christian theology to attack the regime, Marcos has sought his legitimacy in pagan mythology. His official campaign biography, first published in 1964 and since reprinted many times, begins: 'Not often does a man become a legend in his own time... But a persistent legend reverberates in the Philippines... that Ferdinand Marcos has an *anting anting* in his back. The *anting anting* is a talisman... originally the possessions of tribal medicine men'. According to the author, the charm was 'bequeathed to Marcos' by Fr Gregorio Aglipay, a Catholic priest who was vicar to the Revolution of 1896 and later broke with Rome to found a schismatic national church, now part of the Anglican communion. As a reward for the family's loyalty to the schismatic church, Supreme Bishop Aglipay 'before he died, gave his magic talisman to Marcos to protect him during the Battle of Bataan, making an incision in Ferdinand's back with his own hand to insert the amulet'. The charm supposedly gives Marcos supernatural powers: 'Among its virtues, it permits its holder to disappear and reappear at will... Under some circumstances it can restore the dead to life'. In the Battle of Bataan against the Japanese at the outset of World War II, Marcos engaged in such daring exploits that 'he could not have survived without the *anting anting* of Aglipay'.

The regime has used the Philippines' ancient pagan religion to fashion a mythology that makes Marcos seem a divinely inspired ruler. In celebration of the inauguration of 'the New Republic' in 1981, the regime displayed an enormous painting, six metres high and eight metres long, done in Marcos' first term by national artist Carlos Francisco, best known for his historical and mythological murals. Following the President's detailed instructions, the artist Francisco painted a tableau that depicts Marcos' personal vision of his own divine origins and heroic destiny.

At the centre of the mural are the massive heads of Ferdinand and Imelda Marcos nearly two metres high. And looping about the painting's upper boundaries is a ribbon of orange fire that leads the viewer's eye through a series of vignettes of Marcos' life – from origins to Ilocos, through wartime service, to presidential inauguration in 1965. Juxtaposed between Marcos' huge head and several ancient Filipino warriors raising their swords in battle, the fire ribbons trace out a curious form – the figure of a human body with an oval void where the face should be. What is the meaning of this faceless form?

From the mural's structure it seems clear that this humanoid form symbolizes the tradition of heroic Filipino warriors who are divinely ordained to lead the nation in its hour of crisis. At the painting's corners are images of military heroes who became great leaders – the eighteenth century rebel from Marcos' home province Diego Silang, the revolutionary general Antonio Luna, and the World War II officer Ferdinand Marcos. The painting seems to say that the ancient Filipino warriors have released a spirit which floats about waiting for a body to invest. At times of national crisis the spirit takes a body – first Silang, then Luna, and now Marcos. How can we be sure that Marcos is the chosen one? By his works you shall know him. As the vignettes arching above the fire ribbons tell us, Marcos has been tested and anointed by the great men of Philippine history – President Quezon, President Laurel and General Douglas MacArthur. Invested with this ancient spirit, Marcos becomes the chosen leader, beyond the court of the present and answerable only to history.

Through ten years of martial law, Marcos tried to indoctrinate an entire generation of Philippine youth with this vision of his destiny. Under the direction of his daughter, teenagers by the tens of thousands have been organized into Youth Councils and sent off to mountain camps across the archipelago. Through intensive psychological indoctrination they are taught to reject their parents and embrace the first couple. The week-long drill culminates in a candlelight ceremony where massed thousands gather before giant portraits of Ferdinand and Imelda to chant an oath of loyalty to the 'father and mother of the nation'.

At the ultimate level, Philippine politics has thus become a clash between two religious visions – a quest for Christian liberation struggling against the triumph of pagan power. The opposition sees the nation as a crucified Christ, betrayed by the pharisees of the Marcos regime into the hands of American legions. Their goal is a national community based on Christian brotherhood – without poverty, exploitation, or injustice. Marcos, by contrast, demands obedience from reverential subjects like an ancient warrior king. His magical powers and heroism in battle are proof of his legitimacy. Those who doubt that should recall the twenty-seven medals the United States awarded him in World War II and ignore the rumours that most of them are fakes. His advent is the fulfilment of two millenia of Philippine history. Those who doubt that should read the twenty-seven volumes of Philippine history that he is, we are told, writing personally each night after work. Significantly, the Tagalog title of that history, *Tadhana*, means *Destiny*. Since he is the embodiment of the nation's past and the seer who guides its future, the land and all its fruits are his by divine right.

With such a religious view of politics, Filipinos have quite naturally sought refuge in the Church as conditions have worsened under the Marcos dictatorship. Peasants come to their parish priests for protection against violent Army pacification campaigns. The middle class have turned to religious societies for a political forum when Marcos closed Congress and silenced public debate. Manila's elite have used Archbishop Sin as their political spokesman when martial law denied them the right to speak. As military abuse has mounted and the economy slipped towards collapse, Filipinos turned to the Church, as they did to the Communist Party, to express their opposition to the regime. Always a silent power, the Church has been forced to play an active political role by the gathering crisis of the Marcos dictatorship.

The Filipinos were turning to the Church for support just as it was starting to sever its historic alliance with the Philippine state. Over the past twenty years, there has been a fundamental change in the Church's political posture throughout the Third World. But nowhere has the change been more marked than in Latin America and the Philippines. Through three centuries of

Spanish colonial rule, Bishop and Viceroy cooperated closely to win converts for the Church and treasure for Spain. In the sixteenth century Rome and Madrid struck a bargain over Spain's administration of its new empire. The Vatican conceded the Spanish crown special powers over the Church and its colonies – appointment of Bishops, control of Church funds, and use of priests as local colonial officials. In exchange, the Crown became the church's patron and assumed full responsibility for the conversion of the natives.

During the 350 years of Spanish rule in the Philippines, Church and State were one. Parish priests acted as colonial officials in the countryside – collecting taxes, taking the census, and leading local militia to suppress native revolts or battle Muslim pirates from the south. Through their service to the state, the Spanish religious orders – Jesuits, Dominicans and Augustinians – acquired enormous wealth and power. They controlled all eduction from parish primary schools to the university in Manila. Their vast estates ringing Manila totalled 171,000 hectares and occupied up to 82 percent of the agricultural land in some provinces. For over two centuries, the Church dominated the trans-Pacific galleon trade in Chinese silks and porcelains, accumulating great profits. When the first bank in Asia opened at Manila in 1852, the Church subscribed to half the stock.

Although state patronage ended when America took the colony from Spain in 1898, the Church emerged from five years of revolution and fifty of US colonial rule with its religious and economic power intact. Despite a nationalist schism by revolutionary priests and proselytizing by American protestants, about 85 percent of Filipinos were still nominal Catholics. Thus, by the time the Philippines won independence in 1946, four centuries of colonialism had left two powerful institutions – Church and State. As Marcos used his autocratic state to strip rival oligarchs of their wealth and power during the 1970s, only the Church survived with the resources to resist the rise of his dynasty. With a national network of parishes, its own education system, and a majority of the population as its parishoners, the church has the making of a formidable antagonist.

Faced with a choice between a corrupt dictator and a

communist revolution, the Catholic Church has wavered. Its historical conservatism and vast secular interests place it instinctively on the side of the state and order. But its parish priests feel the worsening plight of the Filipino masses and pull it towards opposition.

Left on its own, the Philippine Church hierarchy would probably have remained a bastion of state power as it was under colonialism. In the mid-1960s, however, the Vatican promulgated a series of encyclicals which, in effect, decreed that the Church had a special mission to the poor of the Third World. In his *Mater et Magistra* (1961) and *Pacem in Terris* (1963), Pope John XXIII stated the Church had to apply Christian principles to the unequal relations between First and Third Worlds. The Second Vatican Council, known as Vatican II, approved a new Constitution for the Church (1965) which made a strong commitment to social justice.

Under Pope Paul VI these once radical doctrines became the new orthodoxy. His encyclical *Populorum Progressio* (1967) condemned 'structural injustice', a concept that radical priests later used to justify their attack on oppressive social institutions. With Pope Paul VI in attendance, the Asian Bishops' Conference (1970) resolved 'to speak out for the rights of the disadvantaged and powerless against all forms of injustice no matter from what source such abuse may come'. Under his leadership, the Synod of Bishops in Rome (1971) rejected the idea that the Church should confine itself to a purely spiritual domain and proclaimed its new mission of 'action on behalf of justice and participation in the transformation of the world'.

The consequences of the Church's radical redirection were first evident in Latin America. At the Latin American Bishop's Conference in Medellin, Columbia (1968), the church drew upon the teachings of Vatican II and the Papal encyclicals to declare its advocacy of the poor and oppressed. The Conference provided an opening to the left and stimulated the growth of a radical 'theology of liberation'. Writing in the late 1960s, its leading exponent, Gustavo Gutierrez of Peru, interpreted liberation to mean: 'the political liberation of oppressed peoples and social classes; man's liberation in the course of history; and liberation from sin as a condition of a life of communion of all men with the Lord'.

Fusing Marxism with Christianity, Gutierrez argued that the gravity of exploitation in Latin America justified violent revolution. Since the prosperity of the First World was based on the poverty of the Third, Latin America had become an 'oppressed and dominated continent'. The failure of the democratic reforms of the 1960s had convinced all 'conscientized' groups that 'there will be a true development for Latin America only through liberation from the domination by capitalist countries'. Their natural allies are 'our national oligarchs' who resist any change. Thus, Latin America 'will never get out of its plight except by a profound transformation, a social revolution'. Although a 'more or less Marxist inspiration prevails among... individuals who are raising the banner of the continent's liberation', Christians are moved to 'participate in liberating oppressed peoples' by a conviction that 'the gospel message is radically incompatible with an unjust, alienated society'. In joining a Marxist struggle for liberation one can fulfil the Christian faith. 'Christ thus appears the Saviour who, by liberating us from sin, liberates us from the very root of social injustice.'

The new Church militant first appeared on the field of battle in Nicaragua. Reflecting its Spanish colonial origins, the Nicaraguan Church had remained a bastion of the Somoza family's dictatorship for almost forty years. In the 1930s the Catholic Bishop of Granada had earned a certain notoriety by blessing the arms of US marines on operations against the nationalist guerillas of Agusto Sandino. The upsurge of the Vatican II spirit coincided with the consecration of a liberal, Monsignor Obando y Bravo, as Archbishop of Managua. Soon after his appointment in 1971, he announced the Church's break with the Somoza dictatorship. 'A situation of violence is crushing the masses. I make a clear distinction between basic or institutional violence rooted in socio-economic structures, and the violence of the oppressed which it engenders'.

The Bishop was speaking out at a time when there seemed no end to an intolerable regime. The elder Somoza was a playboy whose appetite for corruption earned him the nickname 'vampire', a reference to his disreputable bloodbank which exported its donations to the United States for profit. Not only was his son and heir corrupt, he was also demonstrating a taste for torture. Despite the regime's obvious degeneracy, the Archbishop maintained a curious faith in his ability to negotiate a new government with the dictator until the day the revolution captured the capital.

While the Bishops remained, on balance, neutral, many parish priests became architects of the Sandinista revolution. A pioneer exponent of the theology of liberation, Fr Ernesto Cardenal, had established a religious community on the islands off the coast in the late 1960s and taught the thousand families who settled there a Marxist-Christian doctrine. As one member of the community later recalled: 'In these Sunday assemblies we talked about the justification of revolutionary violence for a Christian... the image in the gospels of Christ as a proletarian revolutionary'. In 1970 Fr Francisco Meija founded the first organization combining spiritual and class concerns, the Catholic Workers Youth, and was severely tortured by the Somoza regime for his efforts. In remote rural areas where the traditional church was weak, radical priests began to organize a new style of grass roots parish called the Basic Christian Community.

After breaking with the more moderate bishops in 1975, radical priests began to play a key role in bringing the Sandinista revolution to power. In October 1977, the rebel command decided to gamble with a bold strike against the National Guard barracks at San Carlos on the southern border with Costa Rica. Fr Cardenal opened his island community to the guerilla strike force as a training camp and about twenty of his followers later decided to join the attack. As one of these Christian guerillas recalled: 'The Nicaraguan people were involved in a fight against injustice, and to use violence was to be willing to give your life for Nicaragua; it was a violence of love'. Although poorly armed, the small guerilla band scored a stunning success at San Carlos. That victory was the start of an offensive that captured the people's imagination and carried the revolution into the streets of the capital.

As the revolution gathered momentum, the Basic Christian

Communities merged with local Sandinista cells to become the mass base of the guerilla army in both countryside and city slums. On the revolution's southern front, Fr Gaspar Garcia Lavina, a Spanish Sacred Heart missionary, became 'Commandante Martin' and was killed in combat leading his guerilla forces. Announcing his decision to take up arms in December 1977 the priest explained: 'I was trying to salvage the situation in a Christian way, in the pacifist sense, trying to lift people through their own resources or those of the government. But I realized that this was a lie, a big deception'.

After the Sandinista guerillas captured the capital Managua in July 1979, the revolutionary union of Christians and Marxists was consecrated in a new cabinet. The Maryknoll priest Fr Miguel D'Escoto became Foreign Minister, the radical theologian Fr Cardenal was Minister of Culture, and Fr Alvaro Arguello SJ joined the Council of State as the clergy's representative.

While radical priests and parishes helped legitimate the revolution, the Church hierarchy has remained ambiguous. Although Archbishop Obando y Bravo celebrated a victory mass soon after the Sandinista guerillas captured the capital, he had obvious reservations about the new revolutionary government. The hierarchy's uncertainty has been reinforced by the Vatican. Under pressure from Pope John Paul II, the Nicaraguan bishops soon instructed their priests to resign from the revolutionary government, an order they publicly refused. The bishops are still wavering, uncomfortable with the revolution's embrace of radical Christianity but afraid to risk an open break with such a popular government.

The spirit of Vatican II has sparked a similar split in the Philippine Church. With vast temporal resources that made the Manila Archdiocese one of the richest anywhere, the Philippine bishops are not inclined to radicalism and were reluctant to respond to the new orthodoxy. Although their 1971 pastoral letter on social justice spoke of helping the 'economically deprived' and 'powerless poor', theirs was still a traditional view of top-down Christianity with priests dispensing spiritual and material gifts to the obedient downtrodden.

The prince of the Philippine church until the mid 1970s,

Cardinal Rufino Santos, was an unrepentant reactionary who did little to disguise his lack of interest in the new theology. Appointed during World War II, Cardinal Santos was the first Filipino to become Archbishop of Manila and reflected the conservatism of the colonial Church. His patron and predecessor as Archbishop of Manila, Michael J. O'Doherty, an American, was an enthusiastic supporter of the Fascist Party organized by Spaniards in Manila during the late 1930s. When Manila's fascists published a book celebrating General Franco's capture of Madrid, Archbishop O'Doherty wrote an enthusiastic introduction: 'General Franco has been an instrument of Providence for the salvation not only of Spain but of the whole world. Some day the world will recognize its debt to the Great Leader of the Spanish People'. Cardinal Santos maintained the Archdiocese's affinity for conservative Spanish Catholicism and later supported the formation of a chapter of Opus Dei. A lay society of exceptional conservatism, Opus Dei was founded in Spain and its members held key posts in the Franco dictatorship during the 1960s. Today the society's Manila chapter is a bastion of the Catholic right and plays an active role in public policy formation through its think tank, the Center for Research and Communication.

In the mid 1970s, the Manila Archdiocese moved towards the centre when the current Archbishop Cardinal Sin succeeded Santos. Led by Cardinal Sin, the moderate faction now commands the centre of the Catholic Bishop's Conference with about 70 supporters – leaving 15 bishops on the extreme right and some 15 to 17 on the left. Despite keen debate on social issues, all are united in an effort to preserve the authority of the Church and its hierarchy.

While the Marcos regime's authoritarian progress has sparked some sharp conflicts between Church and State, the bishops have so far avoided an open break. Announcing a policy of 'critical collaboration' in 1977, Cardinal Sin made it clear that he was prepared to tolerate the Marcos dictatorship. The regime's increasing repression of progressive priests and their parishioners has, however, strained that tolerance. During the decade of martial law, the Army launched thirteen raids against various

Church offices – a parish church, a convent, several seminaries, two Catholic radio stations and several religious newspapers. In each case the military accused the religious of communist subversion on questionable evidence, prompting an immediate tension in Church-state relations. Ever the politician, Cardinal Sin has managed to mediate each crisis and preserve a working relationship with President Marcos.

His delicate balancing act after the Aquino assassination in August 1983 was a virtuoso performance. After delivering a moving homily at Aquino's funeral which spoke in vague terms of the country's 'tragic condition', Cardinal Sin visited the President to urge formation of a government of reconciliation which would include the opposition. Through such tactical flip-flops Sin evidently hopes to avert violence which might leave an opening for the left. While his political dexterity is most skilful, it is hardly the kind of moral leadership which could command the loyalty of radical priests.

Despite the best efforts of the hierarchy, the radicals have grown in both number and influence over the past twenty years. In the heady days after Vatican II, the younger religious radicals devoted their initial efforts to forging a progressive presence inside the Church. Gradually, a loosely organized Christian Left emerged in the late 1960s among the ordinary parish priests in the southern islands and the religious orders across the archipelago – the Jesuits, the Columbans and smaller congregations. Influenced by the Latin American theology of liberation, the progressives took control of an ordinary diocesan organization, Philippine Priests Inc. (PPI), and began to radicalize many of its 1,500 member priests. At its national convention in 1972, the PPI announced its intention to 'mobilize and organize our people in a well-planned program of protracted and disciplined struggle for liberation'.

The leaders of the Christian Left moved quickly from reform to revolution. On the eve of martial law in 1972, the leading radicals in PPI, Fr Ed de la Torre, SVD and Fr Luis Jalandoni of Negros, organized a smaller, more militant organization, Christians for National Liberation (CNL). The new group committed itself to 'expose and oppose imperialism, feudalism and bureaucratic capitalism' and declared its open alliance with the Communist Party. 'Our belief in Jesus Christ', explained Fr de la Torre in a manifesto he released in 1981 after nine years in prison, 'calls us to incarnate our Christianity, to give it flesh and blood. This we seek in the passion, death and resurrection of the Filipino people – the people's democratic revolution'. For that revolution to succeed, radical Christians must stop religious culture from being 'used by our enemies to mystify and domesticate people'. Once that is done 'we must try to mobilize as much of the Church's resources as we can for the people's struggle'.

When Fr de la Torre and Fr Jalandoni were arrested soon after martial law, revolutionary ideology seemed to lose its influence among the progressive priests. Within five years, however, the rising tide of military brutality and crony corruption forced a growing number of moderate priests into an alliance with the Communist guerillas of the New People's Army (NPA). Significantly, the most radical reaction came in the Ilocos region of northern Luzon, Marcos' home region where crony capitalism held greatest sway. By 1980 at least four Catholic priests were fighting with the NPA in the Ilocos. The Christian Left soon acquired its first martyr.

'Zacarias G Agatep is dead', began an announcement from the Catholic Social Action Secretariat in October 1982. 'He died a revolutionary in his native soil of Ilocos Sur. He is the first Filipino Catholic priest to die, gun in hand, in pursuit of a Revolution'. Fr Agatep began his pastoral career in the 1960s as a moderate, but through his work as chaplain to the Federation of Free Farmers, a church-sponsored union, he was drawn into conflict with the province's warlord Floro Crisologo, then a close political ally of Marcos. He tried to organize the poor tobacco farmers exploited by the warlord's monopoly on the drying and export of the province's crop. When Crisologo's troops burned out the village of Bantay for dallying with a rival political faction, Fr Agatep mobilized Church support for the ruined farmers. For his persistent advocacy of the poor, the priest was imprisoned for four months in 1980 on unsubstantiated allegations of subversion. The Church hierarchy abandoned him to an indefinite imprisonment. When released in honor of the Pope's visit to Manila, Fr Agatep joined the NPA guerillas in the mountains of Ilocos. A few days after the Army placed a price of P130,000 on his head, he was hunted down and killed.

Moderate clergy hailed him as a martyr. Fr Avelino Sapida, Social Action Director, Cavite Diocese: 'I am more proud to be a priest now before our suffering and struggling people... I feel closer to Christ now because of the involvement, immersion and identification of my fellow priests, like Fr Zach, with our struggling people'. Fr Angel Dy, Social Action Director, Bicol Diocese: 'He brought his Christian commitment for social transformation to its logical conclusion. He was a martyr. A Christian nationalist'. Fr Anton Korterik: 'Some will want to forget Fr Zach. Many others hold him in highest esteem as a glowing example of Christ's paradox: "If the world hates you, remember that it hated me before you" (*John*, 15:18)'.

If Fr Agatep is a martyr, then Fr Conrado Balweg is a spectre whose media image haunts the regime. In May 1984, the Manila newspaper *Veritas* carried a photograph of Fr Balweg in the mountains with an M-16 rifle and the banner headline, 'NICARAGUA TODAY, RP [Philippines] TOMORROW?' In a six page interview, Fr Balweg explained that his opposition to the regime had begun in 1973 when his mountain parish in the Ilocos region became part of a province-sized logging concession Marcos gave to his relative and golf-partner Herminio Disini. Balweg's six year battle against Disini's Cellophil Corporation pushed him gradually towards Marxism and the NPA. Intensive logging would destroy the livelihood of the Tingguian tribes who lived in those mountains, and, a Tingguian tribesman himself, Fr Balweg was determined to resist. After his Bishop allegedly accepted a P400,000 'donation' from Cellophil to campaign for acceptance of the concession, Balweg found he could not expect any support from his diocese. Finally, in mid-1979, Deputy Minister of Defence Carmelo Barbero, a native of the area, dispatched a team of hired killers to liquidate Balweg. To avoid a killing which would inflame the logging issue further, the Bishop warned the priest who fled into the mountains to join a band of thirty-two NPA guerillas.

Fr Balweg has made an easy transition from Catholic priest to

Communist guerilla. 'When I was ordained', he told the reporter, 'it was stressed that the essence of the priesthood was offering of one's life with absolutely no conditions. Here in the revolution you can concretely demonstrate that you are ready to offer your life.'

At first the priest found the killing difficult. 'One had to internalize the idea that the soldiers were doing the work of class enemies like Marcos, Enrile, Barbero', he recalled. 'They're the ones I saw in my sights.'

Reflecting on the trauma that followed his first killing, the priest rationalized: 'The experience was very valuable because it became clear to me why we need guns. It's not because you want to kill or because you're a tough guy. This gun is an instrument for higher value. The value of justice. The value of the dignity of man'.

An articulate and charismatic spokesman for the revolution, Fr Balweg's interviews on BBC television and in the Manila press have made his capture an obsession for the regime. The military has posted a P130,000 reward for Fr Balweg, dead or alive. In March 1984 the Army began sweeping the hills with a reinforced detachment and strafing villages from helicopter gunships. President Marcos tried to inspire his troops with a personal visit to the mountain front in July, pinning medals on fifteen soldiers and urging them to fight on. Fr Balweg remains at large.

Lying somewhere on the political spectrum between the revolutionaries and the bishops are the majority of ordinary Filipino priests who are, like Gore, O'Brien and Dangan, progressive but not revolutionary. As parish workers close to an impoverished people, most priests do not share the bishops' complacency or their overriding concern for preservation of Church authority. Although they are, to varying degrees, alienated by the regime's brutality and corruption, they cannot condone the revolution's violence. Determined to help the poor but unwilling to join the NPA guerillas, progressive priests have found a middle way – formation of new social structures that can liberate the poor through non-violence. For them Vatican II and the new social gospel were a call to action. In essence, they are trying to use the wealth and power of the Church to equalize the balance between oppressor and oppressed.

In the decade before martial law, progressive priests were active in the formation of honest trade unions, hoping that industrial action might improve the workers' lot in the Third World as it had in the First. When the unions foundered on the rocks of military repression and internal dissension, the priests introduced 'conscientization' seminars to liberate workers' attitudes from a crippling culture of poverty. From unions and seminars, the progressives advanced logically to the formation of a new style of grassroots parish, the Basic Christian Community. As they moved closer to the poor to share their plight, these priests were soon caught in a crossfire between dictatorship and revolution.

Chapter Two
A Tropical Island

At 5.30 pm on 8 May 1981, a Friday, a blue Toyota jeep drove down a dirt road through the sugarcane fields of Hacienda Esperanza on Negros Island, some 300 kilometres south of Manila in the central Philippines. Riding inside were the driver, the plantation's cashier with the weekly payroll, and its manager, Mr Juvencio Pereche. By all accounts, Mr Pereche had reason to be content with his world. Born the son of a poor plantation cook, he had risen through the ranks to his present position as manager of this 1,000 hectare hacienda and was, at sixty-two, looking foward to the generous retirement his company provided. In a few days he would be leaving for Manila to witness the graduation of his youngest son from the country's elite business school, the Asian Institute of Management.

The jeep drove past fields that were, for this area, uncommonly squared and flat, past tractors pulling exotic new machinery — a rotavator, reversible plow, and a ripper-cultivator. As the jeep slowed to cross the wooden bridge over a deep ravine, the stump of a banana tree fell across the road. The driver braked to a sudden halt. Out of the high cane came six young men, one armed with a .38 calibre revolver, another with a twenty-centimetre knife. The first shoved the revolver into the driver's face and ordered the passengers out.

While two of the gang ransacked the jeep for the P6,000 payroll, the one guarding Mr Pereche with a knife, an unemployed hacienda worker named Jerry de la Cruz, started to lose control. 'What about my educational loans?', he screamed. Enraged, he drove the knife into Mr Pereche's chest near the heart, three times by his own admission and seven times by the cashier's count. He was still flailing away furiously when the cashier shouted, 'enough, Jerry, enough'. Without waiting to find the payroll, the gang scattered into the cane.

Within minutes, Mr Pereche died. Within hours all six of the gang, who lived on Hacienda Esperanza or nearby, had surrendered to police. Interviewed on local radio the next day, Jerry said: 'Why should I have regrets? I would do it again tomorrow'.

What can we make of this incident — a simple matter of robbery with homicide, or just some of the desperate violence so characteristic of life in an impoverished Third World? Why would Jerry, a ordinary young man of twenty-one with his life in front of him, see such a self-destructive act as sensible and responsible?

A month later, I walked down that same dirt road towards the hacienda and into an investigation which has taken over three years and many trips back there to answer these questions. Five years before, in the mid-1970s, I had walked down that road perhaps a hundred times on field research for my doctoral dissertation on Negros. This time I was coming back, I thought, to visit a few friends and spend a few hours taking notes on some of the changes which had no doubt occurred in the intervening years. From the very outset of this journey, however, there had been indications that life on the Negros sugar haciendas was changing beyond recognition. During the hour drive south from the provincial capital at Bacolod that day, I had passed four processions carrying little silver coffins. Times were hard, I thought, and the children are falling first. Walking down the road into Hacienda Esperanza, there were subtle signs of change. The legions of labourers that had crowded the fields five years ago, planting and weeding in disciplined teams, were gone. Instead I saw two heavy tractors chugging through the fields drawing machines labelled 'Hodge Mackay'. Rolling fields had been flattened, evidently to accommodate the new machines.

As I learned that afternoon and in the months to come from interviews with the new manager and his workers, Hacienda Esperanza was at the vanguard of an agricultural revolution. In the midst of the prolonged depression of world sugar prices in the late 1970s, management became desperate for a solution to what was known in Negros as 'the sugar crisis'. When a local farm equipment distributor announced arrival of a new technology from Australia, the Hodge system, that could both cut costs and raise sugar yield, the hacienda placed an order — two complete sets of seventeen implements for the unheard of sum of P 600,000, or A $65,000. The equipment had arrived direct from the Hodge factory in Mackay, Queensland only six months before my visit, but the tractor drivers, trained by Australian technicians, were already producing remarkable results. Flipping through stacks of experimental tables and preliminary figures in his office that first day back, the new manager, exuding an infectious enthusiasm, showed me how the Hodge system had simultaneously slashed his field labor costs by 50 percent and boosted sugar production by over 30 percent.

Everyone I spoke with in the Negros sugar industry in the coming months bubbled with enthusiasm for the new Australian technology. Whether technician, sugar baron or bureaucrat, all were convinced that the new Australian machines would save their industry from shipwreck in the storms of the world market. Within five years, most sugar plantations across the length of the archipelago would be using the new method. At the same time, everyone denied that the change would produce any increase in unemployment among the already impoverished sugar workers of Negros. How, I asked myself, could they adopt a labour saving technology without expecting to displace labour? From my first glance at Hacienda Esperanza's production figures, I was convinced of two things — Australian technology would indeed modernize the Philippine sugar industry, but it would also bring misery for the million poor of Negros who depended upon it for survival.

My initial reaction was simplistic, but, in retrospect, accurate. A Queensland cane farm of 130 hectares can be worked by the farmer and one labourer with a stable of tractors and machinery. A Negros hacienda of the same size is home to 90 manual labourers and a community of 250 to 300 men, women and children. Queensland had shed its sugar workers gradually over half a century as it created this new technology. If the same change were compressed into only five or ten years in Negros, what would happen to the 90 percent of the 180,000 sugar workers who would lose their jobs? Jerry's desperate act was the most visible sign of a society in the crisis. A hundred years in the making, Negros sugar society was now collapsing into desperation, random violence and revolution.

With extremes of wealth and poverty that rival any place in the Third World, Negros is a society that gives new meaning to the concept of exploitation. Negros is what social scientists call a monocrop island; another way of saying that sugar made Negros and Negros is sugar. Driving the coastal highway that rims an island as large as Hawaii or Jamaica, Negros seems, from its beaches to the steep mountain spine in the distance, a sea of shimmering sugarcane leaves. The monotony of dull green is broken with almost geometric regularity by the silver smokestacks of the sugar mills that dot the coastal plain like mooring posts. The province of Negros Occidental, the island's western half, produces over 50 percent of the Philippine sugar crop, the country's leading primary export. Over half of the land in Negros Occidental is planted with sugar and over 70 percent of its workers depend on sugar for their survival.

All of the province's broad plains are partitioned into plantations of 50 to 500 hectares worked by disciplined gangs of wage labourers. Watching the Negros sugar workers toiling in teams under a tropical sun for eight or ten hours a day, I could not help being reminded of those Hollywood epics of plantation life in the antebellum American South. While the people of the plains work for miserable hacienda wages of a dollar a day, the island's mountain spine is home to poor peasant hill farmers who are squatting on small, two to five hectare farms. Not even the hill farmers are free from sugar. Their poverty forces them to work as casual labourers on the lowland haciendas and their farms, most without legal title, are under constant threat of land grabbing by the powerful planters. In Negros, sugar is the original sin that taints everyone who lives on the island — planters, plantation workers and hill farmers. In such a fragile, impoverished society, the mechanization of the plantations, the latest in a long history of First World technological revolutions on this island, has all the makings of a social disaster.

For over a million of Negros Occidental's 1.8 million people the sugar hacienda is a total life support system. Although sugar farms come in all shapes and sizes, most of the province's sugar land, about 70 percent, is occupied by larger farms of over 50 hectares. And there is a certain uniformity to the layout and life on the haciendas, of which Hacienda Esperanza is a fair sample. Lying at the centre of 1,000 hectares planted largely with sugar, the hacienda compound is a self-contained community with its own school, stores, chapel, clinic, housing tract and central administration. The hacienda's 858 residents live in two clusters of small, wooden houses, the larger group separated from the administrative compound only by the width of a narrow cane field. Although these tumble-down shacks offer only 25 square metres of floor space for families as large as ten, water, electricity and primary education are all free, courtesy of the hacienda. Furnishings consist of sleeping mats, worn cooking utensils, a few plates and spoons, and, among the more fortunate, a wooden wardrobe. Most workers own only the clothes on their backs and four to ten malnourished children. Jerry de la Cruz, for example, is the eldest of six children dependent during most of the year on their father's daily wage as a tractor driver, P21 or about A $2.30. Like all workers they survive on endless loans from the hacienda. When Mr Pereche cut the family's credit two years ago before his death, three of the children, Jerry included, had to drop out of school.

A hundred metres and a world away lies the administrative compound. Past the galvanized iron cluster of equipment barns, through the tall, cast iron gates opened by shotgun guards, and down the long gravel drive that cuts across manicured lawns, rises the Spanish colonial Big House, with the manager's residence above and offices below. For the manager or his children, occupancy can be a stepping stone to a brilliant career in Manila. Aurora Pijuan, daughter of the hacienda's manager during the 1960s, broke into the headlines with her selection as Miss International and has continued to make them as movie starlet and ex-wife of the man who dared to marry President Marcos' eldest daughter.

A dozen domestics staff the Big House and wait on its long dining table that serves as meeting place for corporate executives and visiting sugar barons. My first week back in 1981 coincided with a luncheon for fifty in honor of a parochial visit by the Bishop of Bacolod. Seated opposite the young manager, I noted his table conversation was interrupted several times by hacienda workers in tattered clothes shoving bits of paper before him and muttering into his ear. Whether lunch, dinner or corporate conference, the workers came constantly, I later learned, to borrow money against next month's or next year's wages for every imaginable need — a child's visit to the doctor, a mother's burial, a baby's baptism, or a daughter's high school tuition. The ritual was always the same. As soon as each one ascended the grand staircase into the dining room, these grown men would hunch their shoulders, curl their bodies to an adolescent's height and shuffle haltingly towards the manager, who stiffened slightly in sternness. 'Please sir, it is my second child. Three day's fever. I wouldn't trouble you but . . .' With a glance at the paper but without making eye contact, the manager flicks his signature across the debt voucher. Shuffling backward in the same posture of dependence, the worker mutters 'thank you sir, many thanks sir, we won't forget this sir . . .' while the manager continues his dinner-table conversation.

'They may seem weak, even pathetic', said the manager, Antonio Corro, a stocky man of part Spanish descent, over lunch one day when he caught my interest in this ritual. 'But if ever I refused them and a child died, they would murder me. My predecessor, Mr Pereche, made a habit of refusing them, even insulting them. They got him in the end. His killer Jerry is a hero on this hacienda. Hundreds of our people crowded into the town gaol with food, clothes and money the morning after the murder. And they would do the same for my killer'. He was no doubt mindful that Mr Pereche's cancellation of educational loans had forced Jerry and fifteen other students to 'stand by' on the hacienda for two years before the killing, accumulating anger and frustratión. Most workers carry debts equal to three or even six month's wages, and repayment is impossible since about 90 percent of household income goes for food alone. 'They are born in debt, live in debt, die in debt', said Corro.

After Corro's speech and the end of lunch that day, I walked over to the window to breathe deep and shake off the torpor of a heavy stomach on a muggy tropical afternoon. In the high wind the rippling cane leaves seemed, like a wave rolling up a beach, to reach nearly halfway up the slopes of Mt Kanlaon, a 2,500 metre volcano that fills the horizon. As far as I could see in that sharp sunlight, every square metre of earth had been cleared and shaped to suit sugarcane. Without a lifeline from the haciendas, the sugar workers of Negros would surely drown in this sea of sugarcane.

Among all major Philippine crops, sugar has suffered the most under Marcos. But even if martial law had never occurred, the Philippine sugar industry was at turning point in the early 1970s. After sixty years of access to the lucrative US domestic market, the sugar industry had grown into the most powerful, profitable and inefficient of Philippine primary industries. Sugar usually accounted for 25 percent of total exports and the industry's centralized structure allowed an easy translation of export profits into political power. With large farms, mills and work force concentrated in a few provinces, the sugar industry aggregated its influence into a sugar bloc that was able to dictate its terms to a pre-martial law Congress and presidency. By bartering military base concessions for a liberal US sugar quota, the sugar industry was able to increase its exports to the United States throughout the postwar decades. Strained to fill its increased quotas during the 1960s, the industry expanded production extensively by converting marginal lands to sugar instead of intensifying production on existing farms with improved technology. Between 1959 and 1972, the area under sugar doubled from 193,000 hectares to 424,000, while production per hectare dropped from 112 piculs of sugar to 68. In the process of becoming America's major sugar supplier, the Philippines had become one of the world's least efficient producers.

Although the transition had been known for decades, the sugar industry was utterly unprepared when the US quota expired in 1974. Filipino hopes for a new quota concession were crushed when the United States decided, simultaneously with the end of the Philippine quota, to scrap its forty-year-old quota system and purchase its shortfall on the world market. Suddenly, the Philippine sugar industry was forced into a highly competitive world sugar market. With an America quota higher than any other nation, the Philippines was, in effect, a ward of the protected US market and was, by world standards, a very inefficient industry.

In retrospect, the sixty years to 1974 that Negros spent inside the US tariff wall now seems a dream time of affluence for planters and relative indolence for their workers. Profiting from a US quota that usually paid them three times the world market price, most Negros planters abandoned their haciendas to the administration of salaried managers and built lavish sugar palaces in Bacolod and Manila. The averagely affluent planter of the early 1970s sported a late model Mercedes, a teen-aged mistress or two, and an entourage of servants, social secretary and chauffeur. As soon as their annual crop loan was released by the Philippine National Bank, the less responsible would disengage themselves from Manila's social whirl and launch the entourage on a world tour of Europe or America. At the region's annual cockfighting derby I once watched planters tossing bundles of technicolor pesos, worth thousands of dollars, across the ring to settle bets after a single match.

The planters have an image of themselves as both powerful and merciful. During their infrequent visits to the hacienda, they celebrate their beneficence by dispensing loans and gifts to workers who customarily adopt a posture of craven dependence before their *amo*, their master. Watching a Negros planter make a grand entrance into one of Bacolod City's right places, entourage in tow, is to witness the very personification of pomposity. But their wealth is fragile and based on two key factors — access to the US sugar market and their ability to compel workers to accept wages that are the lowest in the Philippines.

Although the sugar workers were indeed poor during the 1960s and 1970s, worse was yet to come. Within two years of the US Congress abolishing preferential sugar quotas many Negros planters were on the brink of bankruptcy. Mechanized Australian planters were spending 2.5 cents to produce a pound of sugar they could sell on the world market for an average price of 3.3 cents. Inefficient Negros haciendas spent twice as much, 5.5 cents, to produce that same pound of sugar. Although Filipino field labor was incredibly cheap at a dollar a day, it could no longer compete with the machine. As their petrol and chemical fertilizer costs soared with the Arab oil boycotts and their income plummeted, planters responded by abandoning the costly paternalism of hacienda life. Like Mr Pereche, most Negros planters abolished many free services, pressed workers to pay their debts, and began slashing the payroll. By the late 1970s, sample hacienda surveys were finding malnutrition, from mild to severe, in all workers' children.

Long known for their servility and loyalty, workers turned militant and joined a radical labour union sponsored by the Catholic Church. Confrontation replaced deference in daily life on the haciendas. Mr Pereche was only one of five planters and managers murdered during this period. One planter, used to disciplining his workers with whip and gun, was hacked to death by ten men armed with cane knives. Another died with twenty-seven stab wounds. Both had arbitrarily withdrawn the workers' privilege of access to small rice plots on slopes above the cane. For two years before his death, Hacienda Esperanza's workers protested Mr Pereche's cancellation of loans and privileges by setting fire to the cane fields. In the weeks before his death the administrative compound seemed ringed in flames as four and five fires a day exploded in the tinder dry cane. The planters responded with repression. Philippine Army death squads roamed the province killing suspected communists and union activists.

President Marcos had responded to the sugar crisis with a characteristic opportunism. Under martial law, the country's major crops — coconuts, sugar and bananas — have been placed under the control of a reliable friend. With the usual rhetoric of reform, Marcos expropriated the planters' profits by creating a government marketing board, the Philippine Sugar

Commission (Philsucom), under the control of his closest crony Roberto Benedicto. Determined to break the power of the sugar bloc, a group that had opposed him before martial law, Marcos began his expropriation by establishing the Philippine Exchange (Philex) in 1973 to take control of all sugar trading. By simply paying the planters far less than the export price, Philex and its successor Philsucom were able to make vast profits for the regime and its cronies. When world prices climbed to P678 per picul in 1974, Philex only paid the planter P134, enabling the government to pocket an estimated P1,000 million which would have otherwise gone to the planters. As the world market price crashed in early 1975 and headed for a deep trough, Philex gradually lowered its price to P79.50, far below the average production cost of P 90. Thus, by 1976 Philippine planters were faced with circumstances that guaranteed them low prices for the foreseeable future. Unless the industry could develop a new technology that would either cut costs or raise productivity, it was faced with certain collapse.

Although Philsucom's chairman Benedicto declared his support for mechanization, its progress was left almost entirely to market forces. Instead of attending to the crisis in cane cultivation, the regime used its capital and leadership to organize a massive expansion of sugar milling capacity. Ignoring pessimistic projections on the future of the world market, Marcos approved finance for seven new sugar mills at a cost of $40 million each. Sited in marginal sugar areas and faced with an uncertain market, the mills seemed certain to fail. Industry observers explain this seemingly irrational decision by pointing out that new mills were controlled by Marcos relatives or cronies and the major equipment supplier, Japan's Marubeni Corporation, was paying kickbacks of 12 percent, or about $6 million per mill, during the period when Benedicto was ambassador to Japan.

Since their establishment over a century ago, Negros' haciendas, operated as agribusinesses, have been leaders in the search for improved production techniques. Negros planters are the only Filipino farmers with a long and consistent interest in tractor mechanization. At century's turn, a small number of

Negros plantations used large steam tractors for plowing, but it was not until the 1920s that tractors became common on the island's sugar farms. The trend toward tractor use for plowing continued after the war and accelerated markedly during the 1960s.

One of the key factors in the spread of tractor tillage during the 1960s was the consulting work done by American Factors Associates, Ltd (Amfacs) of Honolulu. Seeking to upgrade the industry's low efficiency, the National Federation of Sugarcane Planters (NFSP) retained Amfacs to devise improved production techniques and train hacienda managers in their use. Among its recommendations, Amfacs emphasized deep plowing beyond the current depth of 25mm, to 45-60mm. Since this depth was well beyond the water buffalo's maximum of 25mm, Amfacs' method required heavy tractors to break up hard pan and turn the subsoil. Through its extension work in the late 1960s, Amfacs encouraged the use of heavy tractors in the 70 to 120 h.p. range. However, few farmers had sufficient finance for their purchase. There were several abortive experiments with tractor cooperatives in Negros during the late 1960s, but they only succeeded in demonstrating that farm mechanization would not become a reality until each planter could finance purchase of his own tractor. In their time of crisis, wealthy Negros planters would find their finance, ironically, in a World Bank rural credit program aimed at benefiting poor farmers and fishermen.

In recent years, the World Bank has attracted growing criticism throughout the Third World. Nationalists in Asia and Latin America have charged that the Bank's fiscal directives to borrower countries favour multinational corporations and its lending policies favour entrenched elites. Under the leadership of Robert MacNamara in the 1970s, the Bank trumpeted a new policy of people-oriented development. If the experience in Negros is any guide, the Bank's rhetoric is still far from reality. Through ignorance of local conditions and incompetent research into the impact of its loans, the Bank allowed its rural credit program for small farms become cheap finance for the mechanization of large plantations. In short, the Bank has played an unwitting role in the making of a social disaster.

The World Bank, or more correctly the International Bank for Reconstruction and Development (IBRD), was largely responsible for the sudden proliferation of heavy tractors in the Philippine sugar districts during the 1970s. Through its four Rural Credit Programs between 1964 and 1979, the IBRD provided $76 million on a matching grant basis, ostensibly for a wide range of rural development projects, and 'mobilized' a total of $163 million for rural credit operations. The bulk of the IBRD finance, some $56.5 million under the third and fourth loans, was released between 1974 and 1979, the period when the sugar industry was seeking a solution to its chronic inefficiency. Desperate for credit to finance mechanization, the sugar industry succeeded in subverting the World Bank program by appropriating over half its credit facility for tractor purchases by large planters.

After making two relatively modest loans, the IBRD decided to accelerate its rural credit program by releasing a third loan of $22 million in 1974 with an anticipated disbursement period of three years. The Bank anticipated that the third loan would 'finance approximately 8,000 beneficiaries mainly small and medium sized farmers cultivating between 2 and 10 hectares', and serve a range of rural projects such as livestock, fishing, and dairying. About 75 percent of the first two loans had gone to purchase tractors and power tillers for sugar and rice farms, and the Bank tried to avoid repetition of this experience by mandating a 64 percent ceiling on mechanization loans and an 80 h.p. limit on tractors. 'Reflecting the lessons learned under the first and second loans', reads the bank's evaluation report, 'the project aimed at decreasing the share of farm mechanization, gradually shifting lending to other identified needs in the rural areas'.

Despite these restrictions, the Philippine sugar industry succeeded in transforming the World Bank's rural credit program into a tractor finance scheme for large plantations. In only eighteen months, half the projected disbursal period, the entire $47.2 million was loaned out and 63.9 percent of the total went to finance 1,952 tractors. When the World Bank became aware that tractor loans were rising far beyond the target 44 percent of the total credit program, it moved quickly to 'suspend . . . financing of tractors for sugarcane areas'. By the time the suspension took effect, however, the demand for tractors had been so high that the entire credit program had already exhausted its funds. In its evaluation report the World Bank tried to avoid admitting that its loan had become a credit subsidy for the affluent sugar planters by claiming that '62% of these tractors went to Luzon primarily for rice production'. In its commentary on the World Bank evaluation, however, the Philippine Central Bank pointed out that since 'big tractors destroy the hard pan' in rice paddies, 'tractors financed in the Central Luzon region were also largely for sugar farms'.

There were a number of factors which allowed the sugar industry to expropriate the World Bank's cheap credit. Since rural banks, the primary lending agencies, required land as collateral, large sugar planters could outbid small farmers and fishermen for credit. The World Bank's 80 h.p. limit on tractor size provided no restraint since 75-80 h.p. is an optimal size for sugar cultivation. With prices on 77 h.p. tractors rising at 80 percent between 1973 and 1975, many farmers seized the IBRD credit to gain a hedge against inflation. Thus, over the space of a few years, the sugar planters acquired a subsidized tractor finance of some $100 million, a vast capital by Philippine standards.

There are a number of indicators of the dramatic impact that this massive capital had upon the sugar industry. In its own evaluation report, the World Bank notes the decline in the country's water buffalo population from 4.9 million in 1973 to 2.7 million in 1976 and attributes it to rapid spread of tractors and power tillers. In 1982 a private equipment corporation conducted a comprehensive survey of tractor population in the Manapla district of northern Negros and discovered a remarkably high level of mechanization. Among the district's 87 haciendas with a total of 5,029 hectares in cane, there were 113 working tractors, an average of one tractor per 44 hectares. In terms of cane area, 89 percent of the district's total sugar land was serviced by tractors.

Despite its disastrous potential for several million Filipinos, the World Bank remained ignorant of the consequences of its credit program. Showing its sensitivity on the subject, the Bank claimed, without any evidence, that mechanization had not reduced labour demand. 'Although labour requirements for land preparation have been reduced substantially', the Bank insisted, 'increase of labour for harvest and other operations due to a higher land use have more than offset the labour reduced by mechanized land preparation . . .' The Bank did admit that 'under particular circumstances adverse social effects do occur', and ordered a study to accompany its fourth rural credit program in 1977, by which time any adversity would be irreversible. In its review of the World Bank report, the Philippine Central Bank claimed that studies by the International Rice Research Institute had confirmed that labour lost in preparation of rice paddies was recovered in other forms of farm work. There was, of course, one problem with these sanguine conclusions. They were based on detailed studies of rice cultivation, while 87 percent of the mechanization credits were being used for sugar farming. The World Bank's ignorance of mechanization's impact upon the Philippines' 431,000 sugar workers was absolute.

Tractor plowing had created the preconditions for a techno-logical revolution in the Philippine sugar industry but was not a revolution by itself. Even within the existing cultivation system, plowing was but one of many labour intensive cultivation tasks — planting, fertilizing, weeding, irrigation, inter-row tilling, and harvesting. Thus, the social impact of mechanized plowing was relatively limited.

Even with mechanized plowing, the Philippine sugar indus-try's cultivation techniques remained a model of inefficiency. In brief, its yields of sugar per hectare were too low and its costs of production too high. Vaguely, dimly aware that Hawaii and Australia were somehow, someway doing something different, Roberto Benedicto and Philsucom decided that the solution must lie in mechanized harvesting. With the cooperation of Massey Ferguson of Australia, Philsucom experimented with the MF-105 harvester in January 1979 on Benedicto's own plantation, Hacienda Carmenchica in Negros' La Carlota mill district. The study determined that it was not cost efficient to cut cane mechanically even under ideal field conditions. Moreover, there were serious drawbacks. In order to minimize down time for repairs, the MF-105 requires that the small, rocky fields characteristic of much of Negros be land-formed into level, rectangular fields with 400-500 metre furrows. Until the fields can be land-formed for mechanized cultivation, mechanical harvesting will not be cost effective. Philsucom was putting the cart before the horse, or the harvester before the tractor. Its initiative was, over the short term at least, a failure.

Despite the Philsucom failure, conditions in the late 1970s were ideal for a major technological breakthrough. In earlier decades Hawaii and Australia had been forced to mechanize when labour supply declined and labour costs consequently rose to the point that investment of capital in the design and purchase of a new technology was warranted. In the Philippines the economic equation was more complex. Although labour was in surplus, President Marcos had courted organized labour's support for his martial law regime through a series of wage rises and cost of living allowances that doubled labour costs for field work between 1973 and 1980. Pressed by rising labour costs and declining prices, the sugar planters needed a new system of field cultivation to survive. Through its massive infusion of relatively cheap capital, the World Bank had created a sufficient pool of heavy tractors to power any new system of mechanized cultivation. In short, by the late 1970s the sugar industry had both the means and the need for a new cultivation technology.

In the midst of this crisis, the Negros sugar industry began searching desperately for a solution and found it in the canefields of Australia. The story of Australia's technological revolution in the Philippines revolves around two men — the Queensland machine manufacturer Mick Hodge and a Negros plantation manager, Jose Maria Zabaleta. Basque born and Philippine raised, Zabaleta is the very model of the modern Manila executive – poised, multilingual, and well informed on agri-business developments about the globe. After reading an article about my research into mechanization in a Manila financial newspaper, he rang up to whisk me away in his Mercedes for an interview over lunch at the Manila Polo club, a lavish establishment the Filipino elite inherited from American colonials.

As executive vice president of Gamboa Hermanos Inc., a 700 hectare hacienda in northern Negros, Zabeleta made an official tour of Hawaiian sugar plantations in 1975 searching for solutions to his industry's chronic inefficiency. Although he was impressed with Hawaii's efficiency, he realized that its heavily capitalized style of cultivation was utterly inappropriate to the Philippines. Hawaii's plantations are woven with costly irrigation systems. Expensive full-track Caterpillar tractors pull heavy, hydraulic machines that shape the soil after every harvest to suit the cane.

Zabaleta remained discouraged about Philippine prospects for mechanization for some months until he came across an article on Hodge machinery in an Australian sugar journal. Keen to expand his market into Asia, Mick Hodge had already made his first trip to the Philippines in 1976 and offered a free set of implements to a planter south of Manila who agreed to try them on a experimental basis. When Hodge returned to Manila on a follow-up visit a year later, he met Zabaleta and agreed to supply his Negros hacienda with a complete set of seventeen machines and several Australians to train staff.

'The first day an Australian tractor driver arrived on our farm', smiled Zabeleta, 'he revved up the tractor and shot down the rows, spewing dust in every direction. but when he was done the soil was beautifully prepared. I said to one of our drivers — you learn to do that and I will double your wages. And in just two days he did'.

Still somewhat sceptical about the adaptability of the new technology, Zabaleta ordered that only three fields be cultivated with the Hodge system. 'After we planted those first three fields, we could not stop', recalled Zabaleta over dessert. 'The cane was thicker, and taller, and full of sugar. It was beautiful. Within two years we were farming the entire hacienda by the Hodge method'.

Unlike the heavy Hawaiian machines, Hodge's implements

could be pulled by the medium, 75 h.p. tractors found on the larger Negros haciendas by the mid 1970s. By passing a matched set of seventeen implements over a standard width furrow, the Australian method aerated the soil fully, planted precisely, sealed the soil to hold in moisture, and stimulated growth in the months before harvest. Although already an efficient hacienda, Gamboa Inc. increased its sugar yield per hectare by an impressive 16 percent. Not only was the method more productive, it was cheaper. Instead of using twenty to thirty women to crawl back-and-forth down the furrows, planting and fertilizing by hand, the Hodge planter box with two operators does both jobs simultaneously as the tractor churns down the furrow at 15 k.p.h.

'As the word spread in 1979, the visitors started coming to the hacienda – cavalcades of eight or nine cars, Toyota mini-buses full of planters', said Zabaleta over coffee. 'All were impressed. I told Mick Hodge he was on a winner. But he said he would only be willing to sell if he could market the machines in a package deal that would train the planters and their operators to understand the system'.

With Zabaleta as president, Gamboa Inc. set up Scorpion Marketing Corporation in early 1980 to distribute Hodge equipment. One of his first customers was Hacienda Esperanza. Zabaleta visited the hacienda personally and conducted a seminar to convince labour and management of the superiority of the new technology. When the union representative complained that the machines would destroy jobs, Zabaleta snapped back that it was choice of either losing some jobs now or all the jobs later — a logic that Negros sugar unions have generally accepted. Hacienda Esperanza ordered two complete sets of Hodge implements and its impressive results encouraged planter interest.

In August 1981 three separate delegations totalling fifty Negros sugarmen toured the Australian cane fields. They came back convinced that they had seen their future. An editorial writer for the Negros sugar journal extolled the virtues of the Queensland farmer: 'An Australian sugarcane planter, plows, plants, cultivates, fertilizes and harvests his own canes. In one plantation of more than 200 hectares, two brothers and one helper are the only ones working the farm'.

For two years Scorpion Marketing's sales shot upward to an annual total of P12 million, about A$1.3 million, and staff expanded to a peak of ten salesmen and forty-eight technicians. The boom was on. Suddenly, in mid-1982, Hodge sales collapsed. Annual sales figures slumped to P8 million and Zabaleta slashed his technical staff from forty-eight to four, sales from ten to four. When I had visited Scorpion's Negros office in January 1982, floorspace was crowded with dozens of staff and the din of creative chaos reigned. When I dropped by a year later, there was only the office manager and his assistant left to answer my question — what had happened?

'The local machine shops', he replied. 'They are making imitations of Hodge implements with junk steel. They won't last, but they are 40 percent cheaper than our genuine imported models'. Indeed, within fifteen minutes drive north of the provincial capital on the main highway there were four machine shops advertising 'Australian equipment for mechanized farming'. Elsewhere in the province there were another fifteen local manufacturers. Keen to mechanize but unable to pay Hodge's high imported price, planters approached local machine shops for imitations. The shops simply borrowed original Hodge equipment from nearby haciendas, dismantled the machines, and began cutting out parts in sheet steel with an acetylene torch. It had taken Australia fifty years to perfect these machines and Negros machine shops a week to copy them. Moreover, two rival Australian manufacturers, Bonel and Hans Binder of Queensland, had followed Hodge to Negros and were tying up with local distributors to sell their machines at a reduced price.

Although the first imitations were crude copies, several well capitalized Negros manufacturers soon began producing quality equipment. The best of these, Baleda Marketing, was organized by 'Boy' Ledesma, a Negros planter with a degree in mechanical engineering from a top Manila university. In contrast to the crude confusion of the machine shops which have the air of a village fiesta, his factory on the family hacienda near Bacolod is a study in efficiency. Apple micro-computers monitor accounts and production; drafting tables hold plans for innovative designs; and workers use modern machine tools. Although 40 percent of Baleda's parts are imported from Australia, it was able to market a 'basic' five-implement set for P94,000, far cheaper than Hodge's P300,000 minimum for a seventeen implement package. Finding Hodge's machines in certain ways inappropriate for Negros, Ledesma designed his own equipment, reducing machine size to suit the smaller tractors more common locally and combining several farm operations in a single machine to cut fuel costs. Faced with such competition, Hodge slashed his prices by 40 percent in July 1982.

Tested and found efficient in Negros, the new technology spread rapidly across the length of the Philippine archipelago. Finding the competition on Negros too intense, Scorpion shifted its marketing campaign to the Luzon sugar districts north of Manila in 1983. Mick Hodge himself signed an exclusive sales and training agreement with the planters of Tarlac district near Manila. After heavy investments in Hodge cultivation machines and German Claas harvesters, Tarlac is moving quickly towards becoming the first fully mechanized sugar district in the Philippines. By 1986 human hand will not touch soil nor cane in Tarlac. A small Negros machine manufacturer, J C & Sons from the island's north coast, also made major inroads into the Luzon market. By slashing his price to half Hodge's, downscaling machine size to accommodate small tractors, and adding some bits of shiny stainless steel, J C swept through the remote Cagayan Valley northeast of Manila selling P2 million of Australian-style implements in a few weeks, an unequalled record.

Is this story, then, a simple saga of success, a case study of how an adaptable First World technology saved a vital Third World industry from extinction? Unfortunately, matters are more complex. Although almost every one in official positions, from sugar industry czar Roberto Benedicto to his technical experts, have denied from the outset that mechanization means labour displacement, there are now, four years later, clear signs of mass retrenchment. With its access to Manila and diverse job opportunities, the Luzon sugar districts will make the transition to full mechanization without major hardship. The sugar workers of Negros are, by contrast, trapped on a monocrop island without the savings or skills to escape. Like British steam sugar mills in the 1860s or Hawaiian milling factories in the 1920s, Australian cultivation technology is sweeping across Negros with the force of a tropical storm, uprooting the strongest of social institutions and setting them down utterly transformed.

Not only is Negros a monocrop island with little alternative employment, but its haciendas have fostered an attitude of dependence among their workers for over a century. Unlike the sugar tenants of Luzon, the Negros sugar workers are a rural proletariat without the savings, agricultural skills, or the entrepreneurial ability to create a new livelihood off the hacienda.

In 1976 a Ministry of Labour survey confirmed this dependence. After research in all Negros sugar districts, the Ministry found that 87 percent of its workers had free housing on the hacienda; 78 percent borrowed money from the planter; 43 percent of workers were children of sugar workers; and 40 percent had no skills for alternative employment. Even without this exceptional dependence, such a massive loss of employment in the dominant industry on a monocrop island would create major problems. In a 1982 internal memorandum the Ministry of Labour expressed its quiet concerns over the potential of mechanization. 'The overdependence attitude that permeated [the workers] has become a burden to the industry which at this point in time is no longer viable in sustaining the required rate of growth ... One alternative that planters consider to achieve this is mechanization and this is where some social ... imbalances emerge [which] ... would mean *Labour dislocations*, more *underemployment*, and *unemployment*.'

The steady shedding of labour in the Negros haciendas is almost invisible to the untrained eye. With an almost convincing sincerity, Filipino bureaucrats and industry executives told me repeatedly that 'nobody has been fired because of mechanization.' Or, as Philsucom Chairman Benedicto put in a 1980 television interview: 'The idea of massive displacement of labour due to mechanization is a misconception.' They are statements both true and misleading. People are not being fired, they just are not being re-hired. Let me explain. All major Negros haciendas have four categories of workers — seasonal migrants, priority casuals, temporary casuals, and permanent, full-time workers. With a kind of reverse ripple effect, mechanization strips away the demand for most seasonal and all casual work, leaving intact the tiny minority of permanent workers who are, in fact, not fired.

On Hacienda Esperanza, for example, there was a total of 545 workers before the start of mechanization in 1980 — 200 migratory weeders from Negros' east coast, 150 migratory cane cutters from neighboring Panay Island, 45 temporary casuals, 72 permanent casuals, and 78 permanent workers. Three years after mechanization, the hacienda no longer hired 200 migratory weeders, a significant share of the cane cutters, 45 temporary casuals, and about half the priority casuals. The invisible shock waves of labour displacement thus rippled inward – from the hill farms of Negros, to nearby villages, and to the plantation itself – leaving only the tiny minority of 78 permanent workers unaffected. There were no dismissals but there was a great deal of labour displacement. The workers themselves claim that there has already been a marked drop in casual labour for women and children, vital for the survival of workers' families. One field supervisor stated frankly: 'Once this hacienda is fully mechanized, workers in this area will have only two choices – steal or starve. There is going to be trouble.' Once the shock of Mr Pereche's murder wears off and mechanization is complete, only the 78 permanents and a 100 or so migratory cane cutters will remain, less than a third of the original labour force.

There are already signs of a major displacement of hacienda labour in Negros. The province's labour contractors' association reports that the number of migratory cane cutters entering Negros Occidental has declined from 17,000 in 1974 to only 11,000 in 1982-83 as displaced local workers take their jobs. In 1982 a Dutch scholar, Rosanne Rutten, surveyed the impact of mechanization on Hacienda Milagros just north of Bacolod and found it was rapidly eliminating 80 percent of the sugar work. The Hodge mechanical planter was taking almost all casual work done by women and children, depriving desperately poor households of about 40 to 50 percent of their income. A Filipino scholar, Dr Violeta Lopez Gonzaga, surveyed another large hacienda and found mechanization had both increased production by 38 percent and slashed available work by about 90 percent.

The most disturbing results came from research done by the industry itself. In September 1982, the Victorias Milling Co. surveyed twenty-six mechanized haciendas in northern Negros and found the planters had increased their sugar yield by 8.5 percent and cut costs by 12 percent. Mechanization was so successful that the planters were planning to slash their labour force by 89 percent — from a total of 2,355 workers to only 252. 'One of the biggest advantages of mechanization', concluded the study, 'is the substantial reduction in manpower which would mean much less overhead costs for the planters (less housing and house repair & maintenance, less SSS [social security payments], less hospitalization costs and related costs).' In effect, these planters are shifting their investment from human beings to machines. The machines produce more, cost less, and are not inclined to disruptive industrial action. After five years of paying for a machine, a planter has acquired a capital asset, not a social responsibility.

The almost brutal frankness of the planters' response to this survey is revealing. In their public statements Negros planters have expressed sympathy for their workers and denied any plans for mass dismissals. Speaking privately for an internal industry survey, they admitted that they are planning firings that will eliminate 90 percent of their workers. Once retrenched, these 2,000 workers and their dependents will lose their housing, hospitalization, credit facilities and income.

There is every indication that Negros Occidental is heading for full mechanization by the end of the decade. Between 60 to 70 percent of the province's land is now divided among farms larger than 50 hectares and thus capable of purchasing at least a small tractor and a basic set of Australian implements. Once mechanical efficiency becomes the industry standard, smaller sugar farms will be forced to sell out to large haciendas or switch to less labour intensive crops. The future of the Negros hacienda seems clear – 100 percent mechanization, a world market standard of efficiency, and elimination of 90 percent of the present work force.

Like the nineteenth century Scottish tenants driven from the highlands to make way for sheep, the Negros sugar workers are being cleared from the land. Some planters are already offering up to P4,000 cash to any worker who will leave and many are reducing the amount of work available to starve the workers off the hacienda. Other planters are shifting workers' housing out of the central compound to a segregated block at the plantation boundary. The Marcos regime's 'coconut king' Eduardo Cojuangco has been the most ruthless in his approach. Since the mid-1970s he has purchased some 2,000 hectares in Negros' La Carlota district, about 10 percent of its total sugar area, and required eviction of all workers as a condition of sale. The new workers recruited for his estates are housed in a rental subdivision near the town centre and trucked to different farms daily to avoid any identification with a particular plantation. Despite its vast profits from sugar, the Marcos regime has denied the existence of the problem and refused any support, political or material, to the Negros proletariat.

The impact of such massive wastage of employment on Negros must, of course, remain speculative. There are, however, indications that it may well produce a major social crisis. With 70 percent of Negros Occidental's population dependent upon sugar employment, any job loss in such a dominant industry would have adverse effects. The province's young and rapidly growing population complicates the situation further. Like the rest of the Philippines, Negros' population is young with 55 percent below the age of 19 in the 1975 census. While there were 275,000 people in the 5 to 9 age bracket, there were only 33,000 in the 60 to 64, or pre-retirement, bracket. So even to maintain its present miserable standard of living and low nutrition Negros needs massive job-creation schemes, not an uprecedented labour displacement.

Long dependent upon the planters' paternalism, Negros workers lack the skills, savings or alternative employment to survive once they lose the hacienda lifeline. Denying that mechanization has produced labour displacement, the Philippine government has steadfastly refused to intervene. As this gloomy prospect of mass evictions becomes reality, then the million who depend on the Negros hacienda are becoming vulnerable to nature's ancient ways of winnowing surplus populations – violence, famine, and disease. Battling against market forces that are robbing them of their social role and respect, the Negros workers have turned to Catholic priests and Communist guerillas in a desperate quest for survival.

Chapter Three
Social Volcano

It was a most ironic ceremony. In March 1981 the leading citizens of Iloilo City, historic port of the Negros sugar trade, unveiled a bronze statue of Nicholas Loney, a mid-nineteenth century British consul and colonial merchant. 'It is wholly in keeping with the Filipino spirit of hospitality [and] his capacity for recognizing and revering heroes', wrote President Marcos in his message to the ceremony, 'that the people of the city should erect a monument to Nicholas Loney, memorializing his singular achievement that made him Father of the Philippine Sugar Industry'. The British Ambassador, a key figure in the statue's subscription drive, hailed Loney as a model for modern First World-Third World relations: 'His work in the development of the sugar industry and the expansion of the port of Iloilo was a classic example of what is today called "development cooperation", dedicated efforts which worked to the benefit of both Britain and the Philippines'.

The reigning Philippine 'sugar czar' Roberto Benedicto hailed Loney as 'one of the Greats in the Philippine sugar industry'. As heir to Loney's creation, Benedicto's praise was heavy with irony: 'He was certainly our friend and brother, who dedicated the best years of his life to the development and progress of the sugar industry'.

The ceremony's souvenir program carried a brief history of the sugar industry's origins, titled 'Nicholas Loney: Benefactor of the Filipino People'. Loney is credited with raising the city from a swamp, creating the region's modern economy by establishing the sugar industry, and linking the region to international markets. 'He was largely responsible in converting the island of Negros from a sparsely populated, practically virgin island to the country's number one producer of sugar'. As the progenitor of its progress and prosperity, Vice-Consul Loney was the 'best friend' of Negros.

In the Third World where the present is miserable and the future seems uncertain, the past becomes the stuff of bitter controversy. Ruling elites like 'sugar czar' Benedicto often paint a past full of protean ancestors whose great works are used to reinforce their own questionable legitimacy. The dispossessed or their advocates, by contrast, search the past for the original sin, an act of historic betrayal which made the few wealthy and the many miserable.

Thus a reply to this celebration of Loney's greatness was not long in coming. Little more than a year after the statue was unveiled, the Columban missionaries of southern Negros, Fr Gore and Fr O'Brien's order, published their own critical history of Loney's legacy and distributed 10,000 copies across the archipelago. Titled *Social Volcano*, the glossy photo-essay began with an invocation from the *Book of Isaiah*, chapter ten: 'Woe to those who enact unjust statutes, and who write oppressive decrees, depriving the needy of judgment and robbing my people's poor of their rights, making widows their plunder, and orphans their prey!'.

For the Columban priests, Vice-Consul Loney was the author not of progress but of plunder. 'Within thirteen years of his arrival at the Port City of Iloilo on 31 July 1856, Nicholas Loney had killed a city, raped a province, destroyed all local industry and initiative, and had set up an economic system which insured a life of increasing poverty for the vast majority of the people, and super profits for the rich'.

The Columbans insisted that Iloilo City was 'one of the most progressive cities of the world comparing in size to Sydney, Chicago and Buenos Aires' at the time of Loney's arrival in 1856. It was not, as the statue's souvenir program claimed, 'a small town of around 7,000 people'. Iloilo City was 'one of the textile centers of the world' and its 60,000 hand looms produced fine weaves that found markets around the globe. 'Hardly a diocese in Europe or South America was without sacred vestments woven in Iloilo. Fully one half of the available female work-force was employed in the industry'.

As an agent for Manchester's textile factories, Loney pirated the best of Iloilo's patterns and had them machine woven in England at a fraction of the cost of local handiwork. Loney then had the Manchester cotton-goods shipped direct to Iloilo and sold them in the municipal markets at low prices the local weavers could not match. 'In one fell stroke he had destroyed an independent industry and had put an end to a way of life that had developed over the generations'.

As a clever merchant, Loney knew that his region, the islands of Negros and Panay, could not pay for their textile imports unless they exported something. His solution was sugar. 'Loney followed-up his shipment of textiles with another ship loaded with machinery for sugar production', the Columban's counter-history continued. 'The silenced looms had given him an educated elite of small capitalists and an army of hungry and jobless workers for the sugarcane fields. He inflamed the appetites of the elite with stories of the vast fortunes to be made from sugar and gave them generous crop-loans. He led them and their private armies to sparsely populated Negros round the slopes of 8,000 feet Kanlaon [volcano], where settlers from Panay had been farming small but viable lots for generations. But now they were forcibly driven from their land to make way for the invaders, who bought for a pittance or land-grabbed their holdings, and set up the Hacienda or sugar-farm system which lasts up to this very day'.

Not content with rectifying the local hagiography, the Columbans, with a boldness that would cost them dearly, went on to replace it with a demonology. The worst of Loney's Filipino followers was the textile trader Teodoro Benedicto, ancestor of the modern sugar czar Roberto Benedicto. He 'acquired almost 10,000 hectares along the foot of Kanlaon after 1871, by driving out the settlers by force of arms, killing many of them and burning their homes'. After Loney's death from malaria on the slopes of Mt Kanlaon in 1869, men like Benedicto survived him as 'a small dominant class owning all the means of production'. And under the planters' control was 'a large mass of oppressed people sinking deeper and deeper into poverty because of this one-crop, foreign dominated system'.

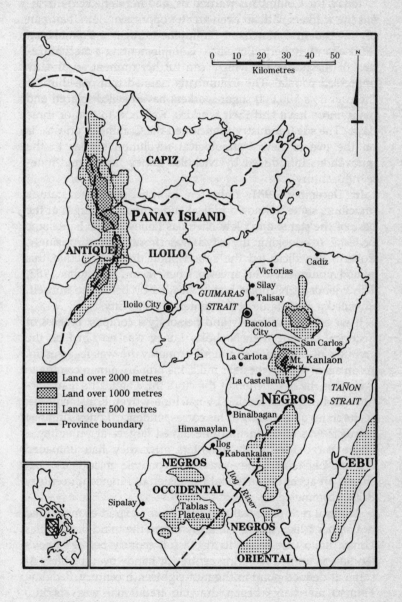

0   10   20   30   40   50
Kilometres

CAPIZ

PANAY ISLAND

ANTIQUE   ILOILO

GUIMARAS
STRAIT

Iloilo City

Cadiz
Victorias
Silay
Talisay

Bacolod
City

San Carlos

La Carlota   Mt. Kanlaon

La Castellana   *TAÑON*
                        STRAIT

NEGROS

Binalbagan

Himamaylan

Ilog
Kabankalan

NEGROS   CEBU

OCCIDENTAL

Sipalay   Tablas
                 Plateau

Ilog River

NEGROS

ORIENTAL

▓ Land over 2000 metres
▒ Land over 1000 metres
░ Land over 500 metres
— Province boundary

Today, the Columbans warned us, another Benedicto threatens the workers with an even greater oppression. As Chairman of President Marcos' Philippine Sugar Commission (Philsucom), Roberto Benedicto is implementing a mechanization of the haciendas which 'can further torment an already oppressed people'. The Columbans claimed that one-third of the country's 500,000 sugar workers have been displaced and many more have had their working week cut to two or three days. 'The sugar industry', concluded the Columban priests, 'is on the eve of new technological revolution similar to the innovations introduced by Nicholas Loney in the mid-nineteenth century'.

In December 1981, only ten months after the statue's unveiling, some unknown radical laid explosive charges at the base of the statue and blew Nicholas Loney off his handsome pedestal overlooking the city's waterfront. Not surprisingly, Roberto Benedicto led the subscription drive to rebuild this ruined monument to his ancestor's benefactor. In October 1983, The Friends of Nicholas Loney, headed by Benedicto himself, unveiled a new statue at the center of Iloilo City.

If we are to so simplify and personify a complex process of historical change, then Nicholas Loney was not, in fact, the architect of the region's modern economy, he was its assassin. As an agent of Manchester's mills, his primary aim in coming to Iloilo was the destruction of the city's thriving textile manufactures and their substitution by machine-woven British cottons. As he states quite clearly in his correspondence, Loney's interest in sugar was an incidental one aimed largely at providing a return cargo for British freighters after they had unloaded textiles. Nicholas Loney was no economic missionary, but simply an agent of the global expansion of nineteenth century British commerce.

Archival records reveal that the region's export economy did not, Athena-like, spring full grown from the mind of Nicholas Loney. Iloilo City began its rise a full century before Loney's landing as a manufacturing centre for handwoven textiles. At some ill-defined point in the mid-eighteenth century, fledgling Filipino merchants began drawing traditional weavers into crude factories where they were able to standardize and accelerate their textile production. Their cheap cottons found markets in China and Java, while their luxurious weaves of silk, cotton and pineapple fibres became the vestments and altar clothes of Catholic Christendom. The commercialization of weaving was a major technological transformation, the region's first, and laid the foundations for a modern economy. No longer a simple peasant society, Iloilo became a city of 70,000 people with wealthy merchants and a large wage-labour force. All of the basic elements that Loney would later need to build the sugar industry – skilled entrepreneurs, disciplined labour, and local capital – had already been created by the textile trade.

The French scholar Mallat visited the Philippines in the 1840s and later published the first systematic survey of the archipelago's weaving industry. 'The province of Iloilo', wrote Mallat, 'is also renowned for its cloth called *sinamays* and *piña* . . .; the combination of their designs and colours is so bright and varied that they have the admiration of the whole world'. Produced at the rate of half an inch per day, the better weaves had 'an admirable beauty which is impossible to imitate in Europe because the cost of production would be prohibitive'.

Although Loney was architect of their demise, he had a high opinion of the local textile merchants and has given us, in his consular reports, the most detailed portrait of their operations. 'Considering that the Philippines are essentially an agricultural rather than a manufacturing region', wrote Loney in April 1857, 'the textile productions of Iloilo may be said to have reached a remarkable degree of development'. His observations revealed a surprisingly modern industry – textiles accounted for over half the region's exports, there were small factories of up to twelve weavers, and merchants used wages and debts to control their workers.

As a dedicated agent of empire, Loney worked with great energy and ingenuity to increase the sales of Manchester cottons. After sending patterns of local weaves back to Lancashire for imitation, he reduced freight costs by arranging direct shipments from England to Iloilo. He then worked through local traders to place British textiles in the town markets. In 1860,

Loney's personal sales of British goods reached $300,000 – considerably more than the total for all importers at the time of his arrival only four years before. Without any government assistance, the vice-consul laid the infrastructure which transformed Iloilo's waterfront area from a fishing village into a modern colonial port within a decade. His effort was an unbroken string of firsts – first waterfront access road, first warehouse, first direct textile imports, first direct sugar exports, first inter-island steam shipping company, first regular international shipping connections.

The outbreak of the American Civil War (1861-1865) produced Manchester's 'cotton famine' and slowed its textile exports, allowing Iloilo's weavers a temporary respite from the inevitable onslaught. In 1862 Iloilo's textile exports reached an historic peak of 696,800 metres. After Manchester's mills revived in 1865, Iloilo's production plunged downward to only 20,400 metres in 1873. Six years later, the British vice-consul reported: 'The trade in *sinamay* fabric, which used to be a great industry in this province, has dwindled down to a mere nothing.'

As the local handicrafts started losing their markets to cheap cottons from the steam looms of Lancashire, Loney convinced Iloilo's textile merchants to abandon the trade and shift their capital into sugar cultivation on neighbouring Negros Island. Loney threw himself into building the Negros sugar industry with the same catalytic energy that had ruined Iloilo's textiles. To encourage the new planters, he offered easy credit for crop-loans and a guaranteed market for their sugar production. As a general merchant, Loney imported from Scotland the first six to fifteen horsepower steam mills for grinding cane, the engines of the region's second technological transformation.

Little more than a century ago the broad western plains of Negros that face Iloilo City across a narrow strait were dense, virgin forests where pagan tribesmen hunted deer with spear. The rapid, almost explosive development of the sugar industry cleared those plains into a patchwork of large plantations. As textile production collapsed and sugar boomed, a demographic tidal wave surged across the strait from Panay Island. In the forty years after Loney's arrival, Negros' population increased from 101,000 to 460,000; its hacienda sugar mills from 7 to 821; and its sugar exports from 48 to 28,750 kilograms.

Like his later hagiographers, Loney rejoiced in the sugar industry's early progress and celebrated his fecund conquest with a joyful poem titled *Ode to the Sun*.

Glow on, thou tropic sun, and ripen the crops
On Negros Isle that grow, and let them bask
In thy warm smile
O! on it beam and quicken every cane
Pregnant with sweetest juice – sweet as the lips
Of the brown maiden whose encircling arms
Oft bind my willing neck the while she rains
Ripe kisses on my mouth! When the long rows
Of purple stalks fall beneath the steel
And yield their sap to the revolving mill,
And bright grained sugar from the Wetzel pour
With crystals, yellow as the golden sands
Of fabled Pactolus, then let me contracts make
And let the prices be tip top – say five and six
Not a cent less, by the Eternal Powers!

The conquest of Negros was more rape than seduction. As planters and peasant pioneers began pushing into the island's interior in the 1850s, the Spanish governor became concerned to pacify the large pagan tribes who still occupied much of the interior. Working through Augustinian Recollect missionaries, Governor Emilio Sarabia, a cruel and violent man, reduced most of the smaller tribes in central Negros for Christ and Spain with a mixture of diplomacy and brutality.

The largest of the pagan tribes, numbering some 15,000 inhabited the foothills of Mt Carolan above the town of Kabankalan in southern Negros. Dispatched into the Carolan hills in 1856 to pacify this large, warrior tribe, two Recollect missionaries quickly established rapport with its chief Manyabog and won his promise to settle in the lowlands once the tobacco harvest was in. Several Kabankalan merchants who had a monopoly on the tribe's lucrative tobacco trade tried to delay their surrender by inflaming Governor Sarabia with rumours of an impending revolt. When a force of 450 Spanish militia invaded their valley, the Carolan tribe fought until their leader was killed and then set fire to their redoubt in an act of mass suicide. Subsequent Spanish military operations – marked by what one Spanish historian has called 'outrages, even abominable crimes' – scattered the tribes and gradually exterminated the survivors. When Carolan became a part of Fr Gore's mountain mission some 120 years later, he discovered some pagan families descended from the survivors of those slaughters.

In the quarter century after the textile trade's collapse, the first pioneers into the forests of Negros were peasants from Panay's weaving towns. They were unable to survive on their small, one or two hectare farms without cash income from women's weaving. Sailing across the strait as families and clans, the peasant pioneers cleared ten hectare farms from the dense jungle. The wealthy Iloilo textile merchants who followed in their wake used capital and legal skills to buy false titles to the peasant farms from a corrupt Spanish regime. Since uncleared land was of little value on a lightly populated frontier, the planters had to concentrate on acquisition of the small peasant farms – by outright purchase of adjoining plots, foreclosure on usurious mortgages at 30 or 100 percent interest, or violent expropriation ratified by fraudulent title.

One of the most spectacular of these land grabbers was indeed Teodoro Benedicto, ancestor of Marcos' sugar czar Roberto Benedicto. With a gang of armed men, Don Teodoro burned out peasant villages, bribed local officials and amassed an enormous property of 11,200 hectares, by far the largest in Negros. In August 1876 some Spanish planters complained to the Governor-General in Manila that Benedicto had acquired 7,000 hectares on the slopes of Mt Kanlaon volcano by 'the expulsion from their properties of poor *indios* [Filipinos] who from time immemorial cultivated small plots of coffee and cocoa sufficient to cover the costs of their basic necessities'. The Spaniards claimed further that Benedicto had grabbed another 4,600 hectares by driving the villagers 'to the mountains with their families where they are relegated to a miserable life'. Since

Benedicto had corrupted the town mayor, the poor had no recourse.

The complaint prompted a formal investigation by the colonial Lands Department in March 1877. One Spanish planter testified that Benedicto had sent the mayor, who was in fact his employee, to evict the villagers, and 'in case the owners refused to turn over their lands they were driven off with violence'. The investigator took testimony from twenty-one dispossessed peasants who claimed that they had migrated from Panay in the 1850s, some twenty years before Benedicto began acquiring sugar lands, and had cleared their small farms from the forest. Once they were driven off, their combined holdings of 256 hectares were a substantial addition to Benedicto's growing plantation.

'In the investigation of the methods used by Don Teodoro Benedicto for the acquisition of lands', the Lands Department ruled, 'there is a criminal liability on the part of him and his accomplices'. The hearing recommended the files be forwarded to the Negros Court of First Instance for trial, but Benedicto used his resources to extricate himself. In the 1896 land survey, he appears as one of the five leading landowners in Negros. Described by a pre-war writer as 'the personification of the grandiose, the ceremonious, the ostentatious', Benedicto built a mansion 'as large as a Cathedral' and died leaving a fortune which laid the basis for generations of family wealth.

While ample land was there for the grabbing, securing labour to work it was more difficult. The Negros planters extended high-interest loans to workers to entrap them in debt which could be passed on to their children. Like *Kanakas* from the Pacific Islands who built Australia's cane farms, the Negros hacienda workers were robbed of their wages with debts, guarded day and night to prevent flight, and worked with whip and club when other incentives were lacking. By the century's turn the Negros plantation had evolved into a social system without parallel in the Philippines or southeast Asia. Unlike the tenanted sugar plantations in Pampanga Province north of Manila, Negros haciendas were cultivated by supervised work gangs paid a nominal daily wage. The Pampanga sugar tenant lived in his own bamboo house, worked four or more hectares as a sharecropper and supplied his own work animals and implements. The Negros sugar worker was a debt slave who owned nothing more than his clothes and cooking utensils. Using their capital and managerial skills as textile merchants, the Negros planters managed their plantations like factories in the field.

The Negros plantation economy was a social system based on coercion and a crude exploitation. An American military officer who served in Negros at the century's turn painted the island's plantation life in the darkest of hues. 'Each hacienda was a community in itself', he wrote, 'a feudal community of which the *hacendero* was the overlord. The hacendero's house, like a baron's fortress of the Middle Ages, stood in the centre of buildings and dependents' huts. Many miles of uninhabited country might separate one hacienda from the next. The labourers, men, women and children might be said to belong to the hacendero, for they were usually so deep in debt for the clothing and food advanced that escape was well nigh impossible'. The officer compared Negros to 'our own South before the war where slavery fostered brutality'. He noted that each hacienda foreman carried a 'stout club made of the heaviest and hardest wood found in the islands' and used it without restraint to inflict injury or death on offending workers. The only alternative for most workers was flight to the remote mountains of southern Negros where Fr Gore and Fr O'Brien would establish missions some seventy-five years later.

By century's turn, there were then three pillars of planter power on Negros – Church, State and Constabulary. The state granted the planters unlimited access to crown lands and placed almost no restrictions in their acquisition by means fair or foul. The state, moreover, made the planters lords over their land and gave them an absolute authority over their workers. The Constabulary defended the plantation frontier from attack by mountain bandits and tracked down workers who tried to abscond on their debts by fleeing back to their home villages or deep into the mountains.

As the third pillar of planter power, the Spanish Church indoctrinated the workers with a theology of subservience. But that was not the limit of its service to the planters. Assigned to Negros in 1848, the Augustinian Recollect missionaries worked closely with the Spanish governors and Vice-Consul Loney to build the island's sugar trade.

Under orders from the bloody-minded Governor Sarabia, Fr Fernando Cuenca hiked the hills for several years in the 1850s negotiating the surrender of the independent pagan tribes who might impede Christian settlement. With his mastery of the local Ilongo language and a certain force of personality, Fr Cuenca won the trust of tribal chiefs along the island's mountain spine from Silay in the north to Kabankalan in the south. If any pagans resisted subjugation, Fr Cuenca executed the Governor's 'barbarous and cruel orders' to deliver the tribes for slaughter by colonial troops. When the governor was finally charged for his crimes, Fr Cuenca committed perjury to defend his friend and was punished with eighteen months' confinement in the Recollects' Manila convent. Upon return to Negros, Fr Cuenca continued to promote the sugar industry by building hydraulic mills in the haciendas and mobilizing his parishioners for forced labour on a road from the sugar town of Talisay to the provincial capital. Although not as keen as Fr Cuenca, other Recollect priests assisted planters with cheap crop loans, corvee labour and moral support. Today the Negros planters still revere Fr Cuenca, along with Vice-Consul Loney, as one of the great builders of their sugar industry.

For these islands sugar was the original Third World sin that tainted everyone who touched it. Both planter and poor suffered, albeit to different degrees, under the sugar export economy. The shift from textiles to sugar produced a marked decline in the standard of living for much of the region's peasantry. During the textile era, most households lived in densely populated villages along the western coasts of Panay Island and enjoyed a mixed cash-subsistence economy that allowed them a considerable independence. While the men provided food by fishing along the coast and cultivating two to four hectares of rice, the women generated cash income for the household by working the two or more looms found underneath almost every bamboo-stilt house.

Once the collapse of textile sales eliminated women's income, many of Panay's peasants were forced to migrate to Negros where they were soon reduced to a life of debt bondage on the plantations. The planters used several devices to burden their workers with debt – lending money at 100 percent interest, giving liberal credit at the plantation store, and then forcing them to sign contracts that made the worker, his wife and infant children responsible for the loan. They were no longer free farmers in control of their lives. The sugar workers of Negros had become debt slaves – barred from leaving the hacienda without a passport from the planter, bought and sold as part of its assets along with the water buffalo or standing cane, and burdened with debts so large that they passed to their children at death. Many of the households that remained on Panay could not survive without outside cash income. Their men had to spend half of each year in Negros as migratory cane cutters, the most exploited of all workers.

The planters had both lost and gained by the century's turn. Plantation sugar production allowed an enormous concentration of control over the region's basic resources, land and labour. Instead of putting out textile work to autonomous peasant households, planters now controlled their labour directly through debt bonding and wages on the haciendas. During the century of textile production before 1850, there had been few farms in Negros or Panay larger than 50 hectares. After forty years of sugar exports, the 1896 census showed that only 324 planters – among a total population of 308,000 – controlled almost 80 percent of the cultivated land in Negros Occidental. While 75 percent of the province's population were landless labourers, a tiny aristocracy of 324 planters owned large farms that averaged 192 hectares each. The gap between rich and poor was wide.

Although the Negros planters of the 1890s were far richer than the Iloilo textile traders of the 1860s, they were now subordinate to European merchants who controlled all sugar exports and finance. As textile traders, the local elite had been dynamic entrepreneurs in complete control of the region's export economy – finance, production, shipping and marketing. As sugar planters, they were reduced to primary producers who now depended on foreign merchants for their economic survival.

The planters' decline was evident in their virtual eviction from Iloilo, a city they had once built and dominated. As the region's sugar exports boomed, the city's waterfront district glittered with the aura of a modern colonial city – a massive row of sugar warehouses, impressive British banks, European merchant houses, Chinese retail shops, smart expatriate clubs, a telegraph office, two Spanish newspapers, and several Lebanese tailors. Despite its modern facade, the reborn city of Iloilo had lost its essential economic dynamism. No longer the home of an independent mercantile elite, Iloilo had become the satellite of the London and New York sugar markets, subject to the vagaries of global trade. Indicative of its weakened economy, the city's population plummetted from 71,000 in 1859 to 43,000 in 1878, a loss of 40 percent. Iloilo was now a cog at the bottom of a global hierarchy of cities. No longer an independent commercial centre, it simply bulked up sugar in its warehouses for export and broke up crates of European manufacturers for local distribution.

Iloilo had become a European city. At the apex of the export economy were two British banks who provided capital at low interest to European merchant houses. The real powers in the region's economy, the European trading houses sold retail downstairs from their shop fronts and ran the sugar export trade from their leather-bound ledgers upstairs – buying crops, booking ships, insuring cargoes and making telegraphic sales in New York or London. Europeans monopolized the import-export trade, reducing Filipino merchants to a petty commerce in personal vice – alcohol, tobacco and gambling.

Although Panay and Negros were obviously more 'developed' in 1890 than they had been in 1855, the region had a far weaker and less resilient economy. The islands had traded their industrial economy for one dependent on sugar production, and were now forced to consume most of their foreign exchange in importing rice and cloth products they had once produced in great abundance. While sugar comprised well over 90 percent of their exports, imports consisted entirely of rice and European finished goods – textiles, steam mills and luxury items. Customs statistics show clearly that these islands were now totally dependent on Europe's economy. Despite all the sacrifices it made to produce sugar, the crop did not repay the region with either profits or prosperity. In 1888, for example, Iloilo port earned P4.8 million in exports (98 percent sugar), but spent P4.7 million on imports – P3.3 million on textiles and P708,000 in rice. Even after a record crop and good prices, the region's trade surplus was still only P100,000. With such a finely tuned balance of trade – raw sugar out, manufactured goods in – these islands could not accumulate any real savings, any significant capital surplus.

Cursed by an ostentatious lifestyle and a fickle climate that periodically ruined their crops with drought, storm or locust plagues, the planters could not save and grew ever more dependent on crop loans from European brokers. In the global commodity trade, profits accrue to the brokers not the producers. European merchant houses controlled over 90 percent of the sugar exports from the port of Iloilo and Chinese brokers had the balance. Naturally, the foreign merchant firms sent their profits home to England or Germany to pay dividends to their shareholders.

A once prosperous region now suffered periodic famines. As early as 1878 the British vice-consul at Iloilo reported that 'many deaths have occurred from starvation' because of an inadequate rice harvest. Five years later another consular report noted: 'The natives having turned all their attention to planting sugar cane and the native rice crop being a failure, a large quantity of foreign rice had to be imported which has caused a great drain on the resources of this province'.

In short, these islands seem to have suffered the sort of historic exploitation that modern Third World leaders cite as they press their demands for First World reparations. Indeed, it is difficult to see any advantages for Panay or Negros in this type of economic dependence. The region had experienced a net economic regression, moving from an integrated industrial-subsistence economy that could feed and clothe itself to dependent, monocrop sugar production marked by mass poverty and periodic starvation. In its export trade the region regressed from secondary to primary production. Stripped of capital and entrepreneurial initative, its economic fortunes would now rise or fall with the rhythm of the world sugar market.

Sugar is an enormously demanding crop that consumed all the region's capital, labour and managerial skills to meet its peculiar demands. Once an island has shaped its resources on the Procrustean bed of cane sugar cultivation, its managers and workers become so specialized that they lack the agricultural skills to experiment with alternative crops. Its costly milling factories, radiating rail grids, bulk port facilities, farm equipment and technical skills can produce only one crop – sugar. As a luxury crop with natural substitutes, cane sugar has suffered an erratic, roller-coaster history of boom and bust. The beet sugar boom in Europe and America in the 1880s ruined the market for cane sugar for many years and still depresses prices, just as super fructose, a corn extract, may do again in the 1980s.

As the most colonial of all Third World crops, sugar has left a string of ruined tropical islands girdling the globe – Cuba, Fiji, Negros, and Java – with a painful legacy of economic redundancy, export dependence and over-population. As the profits flow outward and the sugar industry stabilizes or stagnates, these islands cannot create new industries and new jobs for their swelling populations. They suffer from a crippling inability to find another crop capable of sustaining their legions of unskilled workers. A quarter century after its revolution, Cuba still depends on sugar exports, now to the Soviet Union, for its economic survival.

The Negros sugar workers made one desperate attempt to resist their growing subjugation. Volatile labour relations on the Negros frontier finally exploded in the 'Papa Isio' revolt of the 1890s. Starting as messianic peasant uprising against Spanish rule, the revolt ended in class warfare between workers and planters. The greatest peasant uprising in the island's history began in the slopes of Mt Kanlaon volcano (2,645 metres) overlooking the La Carlota sugar district in 1896.

The movement's leader was Dionisio Sigobela, known as

'Papa Isio' or Pope Isio, a poor peasant who had been born on Panay and later migrated to the La Carlota sugar district at the base of Mt Kanlaon. There are a number of contradictory reports about his early years, but the most authoritative states he was a labourer on Hacienda Esperanza, once owned by Teodoro Benedicto, and fled to the mountains after an attempt on the proprietor's life. Although Papa Isio fused animism and nationalism in his ideology, his movement was above all a class war waged by sugar workers determined to destroy the haciendas and return to small-scale rice farming. In testimony before Congress and in official correspondence, US Army officers later attributed Papa Isio's mass support to hacienda working conditions – debt bondage, low and unpaid wages, and whipping for even minor infractions.

The war began in December 1896 when the Spanish Constabulary received reports that workers were fleeing the haciendas to join Papa Isio's forces in the mountains above Kabankalan. In January 1897 a Constabulary force of twenty riflemen fought 1,000 machete-wielding peasants in two protracted battles, killing 110 in the first and 85 in the second. As the Spanish officers noted in their reports after the first battle, Papa Isio's peasant rebels fought with skill and courage. 'They tried to attack us on both flanks, vanguard and rearguard, cutting off our retreat into the forest and fighting with unusual bravery', wrote the Constabulary commander. 'Even as our abundant [rifle] fire felled a great number of them, they were not dismayed and the place of the fallen was immediately taken by other combatants. This did not stop them from attacking me with greater fury, and with their savage fanaticism they came within ten metres from the barrels of our guns'.

Despite the reverses, Papa Isio and his followers maintained their control over the mountains south of Mt Kanlaon for the next two years and confined their operations to sporadic battles with the Constabulary. As the revolt continued, the Spanish clergy of Negros initiated a subscription drive among the planters to purchase arms for the suppression of Papa Isio's movement. By early 1898 there was, therefore, a predictable symmetry of secular and spiritual allies. On the side of Spain and order were the planters, both Spanish and Visayan, guided by the temporal and spiritual powers of the Holy Roman Catholic and Apostolic Church. And in the vanguard of the revolution were plantation labourers and pagan hill tribes inspired by the spiritual power of a traditional religious figure, Papa Isio.

Despite three centuries of Spanish missionary efforts, belief in the old animist religion remained strong among the peasants of Panay and Negros. Most rural residents entered a Church only two or three times in their lives for rites of passage – baptism, marriage and death. Catholic priests were few and as representatives of the colonial state they were not trusted. The peasants, however, had daily contact with the spirits of the land. Whether plowing a field, digging a well or building a house, peasants were likely to enter the domain of powerful evil spirits who punished transgressors with disease. In this religion, all disease has spiritual causes and the only cure is through a spirit-medium, a *babaylan*, who can contact the offended deity and negotiate a price to remove the curse of illness. After laying out a ritual offering of unsalted rice and meat, the babaylan enters a trance and negotiates a settlement with the spirit while the victim sits by trusting in the power of the pagan priest.

The spirits range from the *kama-kama*, a magical dwarf who covers his pointy head with a large hat, to the *naga*, the great earth serpent who controls a metaphysical cycle of fortune and misfortune. Among the more horrific of these spirits are the *bululakaw*, a crab who lives in the ground and leaps through the sky tracing a rainbow or shooting star; the *mantiw*, a bearded, smoking giant who runs through the fields at night; the *patianak*, a winged creature that sinks its long claws into the womb of a pregnant woman to kill the unborn child; the *kapre*, a ghost who can take the form of a horrible giant; and the *tamawo*, a whitish humanoid that will sicken or kill anyone who interferes with its domain, usually large tropical trees.

Just as there is a hierarchy of spirits, so there is a scale of offerings and spirit mediums. For a child's ailment a peasant might ask an ordinary babaylan to sacrifice a chicken or two. To insure a mine, a bridge or a sugar mill against harm from evil spirits, several powerful babaylan will be called to make a human sacrifice. While Filipinos abandoned regular human sacrifice soon after the Spanish conquest, the belief still persists among peasants that large construction projects which disrupt the geomantic equilibrium of the earth require human blood to propitiate the spirits. In 1976 I interviewed a seventy-five-year-old babaylan who claimed to have witnessed such a sacrifice in 1920 at the inauguration of the Binalbagan Sugar Mill in southern Negros. 'I slaughtered seven black pigs outside the mill near the posts around the edge of the building', he recalled. 'While I was killing the pigs, the machines were turned on and an old Negrito tribesman was thrown into the rollers. I saw him being dragged in by two men and even though the machines were going I could hear him screaming and crying. That Negrito was sacrificed to make sure the milling was good and the sugar would come out'.

More recently, in December 1968 a Japanese technician was crushed to death in the massive steel rollers of a new sugar mill in northern Negros while demonstrating its operations to a crowd of Filipino workers. Many Negros peasants from that area have told me that the spirits of the land snatched the Japanese into the rollers as a blood payment since the management had not yet offered one.

While ordinary babaylan simply intercede with the malign spirits, the greatest, called *dalagangan*, have awesome powers. As the mightiest of pagan priests, they can command the elements, grant immunity from weapons, fly or bring water gushing from the heart of a human corpse. Dalagangan were given the privilege of supervising the Mt Balabago rain ceremony, still the most important ritual in this animist faith.

Our only published record of the ritual is a Spanish account of a tragic incident that occurred in 1874. As they did every year before the monsoon rains, over a thousand babaylan and their followers had assembled at a sacred site near the peak of Mt Balabago in southern Panay. A sacred stream which ran through the site was believed to flow 'always against its natural direction' (i.e. uphill) and thus have the power to carry the ritual prayers 'through the seas and streams of the Philippines'.

Dressed in black tunics and bright red head bands, the dalagangan spent several days reading ritual prayers from an illustrated book 'the size of a Spanish dictionary'. The ritual culminated in a sacrifice of seven pigs by seven babaylan which would draw the monsoon rains across the South China Sea in time for planting. As the ceremony was building to its crescendo, the local parish priest, a Spaniard named Fr Isidro Badrena, OSA, burst into the sacred precinct with a squad of Constabulary and shouted that the ritual was the devil's work. A dalagangan named Dama speared the priest through the heart and armed spectators attacked his escort, killing two and wounding the rest.

A century later, I interviewed an elderly babaylan who claimed that the murdered priest was still buried at the site, something that added to its magical qualities. In the course of my research I met ten babaylan, all of whom claimed to have attended recent versions of the same ceremony. Despite 400 years of Christianity, the blood of black pigs still brings the monsoon rains to Panay and Negros.

In the 1890s, the peasants of Negros believed that Papa Isio had the power of a dalagangan. He carried a sacred *bolo* or long knife, used incantations to grant his followers immunity from weapons, and was himself immortal. One Spanish correspondent who wrote about the revolt for the local press, claimed that Papa Isio had been 'appointed Supreme Hierarch' of the sect on a sacred mountain in Iloilo where the most powerful babaylan gathered every year to bring the monsoon rains.

'Papa Isio is no sort of mortal man', said one of his captured followers to the press, 'and is nothing other than one of the elect, chosen by God to redeem the Filipino people from slavery. He is immortal and cannot be hit or wounded by bullets, possessing a supernatural power which you cannot believe if you have not seen it with your own eyes. So that you will be convinced of his infinite power, let me simply say that he can fly through the air if he wishes and can communicate directly with God with whom he holds interesting dialogues in the presence of all his followers. All of us have seen his aerial vapours, seen God, radiant in his glory, and heard his heavenly words on three occasions when Papa Isio called out the complete holy unction'.

The latent class conflict between planters and peasants of Negros erupted into open warfare in 1898. The outbreak of a nationalist revolution against Spain in the provinces ringing Manila was followed by an American invasion. By August Manila had fallen to the US Army and 350 years of Spanish rule had ended. As Spanish power waned through 1898, the Negros planters forged a brief alliance with the new Philippine Republic. Finding that the surviving Spanish garrison at Bacolod could no longer maintain order, the Negros planters led 7,000 poorly armed hacienda workers in a bloodless march on the provincial capital in November. Assured of good treatment by General Juan Araneta, a wealthy planter, the 200 Spanish troops surrendered. It was not much of a nationalist revolution. The ageing Spanish missionary Fr Cuenca was allowed to keep his parish and Spanish colonials went about their business unmolested.

Shortly after his capture of Bacolod, General Araneta sought to still the class warfare with a comprehensive decree on plantation labour and an alliance with Papa Isio. Issued on 9 December, the decree sought to control workers by requiring all planters to register their men with the local police and issue a travel pass when any left the plantation. Similarly, the treaty with Papa Isio conceded him local autonomy in exchange for his promise to return all labourers who entered his mountain area without passes indicating payment of plantation debts.

The planters soon realized that they would need to replace the Spanish Constabulary if they were to control their rebellious workers. Only a week after capturing Bacolod in the name of the Philippine Republic, the Negros planters wrote to the US commander at Manila announcing that they would 'welcome a protectorate under the great Republic of the United States, placing at once under the safeguard of such a noble...nation the lives and plantations of this collectivity of Negros Occidental'. In February 1899, General Araneta raised the US flag at Bacolod in a public ceremony. Three weeks later, the First Volunteer California Infantry landed at Bacolod to the cheers of enthusiastic crowds. Its commander Colonel James J. Smith, later

Governor-General, was fluent in Spanish and forged a close alliance with the planters' government during his two year stay on the island.

Only two weeks after General Araneta raised the US flag, Papa Isio severed relations and announced that all planters would suffer his vengeance. In his manifesto Papa Isio invoked the 'seven elements' to promise that 'not one of them will escape death by sentence of court martial together with their wives, children, great grandchildren, relations and followers'. From his camps on the heights of Mt Kanlaon, which he called 'Paradise' and 'Calvary', Papa Isio ordered a general uprising of plantation workers on the volcano's western slopes.

With cries of 'equal division of the lands', 'no sugar cane', and 'no machinery', thousands of workers rose up to destroy the plantations and return the land to the small farms of an earlier era. Within weeks the prosperous La Carlota sugar district was in turmoil and cane cultivation had come to a halt. Towns were attacked and razed. Some fifty-six haciendas, mainly Filipino owned, were burned out and twelve planters were murdered. 'The Babaylanes [of Papa Isio]', reported Colonel Smith, 'by specious representations that the lands would be repartitioned among the people, that [sugar] machinery would no longer be permitted on the island, and that nothing but *palay* [rice] would henceforth be planted, succeeded in persuading the ignorant labourers of about fifty haciendas to join them and to destroy by fire the place which had given them employment'.

Responding to a desperate appeal from the planters at the base of Mt Kanlaon, Colonel Smith assigned the bulk of his troops to the area. Pressed by US operations in the La Carlota-Isabela areas, Papa Isio's followers shifted to the north. In July 1899, fifty-five American soldiers with repeating rifles encountered 450 rebels armed only with cane knives. After 'much fighting at close quarters with bayonets and clubbed guns', they killed 115 and suffered only two casualties. A week later Papa Isio's forces launched an abortive attack on the provincial capital at Bacolod. But they were met by several companies of the US Sixth Infantry and lost 170 killed after a 'fierce engagement'.

With the exception of several minor offensives against the

province's southern towns in 1901, Papa Isio and his followers, estimated at about 10,000, withdrew to the vast upland forest covering the southern quarter of Negros. There he tried to establish a utopian community of pagan tribes and escaped plantation workers. His administration of these villages was fundamentally theocratic in tone, combining aspects of both Christianity and animism. In his decree of September 1901, for example, Papa Isio tried to lay a Christian basis for his political decisions, and claimed the power of direct communication with the Christian God. Once after speaking with Christ, Papa Isio told his people: 'The object of the present is to publish the true justice of Heaven and the holy orders of God. For our justice we should be unanimous with this religion. We ought not to turn our backs or desert our Filipino flag given by our Lord Jesus Christ to the just of this land of tears, for which we ought, all of us Christians, to endeavour to resist our enemies the Americans'.

Simultaneously, Papa Isio tried to control his followers with the fear-based loyalty of the animist religion. As he was preparing another assault on Bacolod in 1901, he warned villagers 'that the towns which do not rise up in arms on the assigned day, will be reduced to ashes and all their inhabitants killed, men and women, children and the elderly'.

After several years of relative passivity, Papa Isio mounted his last offensive in 1907. His followers razed the town of Kabankalan in southern Negros, inflicting an estimated P100,000 worth of damage. Despite fears that his attacks meant a revival of widespread uprisings, Papa Isio instead surrendered in exchange for an opportunity to meet with the provincial governor and express his grievances. He was sentenced to death by provincial courts in 1908, but the US Governor-General granted a reprieve. It was feared that Papa Isio's execution would encourage belief in his immortality and spark a revival of the revolt.

The third technological transformation which shaped Negros society followed hard upon the US colonial conquest of 1898. Determined to promote the development of its only major colony, the US Congress conceded the Philippines duty-free access to the American market in 1913, a privilege it maintained until 1974. American sugarmen, mainly from Hawaii, followed the westward march of the US tariff wall across the Pacific, investing large sums to build modern milling factories capable of grinding 5,000 tons of raw cane per day. Desperate to break the ethnic monopoly of Japanese plantation labourers after the Great Strike of 1909, the Hawaiian Sugar Planters' Association struck a classic colonial bargain with Filipino political leaders in Manila. In exchange for mass migrations of Filipino workers, the Hawaiian planters provided capital and technology to build modern sugar mills in the Philippines. In addition to investment in two major mills on Negros, the Hawaiian industry fabricated much of the Philippine milling equipment in Honolulu and dispatched technicians to train a first generation of Filipino operatives.

Between 1912 and 1922, sixteen modern sugar factories replaced the 820 steam and animal powered mills operated by the individual haciendas of Negros Occidental. Under the old system, each plantation had been a self-contained production unit – growing cane in the surrounding fields, extracting the raw sugar in its own 6 to 12 h.p. steam mill, and shipping the bagged sugar across the strait to Iloilo's warehouses in its own sailcraft. But the steam mills produced a crude grade of sugar no longer acceptable to the New York or London refineries. Instead, the planters were now bound to the central milling factories by a grid of steel rails and an iron-clad, thirty-year milling contract. In the La Carlota district, for example, a $6 million factory and its 147 kilometres rail grid replaced 55 hacienda steam mills worth no more than $50,000 each. To pay the factory for grinding their cane, the planters agreed to share their sugar with the mill's management on a 50:50 basis.

While the new mills saved the Philippine sugar industry from extinction, they also deepened the country's dependence on sugar. Philippine sugar exports increased from 157,000 tons in 1913 (worth 15 percent of all exports) to one million tons in 1932 (62 percent of total exports). Of the latter figure, nearly 100 percent entered the US market, indicating a dual dependence – on a single crop and single market.

Gradually, the impact of industrialization was felt throughout the sugar society, changing the patterns of work in all production units – factory, field and waterfront. In Negros, the factories fostered conflicts between all sectors of the sugar industry – planters, millers and labour. As the very richest of Negros planters shifted their capital into the new mills, a once homogenous class now split into rival sectors, planters and millers, with economic interests that were in direct conflict. The split produced political tensions that divided Negros for nearly half a century. As production and prices climbed during the 1920s, the planters came to feel cheated by contracts that conceded the mills vast profits for thirty years. They launched a campaign for legislative intervention that pitted the two sectors against each other. Between 1920 and 1952, the division of milled sugar shifted gradually from 50:50 to 70:30 in favor of the planters. And each percentage point was the object of a bitter political battle.

The construction of the mills also allowed the emergence of labour unions in Negros for the first time. As planters and millers battled over the sharing ratio, the unions played upon the conflict to gather a limited strength. The milling factories, moreover, were something akin to free industrial towns set down amidst the baronial oppression of plantations previously immune to union infiltration. Unlike the haciendas with their quasi-feudal relations, the mills had a proper proletariat of up to 1,000 men. After construction of the new mills, the Negros canefields were no longer a patchwork of isolated plantations ruled by authoritarian planters.

The new sugar mills also encouraged the formation of a radical stevedoring union in the port of Iloilo. As the sugar volume transiting through Iloilo City rose from 2.1 million sacks in 1912 to 10.3 million twenty years later, the demand for stevedores rose correspondingly, swelling the size of the urban proletariat. Denied adequate wages or any social security protection, urban workers formed the region's first modern union, the *Federacion Obrera de Filipinas* (FOF), in 1928. When the Depression lowered all wages and exploded the planter-miller tensions into open conflict, the FOF suddenly gained a mass membership and launched a bold bid to write a new social contract for the sugar industry.

The union's leader throughout its history was Jose Nava, an Iloilo newspaper editor, who remains a controversial figure today, thirty years after his death. Surveying the ruins of their once grand city, Iloilo's modern elite have fashioned a parable which reduced the complex causality of their city's rise and fall to just two men – the heroic Nicholas Loney and the demonic Jose Nava. Her Majesty's vice-consul Loney is revered for raising the city from a swamp in the mid-nineteenth century. Something less than a century later, the union leader Jose Nava is supposed to have destroyed Loney's work of immaculate economic conception by unionizing the dock workers, holding the city to economic ransom, and forcing the flight of commerce to Negros and Manila. The collective memory, like the individual's, is a selective instrument. The city's decline had much more to do with the dynamics of global trade than the personality of Jose Nava.

Led by Nava, their chosen representative, the union membership mounted a series of strikes in 1930 and 1931 which represented a serious challenge to the sugar industry. In May 1930, some 10,000 stevedores struck for twenty days against the city's European sugar exporters, demanding a restoration of the old labour rates. Lacking anything more than a temporary holding capacity at the factory site, the Negros sugar mills could not store their production. Faced with the loss of an entire crop, Iloilo's merchants were forced to capitulate. Nava was suddenly the hero of the masses. Workers from Negros started crossing the strait to join the FOF and were sent home as union organizers.

Encouraged by this unprecedented victory, the FOF launched an industry-wide general strike in January 1931, the first in Philippine labour history, demanding full recognition of the union. During the next six weeks, local union branches managed a series of sporadic work stoppages at the mills, their loading docks and at the Iloilo waterfront involving up to 20,000 workers. At the outset of the strike, the mills met in Negros to plan their response and pleaded with the planters' associations to support the strike-breaking effort. Angered at the mills' refusal to make any concessions over the sharing ratio, the planters announced that they would remain neutral, in effect shifting their support to the union. The mills, however, quickly mobilized Constabulary troopers to break union picket lines. The fighting at the La Carlota Sugar Central was particularly bitter and the Constabulary had to cut through the picket lines with fixed bayonets.

The European sugar brokers tried the same tactics on the Iloilo waterfront but met much stronger resistance. Refusing to discuss the union demands, the export houses placed a panic-stricken call to the US Governor-General in Manila that brought several companies of Constabulary to patrol the waterfront with fixed bayonets. Through the intercession of Cebu City's leading Spanish merchant, some 300 Cebuano scabs arrived in Iloilo to load the foreign freighters under Constabulary protection. Wielding their *caburata*, a lead-tipped rope stevedores used to bind up their guts, like a knight's mace, Iloilo strikers assaulted the scabs and drove them off the docks.

Unable to break the strike, the foreign merchants hit upon a bold solution. If they could not recapture control of the city, then they would simply abandon it. After cabling their insurers in the City of London for permission, the merchants ordered that the freighters be loaded in the open sea off the Negros coast, thus by-passing Iloilo's waterfront completely. The decision was an economic death sentence for Iloilo City. By 1933 only 24 percent of the Negros sugar crop was transiting through its warehouses. An entire city had become technologically redundant.

The Iloilo general strike reveals the industrial impotence of Third World workers. First World unions can capture a key factory, a sugar refinery for example, or its waterfront, and hold the global economy to ransom as sugar freighters back up all the way to the tropics. When Third World workers tried the same industrial tactics from the bottom rung of the world economy, they soon learned that there was a global glut of their product. Their city, waterfront or plantation was, therefore, expendable in a way that a New York sugar refinery was not. If Negros withheld its sugar or its labour became too expensive, then Cuba or

Java would happily supply at the right price. Even if they could withstand the onslaughts of the colonial Constabulary, Third World workers, unlike their First World comrades, could not use trade union tactics to significantly alter their wages or working conditions.

Since the late nineteenth century, an oversupply of most tropical products has depressed their prices to the point that there is very little margin for paying higher wages. Over the past century, the terms of trade have turned gradually against the Third World's primary producers, requiring ever more sugar or copper to pay for the same amount of First World machinery and finished goods. By diversifying their sources of supply for all raw materials – oil, minerals, timber, coffee, sugar – First World buyers have increased competition among suppliers and reduced prices. Thus, if one group of Third World workers were somehow to raise their wages beyond these narrow tolerances, their product could not long compete in the world market.

In an awesome display of power, the colonial sugar corporations had tamed the FOF and broken its radical bid for a new system of industrial relations. Once the merchants understood the threat posed by the new union, they reduced its influence to tolerable dimensions. The sugar industry succeeded in driving the FOF out of its critical areas – the mills, their Negros docks, and the lighters that loaded freighters in the open sea. Unable to recapture the city from militant strikers, the merchants used a new technology, off-shore loading, to rob Iloilo City of its economic function, thereby destroying the union's power to dictate a new social contract for the sugar industry.

Transformed from a militant into a moderate, Nava learned through defeat to tailor his demands to the narrow tolerances of the global economic system. On the Iloilo waterfront the union operated at the sufferance of the foreign merchants and never again launched a dock strike. Building his strength gradually in Negros in the late 1930s, Nava eventually won several contracts at mills in the southern part of the province and used them as a base to launch strikes on surrounding plantations. During this second attempt at organizing the Negros mills, however, Nava was careful in his choice of tactics. Whenever possible he avoided confrontation. The FOF eventually became the largest union in the Philippines, and used its numbers to win some minor reforms and raise wages for its membership throughout the Visayas and Mindanao. But the union abandoned the struggle for a new social contract in the sugar industry, a major redivision of power and profits. It never again challenged the power of the sugar mills and merchants.

The postwar Philippine Republic proved even less tolerant of radical unions. World War II had devastated the Negros sugar industry, destroying most mills and ruining many haciendas. The strain of postwar reconstruction accentuated social conflicts in Negros – planter vs miller, labour vs capital. Desperate for funds to rebuild their farms, the planters intensified their campaign for a 70:30 sharing ratio with the mills. As the planter-miller battle worsened, Governor Rafael Lacson, a wealthy planter, exploited the local tensions and the weakness of the new Republic to become a powerful provincial warlord, the first of a new political type. Appointed governor in 1946 as a reward for his services to the millers' faction, Lacson then broke with his patrons and won election in 1947 as advocate of a planter-worker alliance against the sugar mills. Sensing that the Republic's Constabulary lacked the integrity of its colonial counterpart, Governor Lacson formed a private army of 190 'Special Police' and unleashed a reign of terror that drove his political rivals into exile. The Special Police sprayed the home of one opposition mayor with a .50 calibre machine gun. Another oppositionist was savagely beaten and buried alive in a canefield.

By using his private army to deliver an enormous and fraudulent majority for the winning presidential candidate in 1949, Governor Lacson won a de facto control over the local Constabulary units. With an effective monopoly of arms, the Governor then turned on his original allies, the planters and the FOF. During the late 1940s, Nava and his union had used their political alliance with Lacson to mount a series of militant strikes against the La Carlota Sugar Central. The Special Police had assured a union victory in one strike by simply marching into the mill and beating all the scabs at gunpoint. Through torture and terror, Lacson now suppressed the FOF and replaced it with a series of corrupt municipal unions controlled by his town mayors.

By the early 1950s, however, resolution of the planter-miller conflict allowed imposition of a new social settlement. As the original thirty-year milling contracts approached expiry, the planters finally won their 70:30 milling ratio with passage of the Sugar Act of 1952. Although never enforced, the Act recognized the historic planter-labour alliance by conceding workers a share of the increased benefits. Once the planter-miller breach was healed, the law could now deal with those who had challenged the social order. In 1952 Governor Lacson was charged with the brutal torture-murder of Moises Padilla, a Negros mayoral candidate executed by the Special Police, and two years later was sentenced to death. Similarly, the FOF leaders were charged with subversion in 1951. Two years earlier, Nava had decided to gamble his dwindling political capital on a communist victory and sent his sons into the hills of Panay to join the guerillas. The revolt was a premature one for the island's conservative peasantry and soon collapsed under the weight of a government counter-insurgency campaign. Convicted of rebellion on questionable evidence, Nava was sentenced to death. When he died in prison three years later awaiting execution, the tradition of union militance in Negros died with him.

A century after Nicholas Loney's arrival, Negros Occidental was left with a dubious legacy. After devoting all of its human and material resources to producing sugar for five generations, nobody seriously entertained plans for reducing the dependence on a sugar monocrop. Quite the contrary. When the United States increased the Philippine quota in 1960 after the Cuban revolution, cane fields began to creep up the mountain slopes as Negros strained to produce ever more sugar. All but a very few planters seemed blind to future problems. The province's population was growing at a rate the plantations could no longer absorb. Without some industrial diversification mass misery was inevitable. The plantations were becoming increasingly inefficient and would eventually have to modernize and mechanize to maintain a world standard of production. Once that happened, displaced workers could find no employment in this monocrop island. Without a strong union movement, workers could not win adequate wages to educate themselves or their children for a transition to another way of life.

By the late 1960s, it was becoming clear that the old plantation system, paternalistic and labour intensive, would die before any alternative could develop to sustain the million who depended upon it for survival. Paternalism was, in fact, already breaking down. The planters seemed determined to perpetuate a dead-end industry even if it was no longer capable of sustaining the provinces' population. Without some alternative to the planters' bankrupt leadership, the people of Negros seemed destined for a long, quiet slide into degradation.

Chapter Four
Priests to the Poor

In 1970 when Fr Brian Gore, then a twenty-six-year-old Columban missionary priest, landed in Negros there was little in his background to prepare him for a society and Church in the turmoil of transition. Family and schooling had moulded him into a conventional Catholic. Although his parents came from mixed backgrounds of English and Irish, Catholic and Protestant, both had been raised in the Church and naturally made it a focal point in their children's lives. Born and raised in suburban Perth, Fr Gore finished his schooling in the city's Catholic system. In his third year of secondary school he decided to transfer to the minor seminary where he learned Latin and took the first steps toward the priesthood. In 1962 he entered St Columban's College in Sydney for seven years of conventional theological study to prepare for a career as a mission priest. Upon graduation in 1968, he was ordained, assigned to the Philippines by St Columban's Mission Society, and sent to Manila for a year of language training.

'When I left the seminary I was in the mould of the time', recalls Fr Gore, 'a bit of liberalism but essentially very conservative. I had no training at all in cross-cultural work, and had been prepared just to hand out the sacraments. But I suppose my character is such that I like people. I am more extrovert than introvert. That is what saved me.'

At Easter 1970, Fr Gore arrived in the town of Kabankalan with his suitcases, a head full of conventional theology and a rough working knowledge of the local Ilongo language. He was assigned to the town church as an associate parish priest 'to learn the ropes'.

Lying on the southern edge of the Negros plains, Kabankalan is a sprawling municipality that stretches from a narrow coastal lowland, along the winding course of the Ilog river, and up into rough hills that reach deep into the island's interior. Kabankalan is really two separate towns. As the original Spanish capital of Negros, its town centre, or *poblacion*, is home to a class of wealthy, part-Spanish planters who have divided the prime lowlands into large sugar plantations. Among a population of 72,000 residents, a small group of only forty planters owned almost half the town's cultivated land. While two-thirds of Kabankalan's 4,450 farmers worked less than five hectares, these forty owned haciendas averaging 470 hectares. Residents of Kabankalan for at least three generations, the planters were a closed class bound together by blood, marriage and a proud Spanish heritage. The other Kabankalan was a scattered patchwork of small, five-hectare farms clinging to the barren hills of the island's interior. Often recent migrants, these hill farmers were usually uneducated, impoverished and vulnerable to eviction from their untitled lands.

Like the whole of Negros, Kabankalan was moving into an era of deepening social conflict. Battered by changes in the world sugar market, Negros plantation society began to crumble during the 1970s. As petrol prices escalated and sugar prices plummeted, the planters responded by cutting back on the paternalism that had sustained the island's sugar workers for five or six generations. Anxious to expand their holdings as a cushion against declining income, planters and others of the elite bribed government officials to win title to the hill farms worked by peasant pioneers. Long known for their servility, Negros workers and peasants began to stir in the late 1960s just as the Bacolod diocese was breaking its historic alliance with the planter class.

Like the diocese they serve, the Columban contingent in Negros was coming to a collective decision throughout the 1970s to use their resources to serve the island's poor. Founded in 1918 in Ireland as a China mission society, the Columbans, who soon spread to Australia and America, have always had something of a grass roots image. As a society of parish priests in China, the Columbans had a history of shirt-sleeve mission building celebrated in A. J. Cronin's novel and film *The Keys to the Kingdom*. After their expulsion from China in 1949, the

Columbans moved virtually their entire mission across the South China Sea to the Philippines. Having devoted their youth to the mastery of Chinese, most Columbans were unwilling to tackle Korean and opted for the Philippines where English, a legacy of American colonialism, was widely spoken. The Philippines has become the society's largest mission and today there are 204 Columbans on the archipelago's remote frontiers.

No place in the Philippines needed priests more than Negros Island. Although it was a rich province and 87 percent Catholic, Negros Occidental had only ninety-three priests for 914,800 parishioners, the worst ratio in the archipelago. With one priest for every 14,500 Catholics, Negros had double or triple the ratio of many dioceses. While the older sugar towns in the centre and north of Negros had well established parishes, the Church had almost no presence on the plateau that sprawls across the southern quarter of the island. Today there are twenty-nine Columbans and fourteen Filipino priests to serve that vast area of sugar plantations and rugged highlands in southern Negros.

As the largest and most populous of the towns in southern Negros, Kabankalan became the centre of the Columbans' missionary effort. They staff the main town church, manage a growing network of village missions, and own a Catholic school system that runs from primary to tertiary level. Over the past thirty-five years, the Columbans have become a formidable power in Kabankalan.

Without language training or any real preparation for the Philippines, the first generation of Columban priests in Negros initially accepted their role as one of the pillars of planter power. By the time Fr Gore arrived in 1970 to become assistant parish priest in the large church that dominates Kabankalan's town plaza, many of his Columban colleagues were distancing themselves from the local planter elite who used the Church as a embellishment of their power. 'The enormous extremes of wealth and poverty here in Negros made us all reflect', recalled Fr Michael Martin, the Columban superior on Negros who arrived in the mid-1960s. 'We started to listen to the poor and became aware of the need to study the structures of Philippine society and history.'

The Columbans later participated in such a study. In 1979

Church researchers found that only 1.5 percent of the Negros population owned any land at all. Among a total of 332,000 families in the province, 330 families owned 45 percent of the sugar land, 20 families controlled 60 percent of the fishing catch, and 14 families held 150,000 hectares of lumber concessions. At least 82 percent of the province's 1.8 million people lived in extreme poverty.

A direct man with an Australian intolerance of pretence, Fr Gore quickly developed an instinctive distaste for the town's planter power elite. 'The rich', he recalled in a prison interview, 'want their houses blessed, their cars blessed. They want the priest to spend all his time saying mass every day for their old ladies who then go home and harass their poor maids.'

When he became aware of the social conflicts building in the surrounding· plantations, Fr Gore began to feel the round of Church rituals increasingly meaningless. As a conventional missionary dispensing the sacraments, he noticed that over half his burial services were for infants, most children of poor plantation workers who had died of malnutrition and related diseases. The Columbans, in fact, later retained a sociologist to survey the parish records and found that precisely 50 percent of burials in Kabankalan was for infants below the age of one.

'We would ask the poor parents why the child had died', recalls Gore with an anger still quite visible, 'and the answer would come — "It was God's will". And I would say to them that they should not blame God. It was the planter's will.' Gore is a man with an obvious affection for children. When I was interviewing him in Bacolod prison, a serious expression gave way to a twinkling smile as he interrupted a complex explanation of liberation theology to make Ilongo baby-talk with a visitor's child. His involuntary participation in the slaughter of the innocents filled him with a very deep anger.

Gradually, Fr Gore found it difficult to go on burying the sugar workers' infants during the week and absolving the planters of their sins on Sunday. 'I would look down from the pulpit during the Eucharist as I was talking of Christian love', says Gore with an intense look, 'and see the planters on one side and the workers on the other. And I knew the one was raping the other. By the time I got to the sermon I was ropable with anger. After the mass, the planters would wait outside the Church to argue with me.'

Fr Gore's experience forced him into a critical examination of the Church's close relationship to the planters. 'The social situation in Negros provoked us', he recalls. 'Other people were writing about the theology of liberation in the abstract, but we were dealing with it in reality. It didn't take a whole lot of theology to explain oppression to us in Negros. We were burying a lot of children who were dying of disease and starvation.'

Other Columbans shared Fr Gore's reservations about the role of the Church in Kabankalan and they began a serious effort to extricate themselves from the grasp of the planter elite. After years of reflection and discussion, the Columban priests decided that their services should be used to level, not to reinforce, the town's class divisions.

'The local planters in Kabankalan are of Spanish origins — a head taller and a shade lighter than their Filipino workers', observed Fr Gore. 'The rich sent their children to our schools and the tendency was to make them exclusive. We fought this tooth and nail since we felt it was wrong to have this kind of class division. The high school was integrated and paying for itself, but the elementary school was segregated for the rich. So we Columbans battled the rich to win a partial closure of the elementary school and end the bias. This did not endear us to the local elite.'

The real crisis in the Columbans' relations with the town elite came in the mid-1970s towards the end of Fr Gore's term as a *poblacion* priest. When the municipal judge in the neighbouring town of Ilog died, his family, members of the Kabankalan elite, approached Fr Gore to arrange the usual series of funeral masses to celebrate the deceased's virtues. The judge, however, had been notoriously corrupt and used his office to administer justice for the rich. Knowing the pain his corruption had inflicted on the poor, the town's four Columban priests decided, after much agonizing, that they would deny the judge a funeral mass.

'We refused him a mass,' recalled Gore, his jaw stiffening in recollection of the strain. 'We felt that this man, who had made the poor suffer with his decisions, should not have the Church's blessing. We felt we had to make a statement, so we said publicly that we could not, in all conscience, give him a funeral mass. We were trying to get away from the dominance of money — if you have money you can buy what you want from the Church. Being a judge, the family wanted to put on the big mass to show everyone what a good man he was.'

The family, and the whole of Kabankalan's planter class, were outraged. In their culture, death absolved all terrestrial sins. It was, to say the least, impolite to speak unkindly of the dead. For them corruption and oppression of the poor were a sign of success not of sin. Supported by an outraged *poblacion* elite, the judge's family carried their protest direct to the Bishop of Bacolod, Antonio Fortich. Following the strict letter of canonical law, the Bishop ordered the Columbans to give the judge a funeral blessing. But he could not and did not order Fr Gore to give the funeral mass since that remained the prerogative of the parish priest. 'I was only the assistant priest, but the parish priest was away so I copped it', says Fr Gore. 'There were angry letters in the press and protests on TV.'

As he sat in his Bacolod prison cell a decade later recounting these times, I interrupted the flow of his narrative with an observation. 'Brian, it seems pretty clear to me that you Columbans were taking their Church away from the planters. For generations they have used the Church to make themselves feel moral and righteous in their exploitation of the workers. Now you were challenging their sense of virtue. And you were denying them their Church, their social club with all its lovely traditions and rituals. I doubt very much that you would have made them think. More likely, you made them hate you. Their revenge, in retrospect, seems hardly surprising.' After a moment's silence he continued his story.

Fr Gore began extricating himself from the round of elite rituals to take on the position of Kabankalan organizer of the Federation of Free Farmers, a Church sponsored union of the mountain peasants. The experience of saying mass for the planters in the *poblacion,* the town centre, on Sundays and working with the peasants during the week convinced Fr Gore that his real mission was in the mountains with the poor. 'After four years I decided to say to hell with that *poblacion* Christianity, to hell with being a priest to the planters. Unless you get yourself out of the *poblacion,* you are hemmed in on all sides.'

Fr Niall O'Brien came to the same decision by a different route. While Gore grew up in working-class Perth, O'Brien was raised in upper-class Dublin where his father was Assistant Secretary in the Ministry of Transport and one of the architects of the Shannon Export Zone. While Gore had been groomed for the priesthood since childhood in the Catholic schools, O'Brien had been expected to finish university and follow his father into the professions. After reading a Columban magazine one day in 1957, O'Brien thought missionary work seemed exciting and rang the seminary for the appointment. 'I was attracted by the adventure, crossing rivers on a horse and that sort of thing,' he recalled with an ironic smile in his prison cell. 'I read about people in Korea and the Philippines without priests and thought there were great things to be done.' When O'Brien came home from his interview and announced the decision, his parents were shocked. 'My mother, unlike most Irish, opposed my vocation, and literally fainted away when I first told her.'

If Gore's experience left him a pragmatist concerned with the parish, then O'Brien's background made him a theorist with a taste for theology. Although the Columban seminary in Ireland emphasized the practicalities of mission building, he was intrigued by the ongoing deliberations of Vatican II during his latter years as a student. 'One document that influenced me was that on liturgy which saw it as a weapon in the tool bag of the missionary. Up till then liturgy was developed in isolation. But now it was part of the collective process.'

Fr O'Brien's arrival in Negros as a Columban missionary in 1964 was marked with none of the trauma that Gore would encounter six years later. The sugar boom of the mid-1960s moderated social conflict and the new theology of Vatican II was yet to challenge the diocese. O'Brien's elegant manners charmed the planters and they happily played pious before him. Instead of undertaking parish work which would have forced him to confront the social system, O'Brien continued his interest in liturgy by starting a decade-long project to translate the *Missal* into the Ilongo language. But even this conventional missionary endeavour was infected with the spirit of the new theology. 'I brought in new songs to make the liturgy more Filipino, and closer to the people's needs. The idea was that the people should go to mass to enjoy it and deepen their faith — not because it was an obligation.'

Although O'Brien was making a success of his work as a missionary by the old standards, he found something lacking. 'There was a wall, a glass wall between the priest and the people. We were just not getting through to the suffering of the people.' Inspired by the spirit of Vatican II and a growing sense that there was something wrong with Negros, O'Brien threw himself into the *Sa Maria* movement, a series of intensive seminars for workers and peasants. Founded by a wealthy planter in northern Negros, the Sa Maria movement spread rapidly through the island since the planters supported its conservative Christianity. Indeed, the Sa Maria founder, planter Antonio Gaston, had a long history of organizing lay Catholic societies for the indoctrination of the Negros poor. After the Virgin Mary spoke to him in a dream in 1949, Gaston had founded the *Barangay Sang Virhen* (Community of the Virgin) which taught workers that their poverty was a blessing which would win them instant entry into Heaven. Twenty years later, Gaston launched the more subtle Sa Maria movement to curb a growing workers' militance by teaching Christian passivity — love thy enemy, turn the other cheek.

Despite Gaston's conservative intentions, the movement became an unwitting vehicle for breaking down the very passivity that it was supposed to induce. By simply making workers aware of their dignity as Christians and their potential for self fulfilment, the Sa Maria seminars stirred a subdued consciousness. Once the poor had been brought back into the Church, they would challenge their priests to serve them and not the planters.

Sensing the movement's potential for bringing priests close to the poor, Fr O'Brien became chaplain to the Sa Maria retreat houses at Binalbagan and Kabankalan. He threw himself into the work with an enormous energy. With the help of a close friend, planter Pablo Sola, the municipal mayor he was later accused of murdering, O'Brien supervised the construction of the Sa Maria house in Kabankalan. Through four days and three nights of lecture, seminar and prayer, the Sa Maria sessions tried to deepen the Christian consciousness of the ordinary Negros worker.

'These were a great success', says Fr O'Brien. 'People were queued up 150 deep and threatening suicide unless they could get into the seminars. It was joyful work seeing families reunited and couples reconciled, eyes full of tears and weeping embrace. But then the priests, Filipinos and Columbans, started to criticize. It solved personal problems and dealt with individual sin, but it did not deal with the social sin that is Negros.'

Although O'Brien minimizes the import of his work, other Columbans feel that it made a significant contribution to building a new Church in southern Negros. As long as the priests concentrated on traditional ritual and circulated through the planters' sugar palaces, middle and working class men stayed away from the Church. 'In the old days before the Sa Maria', explains Fr Gore, 'every Church in Negros had a clique of rich old ladies who ran the parish and told the priest what to do. Through his seminars, Niall brought the men back into the Church and unleashed a new energy in the parishes.'

Emotionally exhausted and somewhat dissatisfied after four years with the Sa Maria seminars, Fr O'Brien settled in a large hacienda north of Kabankalan to continue translation of the *Missal* and learn something of plantation life first hand. Reflecting his essential moderation, O'Brien became critical of the plantation system but somehow never stoked the anger that grew in Gore.

After some months of drinking with the workers at night, O'Brien decided that a cooperative farm could improve their lot and in 1973 set one up at Tabugon, the site of his future mountain parish. While other priests were reading the theology of liberation and radical critiques of Third World societies,

O'Brien felt more comfortable with the structural analysis of Fr François Houtart, the Catholic sociologist from Belgium. Although he avoids the rhetoric of the radicals, Houtart is deeply interested in giving oppressed groups 'power through social knowledge'. His mode of analysis, which had a strong influence on O'Brien, taught church workers how to analyze structures of oppression — feudal landlords, foreign corporations, dependent economies and the repressive state — and then teach their conclusions to poor parishioners.

After a decade in Negros, Fr O'Brien was at a crossroads in the mid-1970s. Although he still remained close friends with Mayor Pablo Sola and others of Kabankalan's planter elite, he was now keenly aware that they were perpetuating an unjust social system. With conviction but not in anger, Fr O'Brien decided to leave the lowlands and take up a mountain parish where he could be close to the poor and their problems.

The pressures which drove these two very different men to pull away from the local planter elite were, in many respects, the same as those that pushed the diocese of Bacolod, which includes the whole of Negros Occidental, into an open alliance with the poor. There were two distinct, indeed contrasting, phases in the diocese's approach to the poor. In the decade following the Huk revolt among the peasants around Manila in the late 1940s, the Philippine Church launched a series of conservative unions to contain communism among the working class. Led by Filipino and foreign priests, their Negros branches exhausted most of their energies during the 1950s encouraging the planters to reform themselves. After almost a decade of inactivity in the 1960s, the diocese then resumed its union work inspired by the spirit of Vatican II. Unlike the first worker priests of the 1950s, the radicals of the 1970s were now convinced of the planters' intransigence and supported the poor in a conflict of classes.

The Jesuits were the vanguard of the Catholic union effort during the 1950s. Following the eruption of the Huk peasant revolution in the villages ringing Manila in 1949, the Philippine Army unleashed a repression against all suspected communists. The country's leading labour confederations were outlawed and all serious union activity ceased. Led by an American missionary, Fr Walter Hogan, SJ, the Jesuits seized the opportunity to launch two non-communist unions that quickly became a major force in the labour movement. Most of the new leadership were idealists recruited from among the staff and students at the Jesuit university, Ateneo de Manila. After founding the Federation of Free Workers (FFW) in 1950, Fr Hogan passed the leadership to a young Catholic activist, Johnny Tan. Concentrating on urban industrial workers, the FFW established a reputation for militance with its long, violent Manila dock strike of 1954.

While the FFW was an urban industrial union, the Jesuits' rural counterpart, the Federation of Free Farmers (FFF), was a more conservative organization of tenants and small farmers. Founded in 1953 after the defeat of the Huk revolt and the dissolution of left-wing peasant unions, the FFF tried to offer the rural poor a non-communist alternative. As a landlord's son and Dean of the Ateneo University Law School, the FFF founder, Jeremias Montemayor, was not inclined to militance, an attitude shared by many of the Jesuit priests who worked as his organizers. Funding from the Catholic Church, the US Asia Foundation and Philippine President Ramon Magsaysay, a determined anti-communist, confirmed the union's essential conservatism.

What was moderate by Manila standards could, however, have radical implications in Negros. With the cautious support of Bacolod bishop Manuel Yap, a theological conservative closely identified with the planters, the FFF established a Negros chapter in March 1956. Under the leadership of Fr Hector Mauri, SJ, a determined Italian Jesuit recently arrived from thirteen years as a China missionary, the Negros FFF chapter quickly took a more radical caste than the Bishop had intended or the planters would tolerate. Fr Mauri soon recruited a number of militant working class leaders, notably Jesus Villarosa, a former official of the outlawed leftist sugar union FOF, who had once survived three days of torture by Governor Lacson's 'Special Police'.

Less than a year after the Jesuit's arrival on Negros, the FFF was launched on a collison course with the planters. In an effort to strengthen the union, the Secretary of Labour appointed it to supervise the distribution of the workers' production bonus under Republic Act No. 809, better known as the Sugar Act of 1952. The culmination of thirty years of political struggle by the planters, the Sugar Act was supposed to make the workers partners in production. It stipulated that when planters and millers could not agree on contract terms, the sharing ratio of processed sugar would be automatically raised from 60:40 to a 70:30 ratio in favor of the planters. As a reward for their strong support of the planters' cause, the workers were to be given a share of the profits. Under certain specific conditions, the proceeds from the sale of each sack of sugar would now be divided — 60 percent for the mill, 34 percent for the planter, and 6 percent for the hacienda workers.

By 1957 it seemed certain that the Sugar Act's conditions would certainly apply to the island's largest factory, the Victorias Milling Co. in northern Negros. In what one FFF leader later called 'the swindle of the century', the Victorias Milling Co. defeated the law's intention by offering the planters an enormous P8.6 million bonus to sign a contract which dextrously denied the workers any share at all. Thus, the new division would be 64 percent for the mill, 36 percent for the planter and 0 percent for the workers. The union leaders were outraged. On behalf of the union, the old radical Villarosa began issuing leaflets demanding an immediate payment of P5 million and an annual bonus equivalent to 6 percent of the factory's production. In 1962, the FFF began a twenty-year legal battle for recovery of the unpaid bonus which had then grown to some P60 million.

So aroused, in 1958 Fr Mauri led the FFF on a what would become a frustrating four-year campaign to unionize the haciendas. Tactics ranged from conciliation to confrontation. But all ended in failure. Concentrating on the Silay district in the north and La Carlota in the south, the FFF launched the island's first plantation strikes in over twenty years. When Silay planters used the municipal police to harass union organizers, workers retaliated by setting fire to the tinder-dry cane. In La Carlota the strike became a personal confrontation between Fr Mauri and the president of the district's planters, the elephantine Jose Mapa Gomez. When workers repaid the violence of plantation guards in kind, Gomez denounced Fr Mauri for sending 'bands of terrorists' into his district and mocked the union's ability to make the strike stick. Under pressure from police and security guards, the strike by some 4,000 resident workers in twenty plantations soon fizzled.

A year later, the FFF tried a different tactic by organizing a 'go-home strike' among the migratory cane-cutters, called *sacadas*, from neighboring Panay Island. Despite miserable pay and punitive working conditions, only 750 among the 20,000 sacadas quit the haciendas. It was another failure.

In a tone that mixed pleading, anger and desperation, Fr Mauri addressed a circular letter to the planters in May 1960 urging them to treat their workers with Christian kindness. He warned the planters that 'to deny such natural right to the labourers is a grave sin of injustice which no sincere Catholic should dare commit'. If workers are denied a minimum wage and reduced to misery, then 'they can easily be used by the communists to overthrow our present society, because the suggestion of revolution is always attractive to those who do not own anything and feel exploited.'. Fr Mauri urged the planters to give their workers an anti-communist innoculation by raising wages to 'change our poor and hopeless labourers into self-respecting owners of some modest private property'. He argued that the planters could afford, as 'Christian ideals' demanded, to pay the minimum wage without any real sacrifice. 'It is a responsibility for the Philippines, which is the only Catholic country in this part of the world, to give an example of Christian justice and charity to the surrounding pagan countries.'

When the planters' silence showed that they preferred pagan profit to Christian justice, Fr Mauri launched his final wave of strikes in 1961. They began in frustration and ended in violence. Demanding the minimum wage and union recognition, FFF branches on eleven major haciendas planned to shut down the mill by blockading 600 cane cars. Met with violence and mass arrests, the strikes soon collapsed. Fires were set on a number of haciendas and several were burned to the ground. A few planters punished the anonymous arsonists with mass corporal punishment for all workers. On one hacienda, labourers had to stand in line for up to fifteen hours listening to the groans of their fellow workers while waiting a turn to be whipped or beaten. The Papal Nuncio and the Asia Foundation cut their financial support for the union. Uncomfortable with the FFF's militance, Monsignor Yap evicted Fr Mauri from the Bishop's Palace.

The next year's industrial campaign was a disaster. The collapse was most evident in La Carlota, a district the FFF had targeted for organization. Only one hacienda among several hundred went on strike. On Hacienda Monserrat the FFF suffered a sharp defeat in a certification election. Among 158 workers, 74 voted for the rival PAFLU, 64 for 'no union', and only two for the FFF. On nearby Hacienda Caiñaman 'no union' won a substantial majority over both PAFLU and the FFF. The union's decline would continue until the end of the decade.

Church sponsored union activity did not revive until the spirit of Vatican II infused the Negros diocese with a new enthusiasm for social action. In both its general principles and specific directions the *Pastoral Constitution (Gaudium Et Spes)*, promulgated by Pope Paul VI in 1965 at the end of the Second Vatican Council, seemed an indictment of the Negros hacienda system. 'Since economic activity ... implies the associated work of human beings' said the Constitution, 'any way of organizing it which may be detrimental to any working men and women would be wrong and inhuman'. Property owners were then stewards for the common good: 'God intended the earth with everything contained in it for the use of all human beings ... In using them, therefore, man should regard the external things that he legitimately possesses not only as his own but also as common in the sense that they should benefit not only him but also others'. The document had pointed instructions for the Negros diocese: 'In many underdeveloped regions there are large or even extensive rural estates ... Not infrequently those hired to work for the landowners ... receive a wage or income unworthy of a human being ... Deprived of all security, they live under such personal servitude that almost every opportunity of acting on their own initiative . . . is denied them and all advancement in human culture . . . is forbidden to them . . . According to the different cases, therefore, reforms are necessary . . .'

Not surprisingly, the Vatican soon took a special interest in the Diocese of Bacolod. When the conservative Bishop Yap died in 1966 at the close of Vatican II, the Philippine hierarchy chose a reformer, Monsignor Antonio Y. Fortich, as his successor. A special emissary from the Papal Nuncio told him: 'The Holy Father is making you Bishop of Bacolod to do something for the poor of Negros'.

Bishop Fortich has spent eighteen years implementing those instructions. Rather than confront the planters, he simply withdrew Church support from their social system and channelled its resources towards the poor. Although a child of a distinguished family and the head of a powerful diocese, he has none of the pretence of some from such background and position. I have seen him on pastoral visits to the haciendas, recalling the names of planter and peasant with equal facility and giving the same attention to each.

Monsignor Fortich is generally considered 'moderate' among Philippine bishops, but it is a label that does not do him justice. Moderation midst Manila's insurgent radicalism often means a complacent conservatism, but in Negros it leads easily to bitter confrontation with the planter power elite. The Bishop's common-sense pragmatism in support of his province's poor has, over the years, earned him the undying enmity of the planters. Like almost everyone in Negros, the planters are charmed by an outgoing personality and a self-deprecating wit that frequently wrinkles his deeply lined face. But they also regard him as a dangerous radical and refer to him in private as 'Commander Tony', a *nom de guerre* for an NPA guerilla officer.

The peasants, by contrast, seem to like his easy manner and appreciate his attempts at using Church resources to defend them. Whether bouncing down hacienda roads in his battered VW Beetle or riding the southern plateau on his rangy horse, the Bishop is always on the move seeking out problems and trying to mediate conflict. When the Constabulary reacted to the rise of the NPA guerillas in southern Negros with a random brutality, the Bishop used his office and pastoral visits to shield the poor farmers from military excesses.

Although he is perfectly clear about his anti-communism, the NPA cadres have a certain begrudging respect for the Bishop. He rides unharmed through their vast southern liberated zone since to harm him would alienate many of the NPA's peasant supporters. Hiking through those hills several years ago, I came across an NPA patrol of eight guerillas armed with M-16s. 'Who is that?' they asked my solitary unarmed guide. *'Ang bisita ni Monseñor',* he replied, 'the Monsignor's guest'. Although most Americans off the tourist track are automatically suspected as CIA agents, there were no more questions.

As a non-ideologue, the bishop has maintained a ready rapport among all factions of his divided clergy. Conservatives can decorate the planters' lounge rooms if they wish. Progressive priests can serve the diocese's Social Action Office. Radicals can go to the mountains and work with the poor. Although flexible, Bishop Fortich remains a steward of the Church and sets certain directions for his diocese. Mindful of those original instructions from Rome, he has worked to build up a formidable social welfare apparatus. But he is also a leader of the Church, concerned that it should remain the focal point in the life of his province. He is then something of a clerical 'numbers man'. If the poor are in trouble and need an advocate, then let it be the Church. If a priest like Fr Gore can build a parish of 10,000 dedicated Catholics among half-pagan hill farmers, then Fr Gore will have his unwavering support against any attack.

To guide his diocese safely through difficult times, the Bishop usually avoids confrontation. When his radical priests provoke the planters, he placates the powers by restraining the individual cleric. Once the controversy dies down, the long term program, whether unions or free legal aid, continues. Although he does have long-term goals, he tries to keep just one step ahead of his diocese, moving slowly towards change and alienating as few of the powerful as possible.

'The Church is in a difficult position here in Negros', the

Bishop explained to me in 1982 just as the Gore case was starting. 'There is no middle class and the planters are very proud and sensitive. So every time I make a statement on an issue there is a controversy. The Church has to play a balancing role between the contending forces in society. Both planters and workers are my parishioners. But we also have to be activist in reform of society and political in the sense of working for the good governance of the nation.'

Those who have worked closely with Bishop Fortich claim his office requires a diplomacy that conceals a commitment to the poor. Inspired by the principles of Vatican II, the Bishop is said to have a social democratic vision of Negros as a society of independent small proprietors and farmers.

'You know, you must see my project', said the Bishop waving his cigar for emphasis and interrupting another of my questions about his attitude towards sugar mechanization. 'The Dacongcogon Sugar Mill is really something. It shows what the poor of this province can do if they are only given a chance.' He would send the mill's manager to pick me up tomorrow. Actually, I was on research leave from my university and I had other things to do — interviews scheduled, documents to copy. But it was not polite to refuse. So I wound up spending a week in January 1982 as the Bishop's personal guest at the Dacongcogon Sugar Mill.

The manager picked me up from my Bacolod City boarding house as scheduled and we drove for half a day — south along the coastal highway fringing the sugar plains before turning inland at Kabankalan to climb the bald ridges that ripple across the southern plateau. The Bishop was waiting to introduce me to the factory staff and take me for a drink with the local parish priest, Fr Niall O'Brien. He loaded me with documents on the project and told me the story of how he built a sugar mill for the poor in the mountains of southern Negros.

Soon after his consecration as Bishop in 1967, Fortich began searching for a model project that would in some way help the poor. The provincial governor, the populist planter Ben Gaston, suggested setting up a sugar mill for the peasant farmers of the Tablas plateau, an area he knew from his political campaigns.

After travelling those hills, the Bishop selected the Dacongcogon area as his mill site. A series of upland ridges with few trees and impoverished soil, the area was home to some 13,000 poor peasants who worked farms averaging 9.5 hectares. A group of wealthy planters in the Silay district of northern Negros had ordered new equipment for their milling cooperative and the Bishop approached them to purchase their antiquated machinery for his project. Surprisingly, they refused to sell at any price and said they would rather junk the machines for scrap.

'The planters were afraid that the Tablas Mill would become a model that would inspire a land reform movement in Negros', explained the Bishop, pausing to keep pace with my pen. 'When I started the project, I was attacked as a dangerous radical who had to be stopped. They said I was going to stir up the people to demand land reform.'

Several Silay planters have confirmed the Bishop's story. If he could produce sugar efficiently on small farms of 10 hectares each, then the economic justification for keeping haciendas of 50 to 500 hectares intact would be open to question. Once the sugar workers were convinced that they could prosper by partitioning the planters' estates among themselves, then they might launch a land reform movement like the country's rice tenants. A million members of the Negros working class could win a political battle against a few thousand planters. The hacienda owners were determined to stop the Bishop's project.

In the end the planters' corruption defeated them. When they had decided to start their factory by acquiring an abandoned Puerto Rican mill in 1964, several key directors arranged a $1 million loan to purchase $165,000 worth of equipment. Since the Philippine National Bank (PNB) held the mortgage on the overcapitalized mill, Bishop Fortich simply convinced President Marcos, who was running for re-election next year, to sell the mill to his cooperative. With the Church as guarantor, the Bishop signed a new mortgage with PNB President Roberto Benedicto in December 1968 and took immediate possession of the machinery. 'This is an historic day for the nation', declared Bishop Fortich, 'for small farmers have been transformed into producers for the Philippine sugar industry'.

Unlike its other investments, the Church retained no shares in the Dacongcogon Sugar Mill. Instead the Bishop established the mill as a cooperative jointly owned by the district's small cane farmers and the PNB. From 800 shareholders in 1968, the cooperative's membership grew to 1,929 families in 1979, almost every farmer in the district. Although he does not own a single share in the cooperative and thus has no financial leverage, the Bishop has been elected unopposed as president of both the sugar mill and the producers' cooperative for the past fifteen years.

Soon after the NPA guerillas began operating on the Tablas plateau in the mid 1970s, several of their commanders entered the mill compound to meet Bishop Fortich. 'Monsignor', they said in a serious tone, 'we have checked and found that you have no land here and no personal interest in this mill, so we are not going to interfere'. The Bishop answered the heavily armed men: 'Are you sure about that? How about my dummy, my frontmen — have you checked them?' The guerillas laughed.

Once the financial arrangements were complete, it took nearly two years to move the heavy machinery through the hills and set up a factory in the middle of the mountains. Additional boilers and flywheels, rusting from decades of neglect, were shipped from an abandoned mill site on Mindoro Island, another gift from the Philippine government. 'That huge equipment had to be hauled over rough mountains and across rivers with no bridges', recalls Bishop Fortich. 'As it passed, the people came out to rub and kiss the machines since they could sense it would change their lives.'

Although burdened by a heavy debt from the planters' original inflated mortgage, the mill has made a difference to the small farmers of these remote ridges. Anyone who has ever seen a Filipino peasant sweating down a mountain trail carrying a bunch of bananas or basket of mangoes miles to market for a few cash pesos understands the importance of roads. To haul the sugar cane to the factory the Dacongcogon transport department maintains an extensive network of mountain roads into every village and thus guarantees a cash income for member households. While most peasants pay up to 20 percent interest *per day* on their loans, cooperative members have access to liberal credit at bank rates and have used it to educate their children or upgrade their farms. Much of the mill's staff of technicians, accountants and managers are now children of the original coop. members.

Beginning in 1969 with no capital and no equity in the mill, then wholly owned by the PNB, the cooperative built up an investment of P5.7 million in the mill within only ten years. By 1985 the cooperative should be able to buy a controlling interest in the Dacongcogon Sugar Mill, a company with assets valued at P.11.3 million. As the Bishop finished reviewing these statistics, he made perhaps his most telling point. 'All of that is not too bad for a heap of rusting junk I picked up out of the jungle.'

If this mill is his model, then the Bishop's manifesto remains his *Pastoral Letter on Social Justice*. Published in October 1969, a year after the start of the Dacongcongon project, it was the diocese's declaration of independence from the planters. 'I find it necessary to speak out because of the conditions and problems existing on the plantations in the diocese', he began. By ignoring his previous appeals for justice, irresponsible planters were pushing the workers towards 'those elements who seek to destroy our society by violence and subversion'. If there was to be peaceful change, then the planters would have to cooperate. Citing Pope Paul VI's landmark encyclical *Populorum Progressio*, the Bishop condemned the unjust planters. 'By refusing to allow their workers to live as befits their dignity as sons of God and brothers of Jesus Christ, they debase not only the labourers whom God has put under their responsibility but themselves. They sacrifice their right to be respected as Christians; and their communions and pious acts do not edify but rather scandalize those who should be living by their example.'

The Bishop went on to catalogue the injustice being worked upon the poor. The migratory cane-cutters, the sacadas, are badly housed and cheated of their rightful wages. Plantation workers are not paid the minimum wage and are denied the right to join unions. Land grabbing from the mountain farmers is 'a grave offence against Christian charity.'

'Beloved brethren', the Bishop concluded, 'the position and appeal I have stated here may sound revolutionary to some. It is

Fr Brian Gore in the mountains of Oringao Parish, Negros, delivering a funeral oration for a victim of the Salvatorre sect, 4 November 1979.

The Ilongo epitaph translates: 'Lolito Olempos, Killed by cruel means on October 25, 1979. Photo: Fr Francis Connon, CSsR*

After ten hours of cutting cane in the fields of Hacienda Esperanza on Negros Island these two migratory workers, in their physical prime, have earned US $2.25. *Photo: Alfred W. McCoy*

Central La Carlota, the second largest sugar mill on Negros, was the scene of violent confrontations between Philippine Constabulary and the NFSW, a Church supported labour union in 1982. *Photo: Alfred W. McCoy*

Family collecting cane points for planting, Hacienda Consuelo, La Carlota District, in January 1982. For 12 hours work under the sun by three family members they will earn about US $2.00. *Photo: Alfred W. McCoy*

With a near mechanical precision, disciplined teams of women workers move down the rows weeding the young sugar cane of La Carlota district on Negros Island in February 1983. Although their piece-work wages are only US $1.00 for a day of hard labour, they cannot compete with the new tractor-drawn machines introduced from Australia in the early 1980s. *Photo: Alfred W. McCoy*

On the slopes of Mt Kanlaon volcano in the La Carlota district of Negros Island a solitary tractor now does the work of hundreds of plantation laborers. By plowing, planting and cultivating the cane with precision, these Australian machines have slashed costs and raised sugar production. They are also fast eliminating 90 percent of the jobs for the million Negros poor who depend upon the plantations for survival. *Photo: Alfred W. McCoy*

The mansion of the manager and the hovel of his workers on Hacienda Esperanza in the La Carlota district, Negros Island. From the day the manager was murdered by a labourer named Jerry de la Cruz in 1981, the shotgun guard at the mansion gate has been doubled.

Only 100 metres and a world away, the plantation's cane cutters (right) sleep ten to a room on the floor of an old wooden barracks. Photo: Alfred W. McCoy

In an April 1984 demonstration in Negros, this placard shows the Philippines as Christ crucified with nails labelled PDA (Preventive Detention Act) and 'Amendment 6': the constitutional provision that allows President Marcos to rule by decree. Photo: Tom Fawthrop

Loading cut sugar cane onto a rail wagon, Hacienda Esperanza, La Carlota district, Negros in January 1983. For ten hours of cutting and loading cane, this cane cutter, called a sacada, will earn about US $1.50. Photo: Alfred W. McCoy

In the continuing conflict of Church and State in the Philippines, Negros Bishop Antonio Fortich meets with the Constabulary's provincial commander, Colonel Francisco Agudon, to discuss the case of the Negros Nine in 1983. *Photo: Interim Media*

The trial of the Negros Nine begins in May 1983 with hearings for bail in the Kabankalan regional court, Judge Emilio Legaspi presiding. While priests and nuns crowd the court and thousands demonstrate outside, Fr Niall O'Brien takes the stand. *Photo: Interim Media*

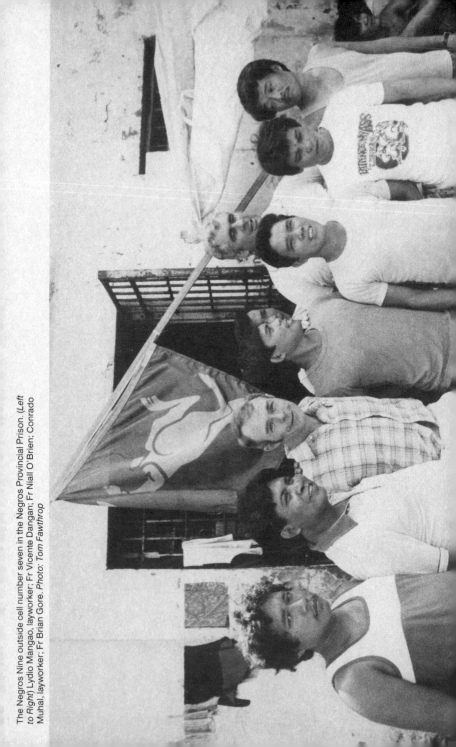

The Negros Nine outside cell number seven in the Negros Provincial Prison. (*Left to Right*) Lydio Mangao, layworker; Fr Vicente Dangan; Fr Niall O'Brien; Conrado Muhal, layworker; Fr Brian Gore. *Photo: Tom Fawthrop*

Demonstration demanding a speedy trial for the Negros Nine, Bacolod City, Negros Occidental, March 1984. To the left are the walls of Bacolod provincial prison and at the rear is the cell where Fr Gore and his co-accused are held.

Photo: Fr Francis Connon, CSsR

A victory and farewell visit to Oringao Parish, Kabankalan by (*left to right*) Fr Gore, Fr O'Brien and Fr Dangan on 5 July 1984 after dismissal of murder charges against them. *Photo: Tom Fawthrop*

Triumphal return to Tabugon Parish, Kabankalan for (*left to right*) Fr O'Brien, Bishop Antonio Fortich (with cigar) and Columban Superior Fr Michael Martin on 5 July 1984 after dismissal of multiple-murder charges against the Negros Nine.
Photo: Tom Fawthrop

Demonstration at Bacolod City, Negros in May 1984 with banner honouring popular leaders executed by the Philippine military – Senator Benigno Aquino, opposition leader; Macling Dulag, Luzon tribal chief; Dr Bobby de la Paz, village health worker; and Edgar Jopson, Communist Party chairman. *Photo: Tom Fawthrop*

May Day 1984, Bacolod City, Negros. Cultural performance by supporters of the National Federation of Sugar Workers before banner reading 'True Unionism!' *Photo: Tom Fawthrop.*

Fr Conrado Balweg, SVD, on patrol with New People's Army guerillas, northern Luzon, Philippines, April 1984. *Photo: Laida Lim Perez, Veritas.*

not so; I merely reiterate the clear teaching of the Church. Let no one be afraid of change or reform; they are needed so justice and love may permeate our society.'

The author of this *Pastoral Letter* and the Bishop's agent for implementing his agenda for reform was the young radical Fr Luis Jalandoni. Child of an old Negros planter family, Fr Jalandoni was a brilliant seminarian and had won the privilege of advanced theological studies in Europe during the 1960s. There he imbibed the ferment of the new spirit in the Church which later crystallized as the theology of liberation. Instead of finishing his degree and earning a ticket to rapid advancement through the hierarchy, Fr Jalandoni returned home to play a catalytic role in shaping new directions for the Philippine Church. On the national level, he founded the radical Christians for National Liberation and was a leading participant in a Marxist-Christian dialogue with the new, Maoist-line Communist Party.

Fr Jalandoni's impact on his local diocese was more profound and lasting. For several years he was Bishop Fortich's close advisor on social questions and, as evidenced by the 1969 *Pastoral Letter*, encouraged him towards a more committed position. He became something of a role model for the younger priests. When money was needed to aid his farmers in a land grabbing case, Fr Jalandoni sold his share in the family hacienda. No member of the planter class, clergy or laity, had ever given up their lands before. As director of the diocese's Social Action Office, he revived the Church's union work. More importantly, he forced seminarians and young priests to confront social issues by encouraging their involvement in his projects. Although softly spoken and of a mild personal presence, Fr Jalandoni's moral example and intellect made him a charismatic figure among the Negros clergy.

Many of the Columban missionaries retain a respect for Fr Jalandoni that borders on reverence. 'He was a pioneer in the church, a John the Baptist figure who inspired us all', recalls the Columban superior Fr Michael Martin. 'He made all us Ministers of the Gospel ask ourselves if we were willing to suffer with the people. Luis was an idol to the priests. I don't want to canonize the guy, but he made decisions that broke the cultural mould — he sold his lands and gave up his chance to study in Europe for higher degrees.'

Inspired by these new theologies, the Church was reaching to the poor at a time when they needed an advocate. By the late 1960s Negros was heading into a period of perpetual crisis. Pressed to fill an expanded US sugar quota after the Cuban revolution of 1960, cane fields began creeping up the mountain slopes to dispossess small farmers. The province's rising population was beginning to squeeze the living standards of both rich and poor.

'When I arrived in Negros in 1970', recalls Fr Gore, 'the hacienda system was already breaking down. A century of sugar had impoverished the people, ruined the forests and destroyed the soil. Sugar takes all the nutrients and the soil had no living organic matter. Only expensive imported fertilizers kept the cane coming up every year. The new generation of planters were more greedy than their fathers or grandfathers. If father had 100 hectares and five or six kids, then each child wound up with only 10 or 15 or 20 hectares — not much more than a peasant. But the children want to maintain the parents' life style. So they screw down the wages of their workers.'

In October 1969, only ten days after publication of the Bishop's *Pastoral Letter*, the plight of the sugar workers exploded into national controversy. After spending his summer vacation working among the Negros cane cutters, Fr Arsenio Jesena, SJ, then a professor at Ateneo University in Manila, published an article in the Manila press, 'The Sacadas of Sugarland'. In its understated style, the article imprinted an image of total exploitation upon the national consciousness. For spending twelve hours under a tropical sun to cut and load 1.5 tons of cane, the sacada was nominally paid about P.2.50, roughly the minimum wage for an eight-hour day. By requiring the sacadas to buy their food from his canteen and then both overcharging and padding their accounts, the labour contractor would reduce their daily income to P.1.00. 'As the day ends, the sacadas slowly drag their way back through the canefields and dusty roads. As they walk on, a cloud of dust would be kicked up by an occasional Mercedes-Benz zooming past as the *hacendero* hurries to an appointment in Bacolod.' At the end of six months under the sun, most sacadas returned home with P30.00 in their pockets, about $10.00.

The problem, Fr Jesena argued, was not the contractor but the planter, the *hacendero*. 'One can, for instance, isolate the case of a well-known hacendero and point out how he goes to Cebu for a cockfight and loses P120,000 there in one day, how he keeps a harem of teen-aged prostitutes in his Bacolod "office", and how his farm is a constant hot bed of violence and labour problems.' Thinking over these contradictions, Fr Jesena reached a surprising conclusion for a moderate Jesuit: 'I saw the injustice of it all, and I began to understand why the communists are communists.'

To still the storm of controversy, the National Federation of Sugarcane Planters hired a Jesuit to catch a Jesuit. With a grant of P97,000 from the planters, Fr Frank Lynch, SJ, director of the Ateneo's Institute of Philippine Culture, produced a report on the Negros plantations that local clergy dismissed as 'sugar-coated whitewash'. By a selective presentation of his team's survey data, Fr Lynch mustered a weak defence of the planters. For example, he argued that only 5 per cent of planters own more than 100 hectares. Yes, rebutted an FFF union officer, but that 5 percent of planters also owns 80 percent of the province's sugar land, a more revealing statistic. The attempted obfuscation of Fr Lynch, SJ, did little to blunt the impact of work by Fr Jesena, SJ.

Within months after the publication of Fr Jesena's article, Bishop Cornelius de Wit of Antique, the Panay province that is home to most sacadas, launched 'Project *Contractista* Elimination'. In an attempt to end the dominance of exploitative contractors, Bishop de Wit used P67,000 of Church funds to make his diocese the province's largest labour contractor. In his haste, however, the Bishop started too late in the season and did not prepare his program properly. By the time his project was underway, only inexperienced sacadas remained in Antique and only marginal haciendas were left in Negros. The project collapsed in a total loss when the Bishop's sacadas defaulted on their advances and fled without finishing the season.

While Bishop de Wit struggled with the sacada problem, Fr Jalandoni was unexpectedly confronted with his diocese's first major case of land grabbing. In May 1970 a group of eighteen settlers from the mountains of Cadiz City in northern Negros called at the Catholic Social Action Office in the provincial capital to complain that they were being driven off their land by the local mayor. Accompanied by heavily armed police, Mayor Heracleo Villacin had marched into their village, bulldozed their houses and drove them off their land at gunpoint. Subsequent research at the Forestry Division in Manila revealed that the Mayor's family had filed a claim for 144 hectares in that village by certifying that it was 'free from squatters'.

The people were determined to fight for the land they had worked for twenty years, but were afraid to press the case while remaining within reach of the Cadiz police. After consulting with lawyers at the diocesan Legal Aid Office, Fr Jalandoni decided to lead an exodus from the mountains. Hiking at night to avoid the police patrols, Fr Jalandoni and five Catholic student activists led the villagers on a long march out of the hills. By nightfall of the next day, the forty dispossessed were dining in the Bishop's Palace and safely housed in the diocesan seminary.

Using Church contacts in Manila, Fr Jalandoni mounted a media campaign that made the 'Cadiz case' a national scandal. Defence Minister Juan Ponce Enrile issued a formal statement saying that the mayor's land grabbing was illegal. Other high officials made similarly sympathetic noises.

But the Mayor was evidently determined to restore his family's declining fortunes. Five days after the exodus, two elderly women who had sheltered the dispossessed told a Bacolod radio station that the Mayor's police were threatening to murder any who tried to return to their land. Several weeks later, the two women, one aged eighty and the other fifty, were found hacked to death. Cadiz police investigated the incident and Mayor Villacin announced it was 'purely robbery killing'.

Despite protests and public outrage, nothing happened. The murders were not investigated and Mayor Villacin, backed by his municipal police, kept the land he had grabbed at gunpoint. Defence Secretary Enrile might denounce the land grabbing but he did nothing. 'The Cadiz land disputes could be a real occasion for restoring faith in our government and our democratic processes *if our leaders will act decisively with real concern for justice and truth'* wrote Fr Jalandoni in frustration. 'This is an occasion for Christian witness, with its risks, with its potential for growth in faith and practical love for others as exemplified by Christ.'

Fr Jalandoni evidently regarded the Cadiz case as a crucial test of the government's integrity. But when the publicity faded, officials turned their attention to other sensations, leaving Mayor Villacin in his new hacienda and the people in Bacolod City. Fr Jalandoni sold his own lands to support them and fight the case. In the end nothing changed. His funds were exhausted and the people were still landless.

Those priests who know Fr Jalandoni well claim that it was the Cadiz case that embittered him towards the government and pushed him towards rebellion. Indeed, his own commentary on the case written two years before he went underground seems confirmation. 'Is this community willing to reinforce the ranks of those who are depriving their brother citizens of the basic right to a share in life and liberty?' he asked. 'The force is sometimes subtle. Sometimes brazen. For those who are willing to examine the evidence, the elements of force are here present. This force will continue and will grow as long as enough citizens allow it to continue unchallenged'. The time would come when Fr Jalandoni would meet force with force.

Like the Cadiz hill farmers, the plantation workers of Victorias district turned to the Church for help and drew the priests into their struggle. As a cost-cutting measure, Victorias Milling Co. forced the field workers on its haciendas to switch from a daily wage to piece-work labour, a de-facto pay cut. Before introducing the scheme, the mill had organized a company union, called PAICLU, to forestall any industrial action. When the new union predictably failed to act on the workers' complaints, several spoke with the mill's chaplain, Fr Luis Iriarte, about this new hardship. The priest preached a strong sermon about workers' rights and was summarily transferred when the company management complained to his order's superior. Before his departure, however, Fr Iriarte urged the workers to continue the struggle by joining the Federation of Free Farmers (FFF).

Only recently revived after a decade's hibernation, the FFF leadership agreed to organize the Victorias workers only if they would willingly participate in a series of labour education seminars. As attendance swelled from only nine workers on the first Sunday to 150 on the third, management intensified its anti-union pressure — requiring Sunday field work, cutting rice rations for seminar participants, and summarily sacking suspected unionists. After several FFF members were fired for refusing to affiliate with the company union, workers from three haciendas approached Bishop Fortich and asked him to intercede. Management replied that it was a dispute between two rival unions and refused to meet with the Bishop.

In August 1971 the FFF declared a strike at the Victorias haciendas, demanding union recognition and an end to the use of piece-work labor to reduce wages below the legal minimum. Citing alleged terrorist attacks in Manila, President Marcos had recently suspended the writ of *habeus corpus*, giving Victorias municipal police the right of summary arrest. Strikers were held for days without charges. Others were pressured with threats of dismissal or coaxed into the rival union by management promises of increased wages. The strike soon collapsed, providing clergy with another example of how the powerful in Negros could bend the law to exploit the poor.

Such confrontation with an ugly social reality did not discourage the progressive priests. Repression confirmed their conviction that Negros was, in the words of Fr Antonio Lambino, a 'structural sin'. The blatant use of force redoubled the diocese's determination to do something for its sugar workers. Within the space of little more than a year, representative poor from each of the province's main areas of employment — hill farmers, cane cutters and plantation workers — had come to the Church with their problems and given its priests a crash-course in the sociology of sugar. The disastrous sacada campaign of 1970 had taught the priests that understanding and analysis were critical for success. Thus, in 1971 the activist priests of Negros stopped to reflect before launching a comprehensive campaign to absolve their society of structural sin. In a series of papers prepared for 'Sugar Awareness Week' in September 1971, the priests of Negros produced a trenchant critique of their society and suggested reforms that ranged from moderate to revolutionary. Theirs was a unique fusion of theology and sociology.

Based on a week-long 'summer workcamp' at a local hacienda, eleven seminarians presented an angry, disillusioned assessment of their own society. A careful survey of income and expenditures revealed that 'the labourers' wages cannot meet their basic necessities'. By toiling in the sun alongside the workers, the students gained their confidence and lost their own 'many wonderful ideas about work'. Children went to sleep hungry, hacienda housing was miserable and the overseer used every trick to cheat the workers of their wages. 'Yes, Lady Poverty could be the sweet bride of a St Francis, but what we had seen disgusted us.'

With drama and teach-in before the hacienda workers, the seminarians drove home the recurrent theme of 'the Christian duty to stand up for and demand their rights'. At the start of these sessions, the workers thought of God as 'someone over and above them; one who is not present in history. They resign to their fate supposedly sent from above and hence they do not bother to overcome their present deplorable condition.'

By the end of the students' stay, the workers were aroused enough to request a dialogue with the owner. Although the owner sat patiently while his labourers voiced out their complaints, the overseer marched into the session half drunk. Brandishing a pistol and waving a list of the many workers who owed him money, the overseer forced them all into silence.

'We cannot overstate the degeneration, the sinfulness of the very structures', concluded the seminarians. 'Structural violence exists, and it impedes man from reaching full development as a human being . . . The Church has to become an institution of socio-critical freedom. In order to assume this task, the Church will have to undergo a radical metamorphosis.'

On a spectrum that ranged from reformist to revolutionary,

the analysis of Fr Ed Garcia, SJ laid claim to the left wing. By encouraging an historic dependence on access to the US market and absorbing capital which might otherwise develop Philippine industries, sugar was 'a servant of American neo-colonialism'. Despite its high profits for the past half-century, the sugar bloc had not invested in either industry or alternative crops. There were two key reasons why sugar is, in fact, a barrier to industrialization. An erratic world market and an inevitable expiration of the Laurel-Langley Treaty with the US means that sugar is not a reliable source of capital over the long term. Secondly, 'prices of agricultural products tend to go lower over the years while prices of industrial products tend to increase'. The sugar magnates seemed determined to perpetuate this system of exploitation. 'They want us to keep exporting sugar, forever hoping and forever working for the extension of the neo-colonial Laurel-Langley Treaty.'

Fr Garcia concluded his historical critique of the sugar industry with a call for revolution. 'Can we, the people, tolerate any longer the oppressive structures that have led to the depersonalization and dispossession of countless Filipinos? Can we achieve the total liberation of the whole man unless we realize a rapid and radical social revolution?'

In his discussion of a social action program for the Bacolod diocese, Fr Luis Jalandoni presented a program that was still surprisingly reformist. 'Every aspect of life [in Negros] is marked and affected by the great gap between rich and poor, between the politically powerful and the politically powerless. Such a situation as we now have contradicts the brotherhood professed by us Christians as basic to our faith; it contradicts the Eucharist.' The diocese's social action program should not treat the symptoms by sticking band-aids on the victims of this structure, but should 'serve the people by working to change the unjust structure'. Instead of setting up its own organizations as it had done in the past, the Church should support 'both financially and morally' the workers' own unions such as the FFF. This suggestion was to become a blueprint for action.

Although the most moderate in tone, the 'social democratic' analysis by Fr Antonio Ledesma, SJ had, over the short term, the most radical implications. He called for the conscientization of the workers to make them 'aware of their social and political rights', and denounced the 'private armies and political dynasties' who denied workers those very rights. Unless those in charge of the sugar industry allowed 'free labour unionism and its sharing of social responsibility' then there would be 'class war' on Negros. Indicative of these tumultuous times, Fr Ledesma was implicitly attacking his own father, Oscar Ledesma, a life-long leader of one of those oppressive political dynasties. As a young planter, Oscar Ledesma had played a key role in breaking the FOF sugar union and went on to become president of the National Federation of Sugarcane Planters and patron of the Manila branch of the Asian People's Anti-Communist League.

Similarly, Fr Ledesma's suggestions for reforms would, if enacted, destroy his own family's wealth. Using four performance criteria, he concluded that the present system of large-scale haciendas was inefficient. First, the distribution of income in the industry was extremely uneven. Moreover, professional incompetence on the part of many planters had produced a constant decline in sugar yields per hectare. Such inefficiency denied workers decent wages and pressed planters to raise production by grabbing more land from poor peasants. Third, the industry has failed to provide full employment for present workers. Once the industry is forced to mechanize to compete with efficient producers like Hawaii and Australia, there will be a 'consequent displacement of many unskilled workers'. Despite the probability of such change, 'no serious effort has been made for the setting up of complementary industries in sugarland'. Only on the fourth criteria, profit, does the industry pass muster, but at a very high price. Profit under the present industry structure is based on access to the US sugar market 'bought at the price of forfeiting our national sovereignty in other areas'.

To end the rule of a corrupt and incompetent oligarchy, Fr Ledesma offered a four part program to build social democracy in Negros. Workers will have to be educated for a 'democratic seizure of political power' that would enable imposition of an 'industry-wide planned economy'. The key to these changes was the one thing planters feared above all — land reform. With an almost catalytic effect, land reform would allow a 'radical transformation of socio-economic relationships'. As the Silay planters had so wisely feared, Fr Ledesma argued that the Bishop's Dacongcogon Sugar Mill 'could well be the prototype of land reform in sugarland'. These changes would hopefully spark 'a social revolution in sugarland where equality of economic and political opportunities will have become a reality'.

Despite clear differences in ideology and tactics, these papers became a collective blueprint for social action. Following Fr Jalandoni's suggestion that the Church collaborate with the workers' own organizations, the Bacolod diocese allied itself with two unions in a systematic attempt at social reform. The FFF would be revived to organize the hill farmers, while a new union, the National Federation of Sugarcane Workers (NFSW), would organize labourers on the lowland plantations.

Church involvement roused the FFF from a decade-long hibernation. Infused with Church funds and the support of activist priests, the FFF moved down the island's mountain spine organizing chapters in remote peasant villages. As provincial chaplain to the FFF, Fr Jalandoni played a key role in recruiting younger priests to support the union parishioners. In the effort he worked closely with Fr Hector Mauri, SJ, now mellower and more knowledgeable after fifteen years in Negros as a union organizer. During the 1950s his efforts for the FFF had found little response, but by the early 1970s an epidemic of elite landgrabbing had made the hill farmers eager for union support. As the two moved through the south in 1971 recruiting FFF organizers, Fr Jalandoni asked Brian Gore to serve as chaplain of the union's Kabankalan chapter.

Frustrated by his role as priest to the planters in the town centre, Fr Gore seized the opportunity to begin travelling the hills that ringed the sugar plains of Kabankalan. His grandfather had been active in Western Australia's early railway strikes and Fr Gore found union work among the farmers sympathetic to his basic values. In contrast to his adversary relations with the planter elite, he got on well with the peasants. His direct, outspoken manner, which alienated the planters, sparked a certain trust among the poor hill farmers.

As Fr Jalandoni was radicalized by his involvement in the Cadiz landgrabbing case, so Fr Gore's ideas about his role as priest would be transformed by his work with the farmers of Kabankalan. Through his close contact with their miserable lives, Fr Gore would be forced to confront the 'structural sin' that is Negros. Like others before him, he would find that the naked exploitation violated every Church teaching on social justice. 'I suppose I have a strong sense of justice in many ways', Fr Gore explains. 'Once I got the language and got to know the people, which took a few years, I got to know that they were being screwed'.

As chaplain of the FFF Kabankalan chapter, Fr Gore was the liason between Church and union, a task that mainly involved providing money and manpower for the organizers in the hills. Most importantly he used his prestige as a priest to shield the union at times of confrontation with planter power. Soon after affiliating with the FFF in 1971, Fr Gore was confronted with a land grabbing case in Bayhaw village, later the site of Mayor Sola's murder, that illuminated the full meaning of 'structural sin'.

Fr Gore became involved in the Bayhaw case when the FFF sent word that five members had been arrested resisting eviction from public lands they had worked for generations. One of Mayor Sola's cousins, Mrs Agustina Rubin Ladrido, had somehow won a title to 30 hectares in Bayhaw village and sent the town police to enforce her claim. In the ensuing fracas, Mrs Ladrido had five peasants jailed on charges of malicious mischief. With the help of diocesan legal aid lawyer Frankie Cruz, Fr Gore had the parish stand as guarantor and bailed them out of the town jail.

At first the Bayhaw incident seemed a text book case of exploitation — a grasping planter stealing land from poor peasants. But matters were, as Fr Gore found out, more complicated. Mrs Ladrido was president of the Legion of Mary in his parish and seemed a kind woman inclined to do the right thing. Her deceased father had filed the claim many years before, when she had been studying in America. Soon after her return to Kabankalan, she suddenly became burdened with responsibilities. She had married late and had her own family to provide for. Her brothers were gamblers and had dissipated the family's property and wealth soon after their father's death. For the peasants these thirty hectares were their livelihood. For Mrs Ladrio they were a chance to revive her family's failing fortunes and maintain her position among the town's elite. 'She was torn', explains Fr Gore, 'between doing what was right for those people and her responsibility to her family to claim the land.'

The union's intervention frustrated the land grabbing attempt. Once the church interceded, it was clear to Kabankalan's elite that Mrs Ladrido's thirty hectares would cause great controversy. Mayor Sola felt his cousins had handled the matter badly and refused to use his power and police on their behalf. 'I told them to get that fixed up years ago', he told Fr Gore, 'and now it is an impossible mess'. Today the charges of 'malicious mischief' remain listed on the local court docket and those farmers remain on their land.

Although the union had some successes in blocking elite land grabbing, Fr Gore was becoming dissatisfied with the work. 'The FFF used to go into a mountain village and right away say, "we have a lawyer and we'll help you get your land". There was no emphasis on getting land through community action', says Fr Gore. 'The union appealed purely to the individual aspirations of people instead of trying to form a community. Many rich peasants joined the FFF, became *barrio* [village] councillors, and used the union to get power and land.' The union leadership was trying to strengthen the poor villagers by winning legal title to land, political power through local elections and wealth through marketing cooperatives. By offering its services to individuals, however, the union fostered the formation of a new local power elite of rich peasants. That was not what Fr Gore had in mind.

The activist priests tried to avoid the same mistakes when they organized a new union for the plantation labourers, the National Federation of Sugar Workers (NFSW). Under Fr Jalandoni's master plan for social action, the established FFF branches would organize the hill farmers while a new union would undertake the far more difficult task of mobilizing the plantation laborers. A product of the diocese's critical study of the sugar industry in 1971, the NFSW was initially led by three Church activists — President, Ed Tejada, a Catholic student leader recruited by Fr Jalandoni; Board Chairman, Fr Edgar Saguinsin, a young diocesan priest; and spiritual advisor, Fr Hector Mauri, SJ, a veteran of many union disasters. Through his past defeats Fr Mauri was well aware of the way that worker attitudes, reflecting the island's culture of poverty, could ruin a union from within — pretence and opportunism by the leaders and vacillation, defeatism, despair and distrust by the members.

Instead of plunging immediately into the usual round of pickets and petitions, the NFSW leaders decided that all members would have to be 'conscientized' through a five day self-awareness seminar. Led by priests, nuns and Catholic layworkers, these sessions tried to make workers aware of their human potential and break the servility ingrained in them by hacienda life. By observing participants carefully, the religious took care to select leaders with both potential for growth and certain moral qualities.

Fr Mauri had a unique ability to convince capable men that his work should be theirs. After talking with Fr Gore and Fr Martin about likely NFSW leaders in their area, he took the bus to Kabankalan and walked into the town hall to speak with a bright young civil servant, Bobby Ortaliz. 'Lets go out for coffee. I want you to do something about your convictions.' A graduate of Fr O'Brien's Sa Maria seminars, Ortaliz had been active in the Kabankalan parish choir. After rising rapidly through the ranks to become president of the NFSW, Ortaliz moved on to Manila as an executive in the *Kilusang Mayo Uno* (May First Movement), the national labour confederation that has challenged Marcos' control of the union movement.

Despite the careful preparation, the new union's year of industrial action before martial law in 1972 met overwhelming planter resistance. In its strike at Hacienda Taburda in the La Carlota district, the new union had its first taste of the planters' unrestrained violence. After completing a four-month conscientization seminar, some seventy workers from Taburda, a 280 hectare hacienda, joined the NFSW in November 1971. When he learned of the new union, the owner's son, Joselito Vargas, marched through the residential compound with a squad of security guards threatening his workers at gunpoint. Several weeks later, Vargas packed them off to town in a truck and made them sign declarations retracting their NFSW membership before the municipal judge. Vargas announced publicly he would shoot Fr Mauri and Fr Saguinsin if they persisted in agitating his workers.

When workers staged a demonstration to protest against the plantation's non-payment of their social security contributions, the owner, Angel Vargas, reacted by forming a company union. After forcing his workers to join, Vargas awarded the new union a closed-shop bargaining agreement. In March 1972, the planter dismissed all NFSW members and recruited a new group of workers to replace them. Although the NFSW filed an unfair labour practice case before the Court of Agrarian Relations, management's procedural delays blocked any action for five months. By then four infants had died of slow starvation.

The day after President Marcos declared martial law in September, the planter hired Sgt George Presquito, later notorious as leader of a Constabulary death squad, to drive the NFSW workers out of the hacienda housing compound. Accompanied by the local police chief and two soldiers, Presquito administered a savage beating to a male organizer while his fellows ransacked the house of a woman leader. Several union leaders were arrested without charges and many workers were driven off the hacienda. While the case dragged on through the courts for the next three years, most workers drifted away to other jobs and other towns.

President Marcos' declaration of martial law in September 1972 was a major blow to the Negros union movement. All strikes became illegal and the Constabulary, long an ally of the planters in Negros, was given arbitrary authority to resolve union disputes. Indicative of its future sympathies, the Bacolod detachment soon raided the Catholic Social Action Office with an order for the arrest of Fr Jalandoni. Faced with the prospect of torture and indefinite imprisonment, Fr Jalandoni decided to go underground with the New People's Army (NPA). Reportedly under pressure from the planters, Bishop Fortich had tried to restrain Fr Jalandoni's radicalism just before martial law, perhaps pushing the young priest further left. 'It was a time of confusion', recalls Fr Gore. 'Some people in the Christian left were saying the revolution was only a year away.' In the midst of such uncertainty, Fr Jalandoni's decision came as something of a shock to the progressive priests. 'Some of us felt disappointed that he quit the legal struggle and left us, in a certain sense, orphans', said Fr Gore. 'He was the leader in this field and had gotten us Columbans involved in land cases. We knew that there had been a breach with the Bishop, but if he had stayed we would have supported him.'

For the next year, Fr Jalandoni moved about Negros and the Visayas, doing propaganda work and trying to forge a Christian-Marxist alliance in support of the revolution. While underground, he decided to end his career as priest and married a former nun. Surfacing frequently to meet with clergy and layworkers, Fr Jalandoni was soon captured not far from Bacolod. Monsignor Fortich interceded with the military and Fr Jalandoni was transferred to the Bishop's custody. He soon fled into exile with his wife and now works in Holland as international coordinator of the National Democratic Front, the Communist Party's mass organization.

In his declaration of martial law, President Marcos promised 'reform to remove the inequities of society' and 'the clean up of government of its corrupt and sterile elements'. In his later broadcasts, Marcos promised 'a revolution from the centre' that would bring justice to all Filipinos. In fulfilment of the president's promises, the Negros Constabulary formed Task Force *Bagong Pag-asa* (New Hope) to investigate all workers' complaints. Fr Gore decided to test the new regime by taking the Hacienda Union case to the Task Force.

'We were willing to give him a chance and see if Marcos was really as interested in helping the poor as he said he was', says Fr Gore with a slight smile. 'As far as I was concerned, this was a real test case for Marcos and martial law — and they failed.'

The case had started a month before martial law when thirty-eight workers from Hacienda Union on the Kabankalan plains approached Fr Gore to complain that they were not being paid the minimum wage. Once the new Task Force was established, he advised them to file a case which they did on 13 November. Four days later three labour inspectors visited the hacienda to check the payroll. Typical of the town's planter elite, the owner, Delfin 'Baby' Dinsay, who was Mayor Sola's godchild, reacted angrily to this interference and summarily sacked all complaining workers.

A long round of lies, evasion, threats and intimidation ensued. At the hearing on 14 December, Dinsay presented a payroll showing full payment of the legal wage and forged workers' signatures. Under pressure from the Task Force, the planter agreed to rehire his workers, but for the next four months offered only occasional casual work. As frustrations mounted, Fr Gore asked the NFSW to represent the workers. The union won a new hearing in March 1973. Although the NFSW auditors calculated the back wages at P129,000 the Task Force estimated only P49,000, a figure the workers accepted to facilitate a resolution. When the Task Force ordered payment, the planter refused, pleading poverty. Suddenly, it became evident that the Task Force had no legal authority to enforce its decisions. Four months with little work or income had been for naught. The entire case was transferred to yet another bureaucracy, the National Labour Relations Council (NLRC).

While the proceedings dragged on, the planter began applying extra-legal pressures. Through his contacts, Dinsay arranged for the local Philippine Constabulary (PC) detachment to pressure the strikers. One worker claimed: 'The owner himself brought the PC to harass us. The PC said things like — "if you don't stop complaining to the Task Force, all of you who work here will die or be put in the stockade". We were terrified and one of us fainted and wouldn't leave the house so great was the fear.'

After the final Task Force hearing, Dinsay dismissed all thirty-eight complainants and blacklisted them among his fellow planters. Many of their children were forced to drop out of school and their families began showing obvious signs of malnutrition. After ten months of no work, sixteen of the more desperate were allowed to return after authorizing the hacienda to deduct 10 percent of their wages for 'a long overdue account'.

But thirty of the original strikers persisted, and the case dragged on month after month through more than twenty hearings and postponements. Dinsay's obsessive refusal to accept any settlement began to disturb even the most conservative planters. Sensing his godson's potential for violence, Mayor Sola warned that he must not, whatever else he did, harm the priests. 'Some of the planters started telling Dinsay', recalls Fr Gore, ' "Just pay the workers, it's only a small amount. You're going to stir up a hornets' nest by fighting them so hard for so little." But these were the more intelligent planters.'

As the case crept through its second year, Fr Gore tried to short-circuit the bureaucracy by taking it to the Church-Military Liaison Conference in Bacolod for immediate adjudication. Accompanied by union officials, Gore met with Lieutenant Colonel Meliton Goyena, the Constabulary commander for Negros Occidental.

'I explained to Colonel Goyena that it was really an open-and-shut case', recalled Fr Gore in a Sydney interview after his release. 'The hacienda had not kept payroll records, in itself a serious infraction, so there was no way the owner could dispute the workers' demands for P68,000 in back wages. So Goyena offered a settlement of P5,000. I was angry at the suggestion and replied that it wouldn't even cover the fares from Kabankalan. Then I snapped — "if that is all you can offer these people after twenty months of no work and hunger, then in good conscience I cannot bring people to see you in the future". Colonel Goyena exploded and shouted: "If you turn people against the government, I'll cut your throat".'

As parish priest of Kabankalan, Fr Gore had embittered the town elite by taking their Church away from them. As union chaplain, he had alienated a rising military officer. Lieutenant Colonel Goyena soon became General Goyena. Ten years later when Fr Gore was charged with murder, he was on the headquarters staff of the Constabulary's commandant, General

Fidel Ramos, as special advisor for Negros. Fr Gore had made an enemy in high places.

Martial law was the death of the Federation of Free Farmers (FFF) as a militant union. Its national president Jeremias Montemayor declared his fervent support for President Marcos' 'New Society', alienating the union's dominant left wing. In Negros, religious activists, the real strength of the provincial chapter, resigned in disgust. Moreover, the Negros Constabulary made a crude identification between the FFF and the NPA, a self-fulfilling prophecy that soon drove many union leaders into the hills with the guerillas.

Although there is no firm evidence, events themselves suggest that the Constabulary's regional headquarters in Cebu may have ordered a death-squad operation against the FFF in the months after martial law. Across the southern plateau where the union was strong, Constabulary troopers surrounded villages, firing their rifles into the air and demanding peasants come forward for identification. Any with known union involvement were frequently taken away for interrogation and indefinite imprisonment. During these same months Sgt George Presquito began his six year reign of terror in southern Negros.

Until his violent death in 1978, Sgt Presquito was the most notorious of all the death squad commanders who enjoyed immunity under martial law. Child of a planters' lawyer, Presquito spent the years after high school during the 1960s as the leader of a group of thugs who hired their services to planters in the La Carlota district. After joining the Constabulary in 1969, Presquito was assigned to its Criminal Investigation Service (CIS), a special unit operating outside the normal chain of command. In August 1972, he won notoriety when he summarily executed two members of the communist *Kabataan Makabayan* (Nationalist Youth) who had surrendered to him near Kabankalan.

After martial law, Sgt Presquito abandoned any pretence of regular military service and recruited a ten-man squad of professional killers. His group moved through the hills raping, torturing and killing without restraint. With long hair, beard, and black motorcycle, Sgt Presquito basked in the fear and revelled in his role as killer. The refusal of regular military officers to investigate the many complaints against him indicate that he indeed had a licence to kill.

On 3 December 1973, Ofelia Cana and three other FFF organizers were conducting a seminar for peasant farmers near Candoni, the epicentre of the Tablas plateau. Only nineteen, she was a key organizer in the area and had worked closely with a Columban missionary, Fr John Hynes, to build the local FFF branch. An unidentified Constabulary squad raided the village and executed the four organizers. The corpses were displayed in front of the Candoni town hall with a sign — 'This Is What Happens to NPA'. The embalmers later counted 147 bullet wounds in the four corpses. An unknown number of FFF members — a dozen, maybe two dozen — died in like manner on the southern plateau.

Once they had recovered from the shock of martial law, Church activists in Negros decided to concentrate their energies in rebuilding the National Federation of Sugar Workers (NFSW). In the months before martial law, the union had been building towards a major strike in Negros and Panay. Now that strikes were banned, it had to reorganize and adapt to the new system of forced arbitration. By 1974 the union had 8,000 members, largely in Negros, and chapters in eighty-two haciendas. Reflecting the industry's hostility, the NFSW had a signed collective bargaining agreement with only one hacienda. Marcos' new arbitration procedure was clearly biased against the unions. Of the sixty complaints the NFSW had filed for sugar workers by early 1975, only two had been settled amicably and the rest had either been dismissed or were hopelessly mired in procedural delays.

After two years of unrelenting defeat in the plantations, the NFSW made a major bid to win control of a sugar milling factory. Although the year-long battle to organize the Binalbagan-Isabela Sugar Co. (Biscom) ended in failure, it nonetheless established the union's credibility with the sugar workers of Negros. Long used to corrupt union leaders who grafted their dues and did deals with management, workers were convinced after the Biscom strike that the NFSW was a genuine union. The Biscom campaign became a battle of brothers — Biscom manager Gregorio Saguinsin versus the union chairman Fr Edgar Saguinsin. Neither wavered in the pursuit of their responsibilities. Manager Saguinsin used threats, intimidation, and bribes to break the NFSW. Fr Saguinsin used the full resources of his church and union to defeat the company. Significantly, the strike saw the first involvement of nuns in Negros union campaigns, a change that would greatly expand the base of Church support for the NFSW.

The union began its campaign at Biscom with a series of intensive conscientization seminars from January to May 1974. Led largely by priests and nuns, the seminars lasted three days for some 190 prospective members and thirty-five days for twenty-seven selected leaders. When the union petitioned the Court of Industrial Relations for a certification election in April, Biscom management unleashed a concerted campaign to break the NFSW. In the month before the election, workers were threatened with the severance of educational loans for their children and the loss of off-season employment. The union countered with a letter of support from sixty-one parish priests. Despite the pressure, the NFSW won 750 votes in the May election — more than the 719 cast for FLO-ALU, the current company union, but a few short of the required majority.

The conflict intensified in the months before the August run-off election. Management officials made personal visits to each worker warning that failure to support the company would lead to dismissal. Shortly thereafter, the mill began selective sackings and reductions of rice rations to suspected NFSW supporters.

June was a month for Communist scare tactics. A Constabulary major denounced the NFSW as communist before an assembly of mill workers and three union leaders were arrested on charges of subversion. The president of the company union, Zoilo de la Cruz, wrote to the Secretary of Defence accusing the NFSW leaders of 'subversive and seditious activities'. The involvement of 'foreign priests' in the union would, he charged, have 'profound consequences on the peace and order of Negros Occidental'. Affirming this crude equation between Church and communism, the mill retaliated against the religious by forcing closure of the chapel in the workers' housing compound. The Columban priest who served as Biscom's chaplain was locked out of the millsite chapel by company security guards.

So pressed, the religious redoubled their efforts on behalf of the NFSW. Despite harassment from company guards, the nuns returned to continue their worker seminars. Seventeen priests said mass for the union supporters at the Binalbagan town church, and the Columbans offered free schooling to the children of dismissed workers. Seeking to neutralize the Constabulary, priests met with the Constabulary's provincial Commander, Lieutenant Colonel Goyena, while thirty-five nuns wrote the Defence Minister denying allegations of communist infiltration of the union.

In the end, however, unrestrained pressure broke the union. Intimidated by the sackings and arrests, NFSW supporters became quiet or joined the company union. When the government held the run-off elections in August, the NFSW boycotted it in protest at the unfair labour practices, thus assuring the company union's victory. Although the women religious continued to file protests with the Manila courts for another year, the NFSW had lost.

As in 1971 when they first tasted repression, the Biscom defeat strengthened the determination of religious activists. The workers had lost, they felt, because their conscientization was not deep enough. Thus, in the year following the strike, priests and nuns escalated their attack on the sugar industry. The Association of Major Religious Superiors (AMRS) — a union of religious orders such as the Columbans, Jesuits, Redemptorists — played a key role in the new offensive. In an effort to understand the dynamics of defeat at Biscom, the AMRS commissioned the Columbans to conduct a comprehensive study of the Negros sugar industry. Through 300 interviews on eighty-three haciendas, the Columbans found that 58 percent of respondents did not receive the minimum wage, 54 percent were denied social security, 90 percent did not receive worker's accident compensation, and 65 percent were not allowed Medicare.

Another section of the report examined the structures of

exploitation in the Negros sugar industry — multinational, national and local. The findings were summarized in a single cartoon. Suspended in a web of Japanese and American corporate interests, the head of the spider-scorpion monster (Philippine National Bank, government and military) reaches out with claws (planters, millers and their company unions) to crush the people — the NFSW union, religious orders (the AMRS itself), Negros women religious (NOWRA), hacienda workers *(dumaans)*, and cane cutters *(sacadas)*.

After reading the Columban study, which ran to 205 printed pages, the national convention of Religious Superiors wrote to President Marcos in January 1975 denouncing the industry. 'While appalled by the terrible conditions of poverty, misery and virtual enslavement of the sugar workers, we are literally shocked at the conspicuous consumption of many rich planters.' The planters had defeated workers' efforts at unionization through a combination of intimidation, dismissals and murder. The religious charged that the real root of the province's misery lay 'in a plantation type economy which perpetuates an outdated feudal system of dependency'. As a corrective, the Religious Superiors urged the president to terminate the 'exemption of sugar lands from the government's land reform program' and break the plantations into 'small-sized farms owned by the workers themselves'. They praised the NFSW and expressed 'confidence in its Christian orientation and leadership'.

The Religious Superiors closed their petition with a warning. 'Like Mt Kanlaon which towers silently and majestically over the lush sugarcane fields of this rich province, there is here a social volcano. Inwardly, hot lava is being formed by the forces of oppression awaiting the time of eruption.'

The AMRS petition — combining allegations of murder and a call for destruction of the haciendas — sparked an eruption of protest among the Negros planters. Under intense pressure, Bishop Fortich released a public statement, read by the president of the planters' association at an industry convention, attacking the report of his own Columbans as 'gross misrepresentations, exaggerations and patent inaccuracies'. The

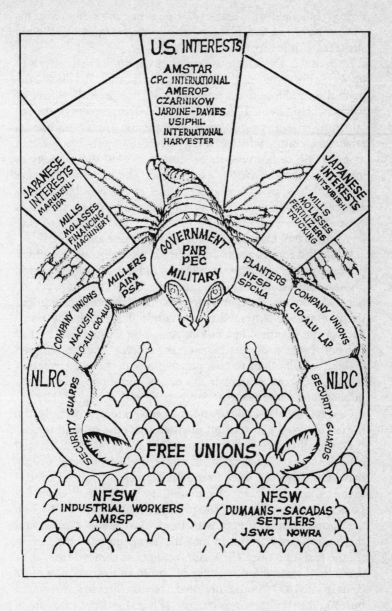

Bishop qualified his remarks, however, by reiterating his condemnation of the 'planters who remain stagnant in the old structure of injustice'.

Undaunted, the Religious Superiors continued their efforts to publicize the results of the Columbans' research. To educate the poor they published a comic book in Ilongo with stories of workers being denied Medicare by greedy overseers or mountain farmers suffering from land grabbing. Unlike traditional religious literature which blamed poverty on moral failings such as gambling or laziness, these stories showed the workers as innocent victims of vicious exploitation. The hacienda overseer is depicted as an evil man who uses every possible trick to reduce his workers to poverty and debt. The moral maxim is clear — if you want justice, don't wait for God to give it to you. Fight these evil men or you will die in disease and poverty.

While the comics passed unnoticed, the Religious Superiors' photo-essay titled *Pastures of the Rich* did not. A series of paired photos contrasting planter sugar palaces with their workers' hacienda hovels, the pamphlet circulated widely throughout the Philippines. Outraged by the continuing attack, the president of the planters' federation, Armando Gustilo, warlord of northern Negros, declared war on the diocese. Planters stopped making contributions to their parishes and declared a boycott of religious schools to punish the orders for supporting such a publication. Although the children of the rich gradually returned to La Salle College and the other religious schools, the breach between Church and planters was now beyond repair.

During this two-year confrontation in 1974-75, a divided church and a decentralized sugar industry were evenly matched. However, once President Marcos centralized control in the hands of his sugar plenipotentiary, Roberto Benedicto, the power equation changed. The process began in late 1974 when the Laurel-Langley Treaty with the United States expired and the Philippines was forced into the competitive world market for the first time since 1913. As world prices climbed from their usual level around 10 cents per pound to an historic high of 67 cents in late 1974, Marcos invested a hastily formed government bureau, the Philippine-Exchange (Philex), with a monopoly over all sugar trading. The new body sold the planters' sugar at P502 per sack but paid them a 'liquidation price' of only P160, effectively expropriating about one billion pesos which it deposited in the national treasury.

Anticipating that prices would keep climbing ever upward to $1.00 per pound, Philex began hoarding sugar in Negros and was caught with some two million tons as the price suddenly crashed ever downward to twenty cents and then ten cents. There it would remain for the next four years, forcing Philex to store mountains of sugar in swimming pools, tennis courts and open roadways. When Philex began paying planters less than it cost to grow cane on most farms, many ceased cultivation and let their lands lie fallow. The area of cane cultivated on Negros dropped 25 percent by 1977, producing severe hardships for the poor who had once worked those fields. The planters simply passed the cost of the government exactions on to their workers, freezing wages and slashing vital benefits. In 1978 a comprehensive official survey discovered that 78.1 percent of all infants in the greater Bacolod area suffered from malnutrition.

In the midst of this crisis, President Marcos activated the Philippine Sugar Commission (Philsucom) and appointed his crony, Roberto Benedicto, chairman. Using his arbitrary authority, Marcos invested Philsucom with an exceptional range of powers — authority to buy and sell all sugar, to set sale price to planters, assume control of any sugar mill, and purchase any company involved in sugar production.

Within three years, Benedicto had translated these paper powers into economic and political dominion. Known popularly as the 'sugar czar', Benedicto soon accumulated enormous private and public assets — sugar mills, transport, warehousing, plantations and banks. On a monocrop island like Negros, unlimited control over sugar meant unrestrained political power. If sugar was king on Negros, then Benedicto was its chief minister. He controlled local officials, dictated to the Constabulary and appointed the provincial judiciary.

As the NFSW and its religious allies continued their mobilization of sugar workers into the late 1970s, they ran headlong into a stiffening resistance. A strike against a single sugar mill now became a strike against Philsucom and an offence to Chairman Benedicto. As a descendant of an old Negros sugar family and a past president of the Philippine National Bank, Benedicto's sympathies lay with the planters. As a nominal member of the Aglipayan Church, a nationalist schism now part of the Anglican communion, Benedicto had no loyalty to the Church nor any particular respect for its priests. Paralleling the growth of Benedicto's power, Constabulary pressure on the union and its religious supporters intensified.

Benedicto's rise and the sugar industry's decline combined to produce a series of ugly incidents in mid-1978. When planters responded to the sugar crisis of the late 1970s by withdrawing land from production, workers suffered and demanded action from their union. Determined to tough out the sugar crisis, Benedicto reportedly gave the Negros Constabulary orders to keep the lid on.

As harassment of unionists and torture of peasants in the south escalated throughout 1978, the Church and its union responded with large demonstrations in Bacolod. On 5 March, 5,000 students and workers marched to protest the Constabulary torture in southern Negros, ending their rally with a mass at the Redemptionist Church decorated with a red banner — 'Stop Terrorism'. The NFSW mobilized 8,000 members for a May Day rally at the Redemptionist Church under banners demanding 'Land Reform in Sugarlandia'. On 12 June, Philippine independence day, another 5,000 led by priests and nuns demonstrated against military surveillance of religious organizations under a huge banner — 'Free the Church, Free the People'. On the thirtieth anniversary of the UN Declaration on Human Rights, 20,000 attended rallies throughout the province.

In an effort to silence the demonstrators, the Constabulary began to direct its attacks against the NFSW. As delegates were leaving the union's national convention at Bacolod on 30 June, fifteen members of a northern Negros delegation were detained and interrogated for several hours at Constabulary headquarters. Southern delegates were arrested and photographed by the Hinigaran detachment. They were held for a day without charges and were told that 'they were just being fooled by priests like Father Saguinsin'. Three days later, the NFSW chairman, Fr Saguinsin, wrote to the Constabulary commander denouncing the incident as 'another ugly stain on the military's not so popular image'.

This harassment was prelude to a major confrontation between Church and Constabulary. What became known as the 'Bago incident' began on 19 July when thirty hacienda workers began planting food crops in an unused canefield. The sugar crisis had forced many planters to cut back on cane cultivation, leaving their workers without sufficient income to survive. These thirty belonged to a *Panimbahon* prayer group headed by Fr Woodrow Gubuan, a parish priest, and had reportedly discussed the morality of allowing land to lie fallow when many were going hungry. The workers had offered to share the harvest with the owner, Angel Araneta, but he refused, not wanting to risk his exemption from land reform as a sugar producer. With the encouragement of their priest and the NFSW, the workers ignored Araneta's refusal and planted the fallow fields to food crops.

Seeking to avoid an eventual confrontation, the NFSW convened a 'dialogue' between all parties at the Bago City Social Hall on 30 July. With its implicit threat of a unilateral land reform by the NFSW, the incident had heightened social tensions throughout the province. The meeting attracted an audience of influentials — NFSW President Ed Tejada, Bishop Fortich, the Bago City mayor, the City police chief, and Constabulary Colonel Arcadio Lozada.

'If no agreement is reached blood will flow', said Fr Saguinsin, the NFSW chairman, in the prosecution's record of the events. 'And Mr Araneta can kill the workers with the help of the PC [Constabulary] and the Police and the military and if so the workers will not stop to look for Mr Araneta and kill him.'

Again according to the prosecution's version, the workers' local leader, Nena Rico, spoke next. 'We will not vacate the land, we will die and fight rather than give up the land. It is useless to bring complaint to the government which is only the tool of the rich people, specially under martial law.'

As soon as the applause died down, Colonel Lozada stood up

and announced that all NFSW members, including Fr
Saguinsin, were under arrest on charges of subversion. Troops
moved into the hall and 129 men, women and children were
herded off to detention at gunpoint. The women were released
the next day and Fr Saguinsin was placed under the Bishop's
custody. But the men remained in the stockade, where many
were tortured, until an international protest movement forced
Marcos to order their release on bail. The Constabulary filed
sedition charges against all arrested and the case of *People vs Fr
Edgar Saguinsin et al* started its long grind through the courts.
With strong international support and capable legal representa-
tion by ex-Senator Jose Diokno, the defendants won an
eventual dismissal.

The Constabulary maintained its pressure on the NFSW and
coordinated an effort by mayors, planters and local police to
break the union. In March 1981, for example, the Constabulary
warned the mayor of Magalona in north Negros that Fr
Saguinsin would be launching a membership drive in local
plantations. The mayor sent out a circular letter telling planters
that 'Father Saguinsin is notoriously well-known for his radical
views on labour'. Workers were to be warned against his 'evil
design' and advised not to be 'exploited of their hard earned
cash' which would allow 'Fr Saguinsin to live in ease and
comfort'. Similarly, in November NFSW members at a hacienda
near Bacolod were met by a phalanx of fifteen Constabulary
troopers in full battle gear when they arrived at a conciliation
meeting to complain about non-payment of the minimum wage.

Military pressure became so intense that Fr Saguinsin was
forced to move into the Bishop's palace under virtual house
arrest. Using an invitation to a labour seminar in the US as
pretext, he left the Philippines in mid 1981 and has since
remained in exile. His flight banished the last of the leading
worker-priests from Negros — Fr Jalandoni to Europe, Fr Mauri
to Manila and Fr Saguinsin to America.

'The Church will not hesitate to take up the cause of the poor
and to become the voice of those who are not listened to when
they speak up, not to demand charity, but to ask for justice.' So
spoke Pope John Paul II in his address 'To the People of Sugar

Plantations' during his pastoral visit to Negros in February 1981. Although a social conservative known for his stand against activist priests in Latin America, the Pope's moderate message outraged the Negros planters. The Pope's Statement was, as he made quite clear, little more than an affirmation of all the Church encyclicals on social justice since *Rerum Novarum* ninety years ago. To the absent planters he said: 'It is not admissable that people who work the land must continue to live in a situation that offers them no hope for a better future'. Citing the *Pastoral Constitution (Gadium et Spes)* proclaimed at the end of Vatican II, the Pope added: 'The landowners and planters therefore should not let themselves be guided in the first place by the economic laws of growth and gain ... but by the demands of justice and by the moral imperative of contributing to a decent standard of living ... for the workers'.

Turning his attention from the absent planters to the throng of peasant and sugar workers who had walked for days to be with him in Bacolod, the Pope said: 'To all the sugar cane workers I say ... never forget the great dignity that God has granted you, never let your work degrade you'. To the delight of the thousands of NFSW members in the crowd, he added: 'It has been the constant teaching of the Church that workers have a right to unite in free associations for the purpose of defending their interest and contributing as responsible partners to the common good.'

The Pope's visit was both triumph and celebration for the activist priests and their peasant followers. Well briefed on the Negros situation by Bishop Fortich, Pope John Paul II had made it clear that the Bacolod diocese's work for social reform had his unqualified support. The social sin that is Negros so clearly violates Church doctrines that the Pope could not have done otherwise.

At a time when Constabulary repression was mounting, the poor and their priests used the Papal visit to demonstrate their strength. Like peasants across Negros, Fr O'Brien's parishioners marched for days in the tropical sun from the far south of the province 100 kilometres to Bacolod to see the Pope. By his words and by his gesture of meeting the widows of Kabankalan layworkers murdered by the Constabulary, the Pope embraced the cause of the Negros poor. Some peasants wept at his words. All felt the collective strength of 750,000 workers and peasants, one-third of the province's population, filling the city's centre with thousands of bright banners for local chapters of the NFSW and the Christian Communities. A year later I asked Fr O'Brien for his impressions of the visit, and his words cascaded out, a jumble of incoherence, to convey a sense of absolute euphoria.

'Once the Pope came and gave his message about the Church aiding the poor, that was the end of planters' closeness to the Church', explained Fr Gore. 'There were half-a-million people in Bacolod plaza to hear his message. Their maids were in the plaza to see the Pope, but the planters stayed home. The planters wanted to be a part of the Church, but they cannot lead this new Church. The Church they want is one that tells the workers not to steal from your *amo* (master). Once the Church says all men are brothers, the planters can't accept that. If they accept the workers as brothers, then the whole system would break down. They want to cavort with the Bishop chatting in Spanish.'

'The Holy Father's statement on social justice aroused the anger of the planters', Bishop Fortich recalled several months after the visit. 'That night Armando Gustilo, president of the planters' federation, called me on the phone. He was shouting: "So you want war, do you Monsignor? Well, we'll give you war. All out war — if that's what you want". You see, the older planters are very proud and very conservative.'

If Gustilo's telephone call was a declaration of war, then the first battle was fought at the La Carlota Sugar Central. Mobilizing the full resources it had accumulated in its ten year history, the NFSW mounted a ninety-six day picket in what became the Philippines' longest strike since the declaration of martial law. Despite four years of constant Constabulary harassment after the 'Bago incident' of 1978, the NFSW had grown into a union of 40,000 members in six provinces. Its controversial campaign for land reform in Negros continued to win support and it enjoyed a growing reputation as a working class advocate. The union gambled all the resources and reputation it had won in ten year's of struggle on the outcome of the La Carlota strike.

Although the NFSW founded its first local chapters in the haciendas of La Carlota's milling district in 1971, its leaders waited another six years before trying to organize the mill workers. As officials of the mill's existing union, PAFLU, developed an overly cosy, and some suspected corrupt, relationship with management, workers from Central La Carlota began joining the NFSW. In November 1977, the NFSW decided to challenge PAFLU for control of the mill and petitioned the National Labour Relations Council for a certification election. After twenty months of procedural delays by PAFLU and management, the NFSW won 52 percent of 1,032 votes cast and the right to organize. Another sixteen months of procedural delays followed until November 1981 when Central La Carlota finally signed a bargaining agreement with the NFSW. It was a major victory for the union. After ten years of failed strikes and elections, the NFSW had finally won control of a major sugar mill.

As soon as it had secured recognition, the NFSW used a new weapon to press its demands against the mill — the strike. President Marcos had rescinded martial law earlier in the year and unions were free to strike for the first time in a decade. Only two days after the bargaining agreement was signed, the union launched a lightning strike demanding, most importantly, promotion of long-term casuals to permanent status and payment of the thirteenth-month bonus ordered by President Marcos in lieu of a wage rise. Stunned, the management capitulated in two days. It conceded most demands immediately, but won agreement from the union that the thirteenth-month bonus be delayed until the Supreme Court clarified its applicability in a pending decison.

Two weeks later the Court ruled in favor of the bonus. When management still refused to pay, Central La Carlota's workers voted overwhelmingly to strike. After a compulsory cooling-off period, the workers walked out on 28 January, 1982 at the height of milling season. For much of the next three months, the picket lines outside the mill became a twenty-four hour celebration of Christian community. Among the mill's 1,200 workers, about 700 stayed with the strike until the end. Those militants slept on the picket lines with their families and ate their meals at a communal kitchen supported by Church funds. Life on the picket lines was celebrated with Christian ritual. During the strike's heady first days, 550 NFSW workers from north Negros arrived to demonstrate their solidarity. Fourteen Catholic priests co-celebrated mass for the pickets and read a manifesto of support from eighty-two priests. When a striker's one-year-old child died after being refused treatment at the company hospital, workers built her a coffin on the spot and held a two-day wake on the picket line.

The first round of repression came on the twenty-sixth day after the courts ruled the strike illegal on a technicality. Supported by troops in full battle gear, a fire truck sprayed the workers with high-pressure hoses, knocking several into the river. After a round of tear gas, a second fire truck opened up with a noxious pink chemical that induced vomiting and fainting. That night one worker died in his sleep from the poison. Over the next two days, company security guards patrolled the area, press ganging skilled workers and forcing them into the mill at gunpoint. Rather than break the strike, some 650 workers fled to Bacolod where the Benedictine Sisters provided them with food and shelter for two weeks. The Christian community persevered and priests continued to co-celebrate mass with the workers. One preached a sermon on the theme: 'The Devil today has no horns, he wears a *barong* [dress shirt] and drives a Mercedes-Benz'. On 3 March, some 100,000 workers, the second largest demonstration in the province's history, staged a mock funeral for a coffin labelled 'justice' on the plaza before the Bacolod Cathedral.

Rested and spirits restored, 500 strikers returned to the picket lines outside Central La Carlota on 10 March. On the first day back, security guards fired into the picket line, wounding five. The line held and two days later blocked cane trains from entering the mill. Responding to appeals from the mill's owners, close cronies of President Marcos, the Constabulary mobilized an operation to break the strike. At dawn on 14 March, 500 soldiers in full battle-gear, backed by 300 security guards, faced 600 unarmed strikers. There was every indication that the troops were ready to open fire.

At 7.00 a.m. Bishop Fortich arrived from Bacolod and spoke briefly with the Constabulary General in command. 'What do we have here, El Salvador?' He then approached the workers who applauded him warmly. The Bishop explained the obvious: the military were ready to shoot and the strikers would have to let the cane trucks enter the mill. In its final report on the strike, the union's La Carlota chapter commented: 'They had to agree and to accept what he told them for after all he was their Bishop and they hoped that somehow next time the Monsignor will help them in another way as he was always wont to help, he being their shepherd.'

Although no longer able to block the milling, some 600 strikers maintained the pickets for another six weeks. A company of 175 battle-hardened Army regulars from Mindanao remained camped at the mill to prevent pickets from disrupting operations. As the milling season finished and the union exhausted its funds, the NFSW leaders announced that the communal kitchen would close on 4 May. The strikers were broke. Their children had been suspended from school when the mill cut off their education grants. All were blacklisted throughout the province. It was a bitter defeat.

Despite the defeat, the strike remains a tribute to the union's strength. No other union in the history of Negros had ever instilled such loyalty and militance. Through their conscientization seminars, the religious had succeeded in breaking the cycle of despair and fostering a new awareness among the workers. This brief discription cannot do justice to the physical and psychological punishment those workers endured for ninety-six days — hunger, tropical heat, beatings, tear gas, poison chemicals, the fear of death, and the threat of permanent unemployment. Still, they persisted.

I met some of these union militants a year later and their determination was undiminished. They had a clear understanding of how their sugar society had stacked the odds against them. But they had faith that someday, somehow they would defeat this 'system of injustice'. Ten years ago when I first lived at Central La Carlota for several months, I was appalled at the culture of servility I encountered. Workers were cowed. Many seemed reluctant even to make eye contact with their superiors. Like hacienda labourers, they curled their bodies into a posture of deference, bowed their heads, and spoke in an embarrassed mumble. These workers could now look their superiors in the eye without any trace of shame. Although the Church and its unions have lost one strike and a great deal of prestige, they may have won a more lasting if less tangible victory — they may well have liberated the consciousness of an entire class.

Chapter Five
Mountain Mission

After five years on Negros, Fr Gore's missionary career was at an impasse. His patience with the planter elite was exhausted and he had begun to doubt the value of serving the sacraments to people living in a state of 'structural sin'. The feeling was becoming mutual as the planter elite grew tired of Fr Gore's criticisms of what seemed to them a time-tested social order.

Through conversations with fellow Columbans, Gore found that Fr John Brazil, an Irish missionary, shared his views. Together they approached their superior, Fr Eamonn Gill, and asked permission to be released from conventional parish duties to experiment with a new kind of mission to the mountains. The conservative minority among the Negros Columbans, a group of seven the majority called 'the Black September', objected strongly and grumbled about 'getting the priests back in the parish'. But Fr Gill had served as a parish priest on the Tablas plateau where his involvement in landgrabbing cases had made him sympathetic to the plight of the poor hill farmers. In 1975 the Columbans released the two priests from regular duties and assigned them the newly created parish of Oringao, a rough highland district that began in the foothills fifteen kilometers southeast of the town and extended to the high ridges at the island's centre.

'When John and I went to Oringao we were convinced that we were not going to do what we had been doing with the sacraments', said Fr Gore in a brief interview between tea with a justice and dinner with the Archbishop of Sydney. 'We also wanted to respond to the crisis of the poor by getting them organized to serve themselves. Most of our work up to then was basic training for children – catechism, communion, schooling. We were tired of the numbers game – getting masses of people into catechism classes and into Churches, getting them cleaned up for Heaven. As [Fr] Mickey Martin once said – "shoving the sacraments down their throats". We wanted to break with mass Christianity'.

Lying between the headwaters of the Ilog and Hilabangan Rivers, the parish of Oringao was 150 square kilometers of denuded hills and ridges. It was a frontier area of small farms without roads, established villages or schools. Like most of the island's southern highlands, Oringao has the forlorn appearance of a wasteland – treeless hills covered with brown *cogon* grass, eroded gullies, and isolated, bamboo-stilt houses clinging to the slopes. The foothills were settled by migrants from the island's east coast who spoke Cebuano, another Visayan language not readily understood by the Ilongo speakers of Kabankalan's plains. After the lumber companies had stripped the hills of their timber in the 1950s, the Cebuano migrants moved in one by one to occupy small five and ten hectare farms without bothering to file for legal title to the land. Many of the migrants had been driven off their lands in northern Negros by expanding plantations during the sugar boom of the early 1960s. Oringao was their last chance to survive as independent small farmers.

The high mountains about five hours hike from the settlement at Oringao were inhabited by pagan Filipinos and black aboriginals, descendants of the few who survived the Spanish slaughters of the last century. Lying on the northern fringe of the new parish, Carolan district was the place where the Spanish priest Fr Cuenca had betrayed the largest of the pagan tribes into a massacre by the colonial Constabulary in 1856. Fr Gore was, in fact, the first missionary to hike these hills since Fr Cuenca's unfortunate visits 120 years before. Most of Fr Gore's new parishioners were still marginally literate and were either half pagan or still animist. He took delight in introducing the aboriginals to the modern world. 'They had never left the mountains in their lives', he recalled smiling. 'Kabankalan was an amazement for them – it seemed like New York. They spent hours staring at the huge ocean'.

Since a conventional church would have only reached a

fraction of the 12,000 parishioners scattered over a large mountain area, the two priests were forced to experiment with a new style of parish organization, the Basic Christian Community. Like a few other innovative priests in remote areas of the Philippines, they began to develop a decentralized parish based on priestless prayer groups of thirty to fifty people. Although the Christian Community has since become one of the building blocks of the Philippine Church, there were no ready models in the mid 1970s. Through experimentation and interaction with their parishioners, the two priests participated in the creation of a Church responsive to the particular needs of their parish. Their innovation created a new model for parish work that soon spread throughout the Negros diocese.

At the outset, Oringao was a parish in name only. There was no local government and no Church. The only focal point was a weekly market at the Oringao settlement where the two priests set up a small chapel to serve as a base for operations. A strong man of great vigour, Fr Brazil began hiking the hills to say mass at the annual village fiestas, the only contact most hill farmers had with the Church. He agreed to return for the next year's fiesta only if the people would set up their own prayer group *(panimabahon)* and send its leaders to the Oringao chapel for training seminars. Since people had some previous Church contact through Fr Gore's work with FFF and Fr O'Brien's with the Sa Maria movement, they were receptive to the suggestion.

These two-day seminars were the key to the construction of a new parish. Assisted by priests and nuns from elsewhere in the diocese, Fr Gore put each group of twenty-five participants through twelve intensive sessions focused on concepts of community and human dignity. In one exercise, the seminar leader would cut a pie into twenty-two tiny pieces and three large slices for the better off. 'We would really lay it on', says Gore smiling faintly, 'and give those with the large slices the royal treatment – a big glass of juice, a serviette. After the pie was eaten and the people angry, Fr Gore would drive home the point. 'I would ask if society were just if it were organized the same way – a few got all the land, all the education? When I asked how to change this inequality, they would say "time will change society". And I would answer: "Bloody Hell! You have to change it".'

Another exercise involved giving each participant a sheet of paper with instructions to do whatever they wanted with it. In every group one or two of the peasant participants would strain to crush it into a tiny ball. 'When that happened', Gore recalls, 'I would ask why. Usually they would say something very revealing of their sense of oppression: "That is the way I feel – crushed in. When I go to the *poblacion* [town centre] with no shoes I am treated badly in the *municipio* [town hall] because I have no land, no education". Then we would talk about that and make it the focus of the session. It was the reverse of the passive banking method of education – teacher hands it out and the student deposits it in his mind'.

Through such 'conscientization' Fr Gore and his co-workers tried to teach the peasant parishioners that they were not merely passive objects of history, but subjects of history who could shape their own destiny. In the broadest sense these seminars were a practical application of the theology of liberation which was then developing among radical clerics in the Latin American Church. 'We tried to give the people a sense of self-worth and dignity', he explains, 'for without that they could accomplish nothing. The seminars had an enormous impact. For the first time in their lives, these poor mountain people realized that they were not the shit of the earth'.

Once the seminars had trained qualified leaders, Fr Gore began transferring control of the parish to local Communities of about thirty families operating as mutual-aid groups. After building an embryonic network of Communities, the priests then tried to devise ways to strengthen the internal unity of each. 'Gradually, we tightened up the participation. You could not just pay P5.00 for a baptism. You have to present your child to the Community for approval'. Eventually, forty to fifty Communities with some 10,000 members were organized into six regions, called *centros*, which in turn sent representatives to the Oringao parish council, the apex in the bottom-up hierarchy.

As their Communities gained strength and their leaders confidence, authority began to flow upward from the people to the parish council where the priest sat as just one member – a complete reversal of the top-down hierarchy in a conventional parish. In a fundamental sense, people were learning to take control of a key institution, the church, and break their passivity, their deference before a traditional authority figure, the priest. The established pattern of Church authority from Pope to Bishop to priest was now implicitly challenged by the rise of a parish structure based on popular control

'For the first time we gave the people an experience in democracy', explained Fr Gore over coffee one sweaty morning at Bacolod prison. 'When we had a referendum for all the Communities we found all the usual election anomalies – votes without elections, fraudulent ballots, all the tricks. After that first disaster, we started to reform – secret ballots in the Communities instead of a show of hands, and a group to check results, our own little COMELEC [Commission on Elections]. In short, we gave them a real education in democracy – discussion, common decisions, and helping each other in concrete ways'.

After his experience as a union organizer in these hills with the FFF, Fr Gore was careful to encourage a genuine democracy by barring local elite from leadership in the Christian Communities. He was concerned that the rich peasants and local merchants would 'use the position to consolidate their control over people. People whom they previously controlled economically, they will now control spiritually'. Through his organization of the parish, Fr Gore was introducing the first community organization into an unshaped society. He was determined that he would not contribute to the emergence of a local power elite which, like the planters of Kabankalan's *poblacion*, used the Church to reinforce their economic and political power.

In selecting lay leaders, the two priests avoided the richest and poorest, instead favouring middle peasants with enough land for independence but not enough to dominate. Their method was a practical application of the 'structural analysis' taught by the Belgian Catholic sociologist François Houtart at a seminar with Philippine clergy in 1975. So inoculated against control by a small elite, the Communities began to develop an egalitarian spirit and overcome the isolation of the mountains.

'We re-introduced the old Visayan custom of cooperative plowing and planting', continued Fr Gore. Groups working together provided a natural security in tough times and allowed farms to keep going if the farmer got sick at plowing and planting time. We tried to enrich the concept of community which was very weak'.

As the parish grew gradually into a self-sustaining network of fifty-two Christian Communities with 10,000 members, Fr Gore became free to shift his efforts into the economic development of these poor highland farms. As this phase of the work began, Fr Brazil went on leave for further studies in Rome and died of a heart attack in Ireland on his way back to Negros. Fr Gore had to give up the comparatively comfortable seminar work at the Oringao Chapel and begin hiking the hills of his sprawling parish. A robust man with a barrel-chested build he learned to walk barefoot like a peasant and use his toes for gripping the mud as he clambered up steep slopes in a tropical downpour. He hiked through the hills for days on end to familiarize the farmers with new new parish projects.

Through his travels and conversations, Fr Gore soon became aware that the key problem facing his parishioners was the poverty of their five or ten hectare farms. On the lush plains of Kabankalan – with its good soil and network of market roads – four hectares was enough to provide prosperity for a small farmer. But in the hills poor soil, inappropriate crops, and the lack of any market roads conspired against him. As he thought through these problems, Fr Gore was determined that he would not play Santa Claus – a white benefactor giving gifts to all the good little brown brothers. He would play a catalytic role, providing information, ideas and seed capital for projects that would enable the poor farmers to help themselves. Most importantly, he would implement each project through a cooperative structure based in the Communities that could continue, once established, without him or any other priest.

Fr Gore initiated a series of projects designed to raise household incomes and thus improve the farmer's chances of survival. He started small with animal breeding. A planter afraid to venture into the hills gave the parish twenty water buffalo in exchange for rounding up a hundred head of his cattle that had wandered off. Instead of simply giving the animals to parishioners, Gore set up a breeding cooperative which dispersed water buffalo to needy farmers. The cooperative also acquired ten breeding pigs to provide piglets for a swine fattening scheme. Working always on a self-help principle, Gore introduced a number of basic development projects through the Communities – duck farming, fish ponds, a credit union and sanitary drinking-water systems. With its profits from these various ventures, the parish acquired a 100 hectare cooperative farm to provide additional income for poorer households and upgrade peasant agricultural skills.

Although these schemes improved peasant life by providing additional household income, they did not confront the basic problem that made these farmers poor – bad soil and bad harvests. Fr Gore contacted an Australian agronomist living in Bacolod City, Basil Rossi, and asked him for suggestions. After surveying the parish, Rossi reported that the soil was severely damaged and would have to be rebuilt with organic fertilizer. Once humus was restored to the soil, then yields would increase dramatically and farmers could prosper on small five-hectare farms. If nothing were done, the soil would degenerate to the point that peasants would be faced to abandon their land. Once the tree cover had been stripped off these slopes, hard tropical rains were leaching the soils of its nutrients. The area was being transformed from a lush rain forest into a tropical desert of bare gullies, calcified hardpan and brown cogan grass.

Rossi had a solution – vermiculture. Imported chemical fertilizers were too expensive for poor peasants. In any case, they would only raise yields for one harvest and could not rebuild humus in the soil. Animal manure was too expensive and not generally available. Earthworm breeding solved all these problems.

'We now have two million earthworms eating their hearts out in clay pots', says Fr Gore with a wide grin. 'They produce four tons of organic fertilizer every week which we can either sell for P4,000 a ton or distribute to local farmers. Worm manure has the consistency of coffee grounds and, best of all, it has no smell. It is a successful organic fertilizer program that both restores the soil and cuts out the cost of imported chemicals'.

As the breeding worms began to fill pot after pot, Fr Gore was forced to hire workers to manage the worm ranch he built near his church. By 1982 he had three full-time workers, fifteen part-timers, and an annual income of P150,000. Fr Gore issued worm pots to his parishioners to breed their own fertilizer and sent an expert to advise them on what additional nutrients were required for specific soil types. By selling the output of the central worm ranch to sugar planters, Fr Gore guaranteed the financial independence of the parish. 'Our experts say that the soil of Negros is dead. The land has no living organisms left and it's only the chemical fertilizers which make the cane come up every year. This organic fertilizer costs half of the price of chemical imports and can raise cane production by 20 percent'.

As the farms began rebuilding their soil with earthworm manure, Fr Gore moved into the second phase of his program, revival of native seed varieties, but was interrupted by his arrest. 'The aim was to save people from paying the high costs for patented high-yielding varieties sold by the multi-national corporations. With improved soil and organic fertilizer, the old varieties should be able to produce as much as the new patented varieties and chemical fertilizers'.

The rapid growth of Oringao's Christian Communities made a convert of Bishop Fortich who had initially been reluctant to encourage their growth in his diocese. 'In early 1978 the Bishop made a pastoral visit to Oringao for confirmations. We took him way up into the mountains and he saw all the adult support and involvement. Thousands turned out to see him. You know, the Bishop is really a numbers man – he likes to see a crowd in church. As he toured, he was really impressed with the Christian Communities and was convinced'. After his return to Bacolod, Bishop Fortich elevated Oringao to the status of a full parish and began to encourage the formation of Christian Communities throughout the diocese.

Fr Gore's partner in this Church experiment was his future co-accused Fr Niall O'Brien who in 1976 was assigned to the neighbouring mountain parish at Tabugon, due south of

Oringao. For the previous five years he had been living on a lowland hacienda north of Kabankalan where he learned first hand of the workers' poverty and poor prospects. He decided to attempt a small solution, a communal farm, which began bringing him to the mountains near Tabugon, the site of his future parish.

'I could remember saying Mass in house after house', he recalled of those days on the hacienda, 'and gathering the people around me. I would be a little bit fastidious over the rules and regulations over getting my Mass correct and making sure of the liturgical set up. But around me was the most excruciating poverty. Suddenly, it began to dawn on me how I had my priorities a little bit wrong.

'In the evening sometimes I would be having a drink with some of the men on the hacienda and they would be telling me the conditions of their lives. We decided together to try a little experiment – a communal farm that brought me up into the mountains. Well this farm spread out and it started other farms, but my heart got caught up with something elsewhere. When I was in the mountains some of the Filipino priests showed me how to start small Christian Communities and advised me to do so'.

Through his continuing study of theology and his contact with the hacienda workers, Fr O'Brien had decided that it was his duty as a priest to devote himself fully to the service of the poor. 'When we join the poor and oppressed in their struggle for life, then we are putting ourselves in the presence of God', said Fr O'Brien, his rapid-fire delivery driving my pen faster across the page. 'St Augustine said, "The Father sent his Son into the world to defend the poor". That summarizes a complex theology so well. At this particular time in human history, the cry of the poor is what must be recognized. To fail to do so is to put the whole human symphony out of tune. The priest is first and fully a Christian. He is more presbyter than *sacerdos* – more a servant of the people than the leader of a cult'.

Their contrasting personalities and backgrounds were well matched. Gore grew up in working class Perth and O'Brien was raised in upper-class Dublin. The Kabankalan elite enjoyed

O'Brien's elegance; the peasants trusted Gore's bluntness. Gore was the pragmatist who pioneered the basic organizational technique for the Christian Communities; O'Brien was the theorist who refined it. While Gore experimented with worms to rebuild the soil, O'Brien wrote a 240-page health manual to teach villagers, who never saw a doctor, self-diagnosis and the use of herbal medicine. The manual identified the plants in pictures, described procedures for preparing medicines and prescribed dosage. The two priests then worked together to distribute herb seedlings to their parishioners. O'Brien's book can reduce peasant dependence on costly imported pharmaceuticals; Gore's vermiculture program can free farmers from the expense of imported fertilizers and patented seed stocks. Both schemes are a pragmatic rendering of liberation theology. Once instilled with self-confidence through 'conscientization', peasants can use such programs to liberate themselves from external exploitation.

After his arrest on charges of multiple murder in 1983, Fr O'Brien reflected on his six year experiment with the Basic Christian Communities in an article for *The Furrow*, a religious journal. Located in the same village as the Dacongcogon Sugar Mill, his parish at Tabugon did not suffer from the same isolation and backwardness as Oringao. Through their membership in the sugar cooperative, O'Brien's 16,000 parishioners were perhaps the most affluent of the peasants on the southern plateau. Tabugon's accessibility, however, created other problems. The Constabulary used the village as a staging centre for its operations against the NPA guerillas, subjecting its residents to harrassment and abuse. These conditions combined with O'Brien's continuing interest in liturgy to make his Tabugon experiment rather different from Gore's work at Oringao.

While Gore had come to Oringao in anger at an unjust society, O'Brien came to Tabugon to try a new theology. Through his reading of the deliberations at Vatican II, O'Brien was convinced that the conventional model of the priest-dominated parish – that he had known in Ireland and found upon arrival in Negros – was passé. Vatican II now required, in O'Brien's words, that 'all the sacraments would be so lucid in their meaning as to be themselves instruments in teaching the Christian life. Mass would be the celebration of community, of thanksgiving and the inspiration for change'.

O'Brien's experience in the Sa Maria seminars had convinced him that the traditional Church was structurally incapable of implementing the new theology. 'Many priests in the parishes complained that the retreat movement had little effect on the chronic social situation. Some went further and complained that the retreats even domesticated people, making them see savlation in purely other-world terms. Where I was in my first parish, I had myself noticed that the sacramental/liturgical approach had very little effect on the people's social consciousness'.

When Fr O'Brien took up his parish at Tabugon, his goal was 'liberation of the whole man rather than saving souls'. As taught by Pope Paul VI in the encyclical *Populorum Progressio*, he would aim for a 'total human development' by creating a network of priestless mini-parishes of thirty families each 'somewhat on the model of the early Christians as seen in *Acts* 2 and 4'. While these local Communities were to become the focal point of life in the new parish, there remained certain rituals, the sacraments, which had to be performed by the priest. These O'Brien altered in a way that de-mystified his role and reinforced the centrality of the nuclear Communities.

The rejection of Satan and his works in *baptism* was given a new social dimension – 'Do you reject landgrabbing and usury?'; 'Are you willing to stand up for your rights?' It was no longer a 'superstitious rite saving us from the wrath of God'. *Confirmation* was to be based on 'the themes of social sin' since it would be 'ridiculous if people confessed personal misdemeanors while being totally unaware of the suffering going on all around them'. Confirmation was now done at age eighteen with the entire Christian Community, not a wealthy godfather, standing as sponsor. *Marriage* was peformed in groups, on set days, for fixed fees – nobody could buy a grand church wedding.

The question of power lay at the core of the new parish structure. Before there could be any change, the priest would

have to divest himself of his authority, a difficult task. 'We
priests are usually very strong individuals so we all have the
problem of learning genuinely to share power', wrote Fr
O'Brien. 'It's an art, it's a discipline, it's a sacrifice, it's a heroic act
of trust. But it has to be done'. The priest cannot simply retreat
into contemplation, but must continue working with the 'core
group' at the apex of the new parish hierarchy. Most importantly, the priest has to ensure that the people's parish council is
not captured by the established elite. 'Some parishes have
parish councils which turn out to be composed of the elite of the
town. Hence it will be against their social interest if the priest
wants to introduce measures which favour the poor. He will be
opposed all the way'.

Structural analysis was required to assure the new democracy.
Working with the Filipino priests from other parishes, O'Brien
found that Tabugon had a pyramid of social stratification that
ran from large landowners, to medium landowners and officials, down to share-croppers and landless labourers. 'We
decided to begin looking for leaders among small independent
landholders and maybe some from the layers immediately
above and below them. We wished to avoid the destitute
because their lives were already taken up with the search for the
next meal – they have little independence of action and can be
easily got at'.

Once mobilized, the people's church was organized to defend
itself against the twin enemies of disease and oppression.
Supported by their Communities, forty paramedics spent three
months studying a medical care delivery system based on three
principles – prevention over cure, herbs over drugs, home over
hospital.

Conscientization taught 'greater understanding of the structures of injustice' and led to the formation of justice and peace
committees in each mini-parish. Instead of relying on lawyers
from the Bishop's free legal aid office, the parish now mobilized
itself to oppose rampant landgrabbing and military abuse. The
Communities made mass marches to other villages across the
Tablas plateau to join rallies against torture and killing. Using
non-violence, the parish confronted landgrabbers. 'The amaz-

ing part is that as soon as landowners and bureaucrats realize that the people will not be beaten under their attacks they more often than not withdraw. We do not propose non-violence as the only way for anyone under any conditions. We proposed it as the way for our Christian Communities'.

Two years after Fr O'Brien came to Tabugon, Fr Vicente Dangan, a diocesan priest, joined his future co-accused in the task of building Christian Communities. A native of Antique Province on Panay Island, he had studied at the local seminary and was ordained only two months before his assignment to Kabankalan. Fr Dangan was a pioneer in integrating Filipino priests into what had been an exclusively Columban mission territory in southern Negros. Responding to the Bishop's call for the formation of Christian Communities throughout the diocese, Fr Dangan built a network of twenty-six in his own parish and counselled Fr O'Brien on the work at Tabugon.

A month after their arrests on charges of multiple-murder, these three priests – Gore, O'Brien and Dangan – sent a circular letter to their 'brother priests' in Negros trying to impart the essentials of their experience with the Christian Communities. Written at a time of intense emotion, the document captures the spirit of their pastoral experiment.

'We believe', they began, 'that the small Christian Community is *incarnating the Kingdom of God*'. But before a group can become such a spiritual community, six essential qualities must be present. The members must share 'not as patron and patronized, not as leader and *sakop* [subject], not as *amo* [master] and *empleado* [worker], but as Brothers of Christ'. Once the bonds of social control are thus shattered, then members can share in a process of genuine dialogue in which everyone participates. Moreover, they have a Christian responsibility 'to remove injustice from their own Community – such as land grabbing, unfair *alili* [interest], unjust division of crops'. Once these barriers are removed, the Community should be able to enjoy the intimacy of 'real reconciliation' and share 'their moments of nearness to God'. But this is not enough. It is wrong if the Community 'turns on itself and thinks only of its own perfection. It must care about what's happening to other parts of

the people of God. It must be concerned. For a Christian there is
no such thing as "neutral". The *Katilingban* [Community] takes
sides with the poor and oppressed everywhere'.

The priests closed their letter with a warning and an
exhortation. "Remember... if your people begin to grow into a
Christian Community, they will take responsibility for their own
destiny, losing the *Bahala na* [God disposes] and *Pagbuot sang
Dios* [by the will of God] mentality. They will question any
oppressor and refuse to be walked on – though their only
weapon is truth, courage and the words of God. Then you'll be
in trouble, but the Gospel and all the Sacraments will come
alive. So be not afraid – remember we have a secret weapon. It is
this: Christ has risen. He is alive and with us as we struggle to
bring about His Kingdom'.

During their first two years, these two mountain missions
were fortunate to remain an oasis of peace midst an escalating
war between communists and Constabulary in southern Negros. As the communist New People's Army [NPA] began
pushing north into Tabugon from their initial bare areas at the
centre of the Tablas plateau, Fr O'Brien's parish was caught in
the crossfire. Unable to distinguish between guerilla and
parishioner, the Constabulary unleashed a random violence
against members of the Christian Communities. Somewhat
later, the resurgence of a messianic pagan cult, the Salvatorre
movement, brought the Constabulary further north into Fr
Gore's Oringao parish. Again unable to distinguish between
pagan and Christian, Constabulary patrols moved through the
hills with torture and murder. In both parishes the Christian
Communities met their enemies, cult and Constabulary, with
the force of a non-violent mass. Their mobilization overwhelmed the Salvatorre cult, but provoked even greater violence from the Constabulary. As the fighting in the south
intensified, many within the Church began to raise serious
questions about Gore and O'Brien's leadership of the Christian
Communities.

'We gradually became aware that we did not have the
ultimate solution to the problem', admitted Fr Gore with a
certain resignation in a prison interview. 'At the outset we did

not realize what we would meet. We got some criticism from our own priests who were further left and sympathetic to the NPA. They told us the only real solution was armed struggle; anything else was pussy-footing around. At first they didn't pay much attention to what we were doing. But once we started showing signs of success we got this reaction quite strongly from priests and movement laypeople in Negros. Our success called into question their decision for armed struggle. We did not say ours was *the* solution. But we wanted to try something which had not yet been tried here – a non-violent means of change'.

Fr Gore's most trenchant critic was not one of Fr Jalandoni's followers on the Christian left, but his own superior, Fr Michael Martin, whom I would classify as moderate, perhaps progressive, but not radical. Like several of the Columbans whom I met on Negros, Fr Martin has been through an intensive process of self-criticism and self-analysis. He seems able to see the implications of an action as he is taking it – as if to envision his self-image in full stride towards him as he takes his very first step. In a modern Church missionaries must be metaphysical acrobats – doing but not doing, leading but not leading, building with great energy only for the sake of giving away. As white men in a brown world, they are not lifetime leaders of the local Church but catalysts of change. Doing their work too well is as bad as not doing it at all.

At least, that is what I think he was trying to tell me in our night-long conversation on the eve of my departure from Negros. After a week in the cell and courtroom talking intensely with Gore and O'Brien, caught up in the drama, convinced of their heroism, I found it somehow unsettling to hear Fr Martin's long and thoughtful critique of his two priests.

'Brian [Gore] thought that Oringao was too poor, too backward for the people to make a choice by themselves for or against the NPA', explained Fr Martin as he tensed his neck or rocked athletically on the balls of his feet. 'He felt they had to go through a period of human development before they were ready to make their choice. And when he was on home leave in 1981-82, his lay leader was very much against the NPA'.

'My objection to Brian's position', Fr Martin continued, 'was that he presumed to make decisions for the people. His parish was very centralized and his key layworkers lived in a central compound around the chapel. Admittedly, the area was a bit backward, but he chose to see it as more backward than it was. The difference between the parishes at Tabugon and Oringao in terms of human development was not all that much. By perceiving the area as more backward than it was, Brian created a parish in which the priest was still the central figure. Niall [O'Brien] was more flexible and open in his style of community organization, but people used to complain that he was much too influenced by Brian'.

'Mind you, there are no two finer missionaries pound for pound than those two. They are men of remarkable intellects and energies, and leave the rest of us gasping to keep up. But that is also a problem. They naturally tend to take on more responsibility and authority in a parish than perhaps they should under the concept of the Basic Christian Community'.

'Brian and Niall tend to have a "messianic" or a Biblical view towards the Church', continued Fr Martin in response to my question about the theological implications of their work. 'For example, the Israelites were oppressed in Pharoah's Egypt so they made the exodus and on the march had a religious experience. Afterwards, it is written up in the Old Testament as God shaping the lives of the passive people. But it was the people who shaped God, or their image of God. Niall, in his article in *The Furrow* [discussed earlier], sees things in terms of Vatican II sending the word to the Church and the Church giving the word to the people. Not so. The people were changing and so the Church had to change with them. Niall and Brian, reflecting their times, sometimes still see things in Biblical or messianic terms of Church and priest changing people instead of being changed by them'.

In the late 1970s, the Tablas Plateau became a battleground between the Philippine Constabulary and the New People's Army [NPA]. The Columban parishes that dotted those hills were soon engulfed in civil warfare.

Two hours drive south from provincial capital, Negros' broad coastal plain of sugar plantations rises into a vast, undulating plateau of forest and small farms that occupies the southern quarter of the island. Long the refuge of unsubjugated pagans and bandits, the plateau was not settled until the 1950s when pioneer families from the sugar districts began clearing small farms of five to ten hectares from the forest. A quarter century later, on the eve of the NPA's penetration, the plateau was still very much a frontier. Isolated farming families suffered bandits, and women walking to and from remote fields were sometimes raped. Cattle rustling and random violence were endemic. Much of the land had been corruptly titled or claimed by wealthy urbanites and landgrabbing threatened the futures of many small farmers. Roads are bad, schools worse, and other services non-existent. There are virtually no doctors, hospitals or clinics. Government was seen as remote and indifferent, if not hostile. Only the Catholic Church seemed at all concerned. In 1969 Bishop Fortich installed his antiquated sugar mill at Tabugon and the Columbans established a thin network of mission parishes, the latest at Tabugon under Fr O'Brien.

Unable to operate in the exposed lowland cane districts or narrow mountain zone to the north, the NPA established its base on the southern plateau in the early 1970s. In September 1971 the Negros press carried its first report of NPA activity in the province under the headline – DO WE HAVE NPA OPERATIONS IN THE MOUNTAINS OF NEGROS? One Kabalkalan resident told of meeting three NPA guerillas who tried to recruit him, and a Constabulary unit had encountered a six-man NPA patrol in nearby mountains armed only with .22 calibre home-made rifles. Eight months later, a captured guerilla told Constabulary interrogators that the NPA, led by members of the Nationalist Youth group, were setting up base areas in the towns of Candoni and Kabankalan in southern Negros.

By the time I visited the area ten years later, the NPA had built up a guerilla force of 100 to 200 men and won the loyalty of the entire district. During a week of intensive interviewing, hiking and driving about the plateau, I met nobody who had anything but praise for the NPA. Led by former university students, the NPA has created an effective government apparatus that provides an order that frontier farmers welcome. Rapists have been shot or buried alive. Stolen water buffalo, a farmer's most valuable asset, are recovered and returned. NPA officers mediate local disputes and prevent conflict from becoming vendetta. Several landgrabbers have been executed as a warning to the rest to stay out of the area. When a lumber company security officer returned to work the 1,000 hectares he had stolen from small farmers, the NPA raided his camp, killing both him and his wife.

One afternoon I happened through a remote hamlet where eight NPA·guerillas, armed with M-16s, were conducting a 'seminar' for the young men of the area. The lectures were something of a morals lesson – respect your parents, don't fight with your mates, no sex before marriage, work hard, make something of yourselves. The NPA impose no taxes of any kind and survive by raising crops in remote mountain fields or by buying their food from villagers.

Not surprisingly, the Constabulary soon began losing the battle for this plateau. In February 1983, the NPA demonstrated its strength by marching 100 well-armed guerillas into the town of Candoni, the plateau's only major settlement. The troops executed two local militia, seized seven M-16s, and six pistols, and occupied the municipal hall for several hours. Candoni is not much – a few shops and wooden houses dotting a concrete road grid. But it was the first time that the NPA have seized a town in Negros.

As the NPA strength grew, the Constabulary command sent in regular and irregular forces to suppress the revolt. After each military operation swept across the plateau leaving its inevitable trail of abuse, the people complained to their Columban priests who demanded that the Bishop file a formal protest. As military operations grew more brutal, tensions between Church and Constabulary in southern Negros mounted.

During the late 1970s, the main object of Church attack was Sgt George Presquito, commander of the local death squad. One of the worst incidents was what one Church publication later called 'the Vilma Riopay Story'. At dawn on 17 July 1977, a group of heavily-armed, masked men under Sgt Presquito's command surrounded a peasant house at Magballo, a village on the Tablas plateau about eight kilometres from Fr O'Brien's parish. 'You are the one we want', said Sgt Presquito pointing to Vilma Riopay, a 21 year old woman who was a 'devoted catechist' in the Columbans' Magballo parish. Despite her father's pleadings, Sgt Presquito's squad drove off with her in a truck they had commandeered from the Daconcogon Sugar Mill. Immediately after the abduction, her father, Domingo Riopay, sought the aid of the Columban priest who spread an alarm throughout the diocese.

Three days later, Church contacts in the neighboring Diocese of Cebu somehow learned that she was being detained by Constabulary headquarters as an 'NPA suspect'. After many attempts, Redemptorist priests and RGS nuns won an interview with a Constabulary colonel who admitted holding Vilma but refused to let them see her. The Redemptorists telephoned Bishop Fortich at Bacolod who wrote his local Constabulary commander pleading that Domingo Riopay be allowed to visit his daughter. Accompanied by the director of the Catholic Social Action Office for Negros, Fr Suplido, Domingo Riopay flew to Cebu City and pleaded for his daughter's release. Since no charges were pending, the Colonel complied.

Noting Vilma's obvious disorientation, Domingo and the religious took her to a Cebu hospital where examination found bruises about the chest and thighs. Her condition was diagnosed as 'acute psychotic reaction'. She later revealed that she had been taken to a 'safehouse' in Bacolod after her arrest where she underwent interrogation and torture – denial of sleep, electrocution, beating about the genitalia and the 'water cure'. A year after the incident, a psychiatrist's report on Vilma read: 'Subject is still found to be suffering from anxiety and tension accompanied by recurrent headaches, insomnia, occasional nightmares, withdrawal from socialization and poor decision and work performance... She might become emotionally invalid for life. Definitely, she could not stand trial in court'. Despite formal complaints from Bishop Fortich, the Constabulary denied any knowledge of Sgt Presquito and no action was taken.

Fr O'Brien and his Communities were outraged by this case and later staged an Easter passion play in the parish Church depicting Sgt Presquito raping a peasant woman. There were other incidents that provoked conflict between O'Brien and the military. 'Presquito killed dozens of people and tortured hundreds around here', claimed one executive of the Dacongcogon Sugar Mill. 'Nobody knew how many. When his men dealt with women suspects, they tortured them badly and sometimes raped them'. Often drunk and always armed, Presquito and his gang roamed the plateau stealing pigs, extorting money and torturing for about three years until his volent death in 1978. Fr O'Brien was not intimidated and joined other priests in mounting an incessant protest against his abuse. There is some speculation that Sgt Presquito may have become such an embarrassment the Constabulary itself liquidated him.

Once Presquito's death squad was removed, regular Constabulary units continued the same style of operations. As reports of abuse accumulated, parish priests protested to Bishop Fortich who used his office as Chairman of the Church–Military Liaison Committee to convene a mass dialogue with the military in the southern towns. Working through their Christian Communities, priests could mobilize crowds of 5,000 to 10,000, an impressive show of non-violent force. Fr O'Brien once marched his parish forty kilometres in the tropical sun to participate in such a dialogue. On another occasion he protested when parishioners discovered several decaying corpses inside an encampment recently vacated by the military.

The situation worsened when 'sugar czar' Benedicto despatched Task Force Kanlaon, the unit that later framed the three priests, to the plateau as his personal contribution to the pacification effort. In August 1982, for example, forty Task Force troops swept the plateau for six days. Their heroics included destroying all the houses in one village, summarily executing two farmers, dismantling several houses for a barbecue, stripping a woman student naked, and stealing one pig, one chicken and P200. The Constabulary's provincial total for 1983 was fifty-four civilians killed and ten missing. The first five months of 1984 already showed twenty-eight killed and four missing. Under such circumstances, it is not surprising that some in the Church may have asked whether non-violence might not have its limits.

Trouble came to Fr Gore's Oringao parish in 1979 when a messianic cult leader named Alfredo Salvatorre wandered into the village to visit a distant relative. A native of Mindanao, Salvatorre received his 'message' from God during a great tidal wave that struck the southern island. Inspired by an ancient Filipino animism leavened with folk Catholicism, he had many of the traits of a *babaylan*, the traditional pagan priest: a one-eyed coconut which held the destiny of the world; amulets that guaranteed immunity to bullets; apostles named Moses and Felipe; and body tattoos in a curious 'dog Latin' that gave him special powers.

Salvatorre revived the ancient animist spirit service, adding some of his own innovations and borrowing liberally from Christian ritual. Every Sunday, he called his followers to the hills where he demonstrated his powers by being struck with a *bolo* work knife. There was no wound. Celebrants formed a circle and passed the magic one-eyed coconut hand-to-hand with great care since its fall would destroy the world in a cataclysm of fire and storm. The sick and the lame came to him and were cured by his magical incantations.

Witnessing his immunity to weapons and his curative powers, the peasants believed and his Salvatorre movement spread north through the mountains as far as Isabela. He soon won about 1,500 believers in Fr Gore's Oringao parish, the heartland of the movement, and another 3,000 to 4,000 members in the mountains further north. Awed by the pagan power of Salvatorre, whom they called 'Papa Pidio' or Pope Pidio, peasants began drifting away from Fr Gore's Christian Communities. Many of his parishioners were recent converts to the Church and had not yet shed their beliefs in the spirits of the land or the babaylan medium who could command them. During the 1890s the great rebel leader 'Papa Isio' or Pope Isio had drawn his peasant legions from these mountains. Three generations later, Alfredo Salvatorre, Papa Pidio, could command the same fear and following.

Like the messianic movements that swept the mountains of Negros in centuries past, the Salvatorre cult soon turned on unbelievers to punish them for their lack of faith. They also began attacking police and Constabulary patrols as oppressors of the people. Papa Pidio protected his followers, armed only with spears and swords, against police bullets by investing them with magical garments and tattoos. A typical Salvatorre warrior wore a white shirt decorated with magical signs – the eye of the Boy Jesus, crosses, pseudo-Latin incantations – and a red bandolero whose pockets were filled with little bottles of oil and weeds, magical potions used commonly by babaylan to ward off evil. Near their hearts they carried a *libretto* full of incantations that seem garbled versions of Latin responses in the old Catholic mass – 'Jesus Acetalum/ausa isla/ama anicuste/Amen Jesus'.

In July 1979, Inspector Leo Quingco and five fellow officers from the Kabankalan Police were on patrol armed with carbines. They were hiking through Carolan village on the northern fringe of Fr Gore's parish. 'We were drinking water when they started coming at us', he recalled in an interview a year later. 'There were about fifty of them waving short swords and spears, shouting *bira mo* ['hit them']. Since they were running and screaming, we had to open fire. We emptied our chambers at them. We were hitting them, we were sure of that. But they didn't stop, so we fled. Not one of them fell.

'After we withdrew, the next patrol of five police encountered them. The unit had one armalite, some Garands and a carbine. As the Salvatorres rushed at the patrol shouting and waving their swords, they opened up with the armalite [M-16] and many of the Salvatorres started falling. They fled with many dead and wounded, leaving two dead on the trail. That patrol met up with ours and we withdrew together'.

Let us all stop for a moment before we go any further with this narrative. I do not want us to fall into the intellectual trap that our white, Western culture has prepared for us. I can see the images forming in our minds right now – the lone white missionary leading his faithful brown flock in a crusade against a fanatical horde of whooping, spear throwing pagan primitives, just like a wagon train surrounded by Indians in old Hollywood movies. Matters were more complex than that. Before we can understand what happened to Fr Gore, we need, as Fr Martin has reminded us, to gain a critical perspective on his work.

The Salvatorres were not simple savages. They were practitioners of an ancient, pre-Christian religion which had survived 400 years of missionary work because it met certain social needs of the island's peasantry. While the Catholic Church remained in the towns and its priests allied themselves with the planters, the babaylan spirit medium lived in the mountain villages and dealt with the people's most basic fears – drought, flood, famine, disease and death. When the planters and the colonial state pressed too hard upon the peasants of Negros, they turned to the most powerful spirit medium, the *dalagangan*, to lead them in revolt – Buhawe in 1887, Papa Isio in 1896, Emperor Intrencherado in 1927, and Alfredo Salvatorre, Papa Pidio, in 1979. The sugar crisis of the late 1970s was pressing hard upon the peasants of plains and hills, creating unemployment, widespread hunger and despair. At this time of crisis, Fr Gore had been in these mountains less than a decade – the babaylan had been here more than a millenium.

True, you might concede, but how can people in a modern world believe in monsters and mediums unless they are ignorant savages? Perhaps my own experience with this ancient religion might provide something of an answer.

As I was finishing the field work for my Yale doctoral dissertation in 1976, I decided that I had to do some research on the babaylan to write about these early peasant revolts. So I observed their ritual sacrifices in Iloilo and Negros and collected information from both peasants and urban professionals about related pre-Christian beliefs – spirits, curse, divination, propitiation and blood sacrifice.

After about five months, it seemed to me that distinctly non-Christian beliefs permeated all levels of society, urban and rural, rich and poor. For three years I had been living quite comfortably here convinced that – despite certain elements of the exotic which I rather enjoyed – I was dealing with people whose Christian values were basically similar to my own. Now I found that a resilient animist religion co-existed with Christianity – weaker in the city but stronger in the countryside.

Despite this realization, I still found it difficult to accept that intelligent people whom I had known for years actually had a deep-seated fear of this awesome array of evil spirits – the *mantiw*, a smoking giant; the *tamawo*, an invisible humanoid who inhabits large trees; or the *patianak*, a winged monster that settles on the stomachs of pregnant women to kill the foetus with its long claws.

My wife was then pregnant with our first born and the delivery was only a few weeks away. My younger brother had suffered Down's Syndrome and I was worried about a recurrence in my own child, although I did not say anything at the time. It was then that I had an awful nightmare which remains a vivid memory. Flying to the Philippines from America in a light aircraft, I stopped over in Japan to re-fuel. There I met an old man who gave me a curious looking rag doll with sun glasses, for good luck he said. The scene changed and sometime later I was living in an isolated nipa hut in the flattest part of the Iloilo Plain that looks across the water to Negros. It was late in the afternoon and massive thunderheads rose grey and awesome to exceptional height, casting a light of dim translucence that brought out the richest hues of rice-paddy green.

As I gazed out the window at this natural spectacle, I saw distant dots descending from the heights at great speed. Their approach exposed their form – horrid looking monsters with long teeth, sharp claws and bat-like wings. They were the baby-killer spirits, the *patianak*. Great flocks of them were screeching out of the sky and dive bombing the roof of my house, then pulling away into the clouds for another descent. I became terribly frightened. There was certainly no escape across that flat plain and it was only a matter of time before they began attacking my flimsy roof. Then I recalled the Japanese doll. I tore it apart and hurled the scraps out the window. As I did so, the monstrous flocks soared off into the clouds and disappeared. I woke and felt fear.

For some days I thought about that dream. Eventually, I came to the conclusion that I had, in a dream state, accepted the reality of this pre-Christian religion. Having come into this society as an adult visitor, I would never know the real fear that comes from a childhood of indoctrination. It could not become a part of my conscious belief system. But I had by then imbibed enough of such fears for them to become a part of my dream

state consciousness. Reflecting upon the lessons of my uncon-
scious, I realized that I had expressed unstated fears for my child
with this vision of the evil patianak. I could now understand
why educated Catholics would still consult a babaylan when
doctors failed and why peasants could follow a powerful
dalagangan when the times made them desperate.

In October 1979, a local landlord in the mountains of Oringao
used the Salvatorre cult to murder a Christian Community
member so he could grab the victim's seven hectare farm. Their
leader Papa Pidio had already been captured and the movement
was breaking up into violent bands. After a ritual execution, the
Salvatorres carved a cross into their victim's forehead and
ordered that his body be left to decompose upon pain of death.
When word reached Fr Gore at his Church, he consulted with
his lay leaders about an appropriate response. Two years ago
some local tenant farmers had resisted eviction and the
landowner, a Kabankalan planter named Ferdie Zayco, had sent
the notorious death squad leader Sgt George Presquito to
resolve matters. Oringao's Christian Communities had mobilized 200 men to confront Sgt Presquito and he fled never to
return.

When the lay teachers suggested a second mobilization to
bury the victim, Lolito Olimpos, Fr Gore sent a circular to all
Communities. 'Lolito's dead body remains by the side of the
road. At the moment, members of Lolito's family spend
sleepless nights in fear and grief, occasionally entertaining
thoughts of committing suicide if only to go near the body of
their loved one. Is this a fitting reward for Lolito's incomparably
hard labour in order to own a small piece of land to feed his
family on? Lolito has not committed any offence to deserve this
kind of treatment. Why doesn't the government put an end to
this? Who will stop these existing wrong doings which prevail
among many of our brothers?'

Fr Gore then issued the call for mobilization. 'Lolito's blood
calls to us from the ground [*Genesis* 4:10] and is calling the
members of the Christian Community and all with good
intentions to unite in getting his body so as to give him a
Christian burial'.

On 4 November, a thousand parishioners marched five hours

through the mountains to the murder site. As they crossed a nearby river each picked up a rock from its banks. On that mountain top where they buried Lolito Olimpos beneath rocks from that river, Fr Gore held an emotional funeral which served to baptize the Christian Communities as a non-violent self-defence unit. That day on that bald mountain Fr Gore became vicar to a Church militant.

Speaking fluent Ilongo in the booming voice that made him such a persuasive preacher, Fr Gore delivered an impassioned sermon. 'My brethren, it is imperative that we must make a vow before the dead body of our brother, that we must continue building up a Kingdom of Christ here on earth, a kingdom of peace where no oppression exists. We must be brave for in the past we were cowards and lacking in our vigilance in defending the life of our brother from these evil men. Now we must repent this cowardice and we must renew our pledge to be ever watchful in the defence of the lives of all our Community members'.

'To all, I am reminding you of the words of Our Lord Jesus Christ, "Those who kill by the sword will perish by the sword". And those who killed Lolito, all twenty-four of them, can never escape the wrath of God, for Lolito's blood that has fallen into the ground is crying out for vengeance. And the Community should heed the cry of Lolito's blood. It is his own voice calling to us from the ground to avenge his death, to avenge justice. From now on we are going to call this the Place of the Skull. This will serve as a monument to his death.'

'Therefore, it is very necessary that we should all be strong and united. If we lack strength and are weak, they will get our leaders one-by-one and in this manner they could weaken our Community. You have seen his bones with his flesh all but nearly decomposed. We must never let them go on with this. That because of our cowardice similar fate will befall other Community members. Therefore, let us all unite. Let us be one.'

When Fr Gore finished, a peasant jumped up on the grave and called out: 'If you will not defend yourselves, who would do this for you? We cannot depend on the authorities. If we are not strong and show our willingness to defend ourselves, they will be able to triumph over us all'.

From the crowd, someone shouted: 'All of us, they have exploited!'

And the crowd answered: 'Let us be one! Let us arise! We'll oppose! The oppressors!'

Another farmer climbed upon the grave: 'Right here on this hallowed ground people from Anahaw, Cabcaban, Bulosan, and Ulugan, let us pledge to be one and fight those evil men!'

And again the crowd answered: 'Let us be one! Let us arise! We'll overcome!'

Another peasant spoke: 'As we turn back to our homes, let us bring with us the memory of this place, the memory of our brother Lolito that we may always be ready to offer our lives in defence of our unity. This we must pledge in memory of Lolito who is buried here in the "Place of the Skull".'

And the crowd shouted: 'People have rights! Let us be one! We'll overcome!'

Over the next few months these non-violent Christian legions marched into Salvatorre villages. Overwhelming them with a show of numbers, the Christians either arrested the Salvatorres on behalf of the police or extracted promises of truce. Once mobilized and militant, the Christian Communities suddenly emerged as a major political force in the mountains – opposing land grabbing, illegal gambling, corrupt local tax collectors and abusive village officials. Without realizing it, Fr Gore had challenged the authority of Kabankalan's Mayor Sola and the planter elite he represented. Once the Christian Communities began to question the integrity of local officials they were threatening Mayor Sola's carefully constructed patronage machine. It became, in the most basic sense, a struggle for power. First, the Columbans had taken their Church away from Kabankalan's elite. And now, Fr Gore was taking the villages, the traditional political power base of the town's elite.

Deflected from their assaults on the Christians, the Salvatorre sect again turned on local police and lowland villages. Several police patrols were attacked by gangs of screaming Salvatorres charging with long knives. As the incidents of theft, murder and assault mounted, Mayor Sola appealed to the government for support. Manila despatched the Constabulary's Long Range Patrol, a unit of thirty crack jungle fighters fresh from the

Muslim wars of Mindanao. Hardened to the point of savagery, the Long Range Patrol often marched with shovels to bury their victims, a habit which makes precise calculation of the number killed impossible. One reliable Kabankalan observer feels that they 'slaughtered dozens of innocent villagers'. The official tally for their few months in Kabankalan was nine villagers dead and fourteen missing.

Prompted by a wave of complaints from the highlands of Kabankalan, Bishop Fortich convened a session of the Church–Military Liaison Committee at Fr Gore's Oringao parish in March 1980. Still militant, an awesome crowd of 7,000 parishioners assembled before a forum of their social superiors – priests, senior Constabulary officers, and local officials – to complain angrily of municipal corruption and military abuse. Used to deference from such 'ignorant' peasants, the Constabulary officers fumed and Mayor Sola exploded in rage. But the Christian Community spokesmen held their ground and the authorities left humiliated.

Their vengeance was swift. Only three days after the Oringao meeting, the Long Range Patrol tortured seven innocent peasants to death. Ten days later, the same troops murdered two lay leaders from Tanawan village, about ten kilometres due north of Fr Gore's parish. The two were arrested at night, summarily executed and buried in a shallow grave. One of the victims, a poor hill farmer named Alex Garsales, was a dedicated leader of the Christian Community who only the day before had been honoured with the role of Christ in the Easter passion play. As a Community leader, he had been arrested three times opposing elite land grabbing in his village. Although less prominent than Alex, the other victim, Herman Muleta, was also active in their local Christian Community.

The Church protested the disappearance of the two Community leaders. The NFSW union chairman, Fr Saguinsin, fired off a letter to the provincial Constabulary Commander demanding their immediate return. A month after the disappearance, Bishop Fortrich convened a dialogue between Church, civil and military officials before a crowd of 4,000 parishioners at Kabankalan. After moving speeches by Alex's wife and children pleading his return, Mayor Pablo Sola rose to speak. He was not sympathetic. 'Why is there trouble? When you organized those Communities, did you ask permission from your mayor? Not at all! Christ organized the Catholic religion, and now we have Christian Communities. Why do we need those? After organizing your Communities in the mountains, then you come here and ask your mayor why some of you are disappearing! Blame the ones who organized you!'

A week later, a farmer plowing a field found the two corpses. Addressing the crowded funeral service in Kabankalan on 17 May, Bishop Fortich urged the people to continue their work. 'The Christian Community of which Alex and Herman were active members, must go on. We Christians should stand up with a firm determination that we cannot, and should not, and must not tolerate abuses of this nature. People of God from Tanawan, continue building the Christian Community for this is the true foundation of your human rights'.

The depth of Mayor Sola's anger was soon revealed when 'the people of Kabankalan' filed a petition with Pope John Paul II for the removal of Fr Brian Gore only a month after this emotional funeral. The document charged that Fr Gore's activities caused people 'to suspect that he has communistic leanings, and under the guise of his office as priest is sowing the seeds of discontent, confusion and chaos among our people, therefore preparing the group for the seeding of communistic ideas'. He was opposing government projects to alleviate the plight of the poor by forming Christian Communities. 'The municipality of Kabankalan was once a very peaceful town before the organization of the *Christianos Katilingban* [Christian Communities], which organization has confused the people in the rural areas'. It concluded with a warning that 'members of our Church are becoming lukewarm in their faith to the extent that a great number of our Roman Catholic population are being converted to other religious sects'.

Although he denied authorship of the petition, a claim that few found convincing, Mayor Sola spoke out strongly on its behalf. 'People here are tired of sermons dealing with the poor and the rich, the haves and have nots, to the extent of dramatizing these words on the altar even on Christmas Eve', said Mayor Sola in a newspaper interview on 30 June. Apparently determined to rid himself of Fr Gore, Mayor Sola enlisted the aid of his friend and political patron, Roberto Benedicto, to press the case with the Vatican. In a later speech before the Negros planters, Benedicto said that he had appealed 'to the highest ecclesiastical authorities' to get rid of those meddlesome foreign priests. Responding to these pressures, the Papal Nuncio contacted Bishop Fortich to express his concern but was assured that the diocese could handle matters.

As the controversy over the petition raged through July and August, Bishop Fortich convened a dialogue of all parties – the Governor, the Constabulary commander, the Columban Superior, Mayor Sola and Fr Gore. When it became clear that only Gore's removal would satisfy Mayor Sola, negotiations broke down. Tensions between Church and State in Kabankalan escalated. Bishop Fortich dismissed the removal petition as irrelevant because Oringao was now a separate parish, but town officials protested that Church boundaries did not matter – the village was a part of their civil jurisdiction. On 28 July, Cardinal Sin, the Archbishop of Manila, played *deus ex machina* by dropping into Kabankalan's plaza in a Constabulary helicopter to lead a rally of 12,000 Christian Community members. Mayor Sola countered with his own rally and drew about 100 people, a failure that left him even more determined. Church and State seemed headed for an open confrontation in Kabankalan until the unexpected happened. On 24 September, Mayor Sola was charged with multiple-murder and the petition campaign suddenly ground to a halt.

The charges arose from the brief orgy of Constabulary violence that had followed the explosive Church-Military meeting at Oringao on 26 March. Three days after the meeting, the Long Range Patrol had arrested seven innocent villagers who had no contact with the Christian Communities, and brought them to Mayor Sola's hacienda where the days of torture began. The logic of their persecution remains a mystery. They were not Salvatorres, were not even members of Fr Gore's parish, and were arrested at a wedding party ten kilometres from Oringao.

Several Filipino priests whom I interviewed offered a socio-logical explanation that I find convincing. Since the arrests came only three days after the Oringao meeting, Mayor Sola and the Long Range Patrol may have been willing to strike at any target for revenge. A patriarchal planter of the old school, Mayor Sola was outraged that any peasant would dare to speak to him as Fr Gore's parishioners had done. Any worker who came to him hat in hand muttering for mercy would never be refused a loan. He loved filling his lounge-room with his workers sprawled at his feet watching his television and laughing like little children. But he could not tolerate disrespect and would explode in a fit of temper when not treated with the deference he demanded. For such a proud and sensitive man, the peasants' assertiveness at Oringao would have been a severe emotional shock that demanded revenge.

After three days of continuous torture, the seven innocent peasants were hog-tied and buried alive in a cane field only 150 metres from Mayor Sola's front door. Unknown to either the mayor or the troops, some peasant watched the burial closely that night and marked the spot – sighting from the road to a tree on the horizon and counting the cane furrows to the grave. The news somehow reached the Columban priests in Kabankalan and Bishop Fortich began pressuring the Constabulary for an investigation.

On a dark, moonless night five months later, a Constabulary captain jumped from a moving vehicle to avoid attracting attention from anyone in Mayor Sola's house. Sighting from the spot on the road to the tree on the horizon, Captain Robelito Comilang, Constabulary commander for southern Negros, counted the furrows as he crossed the canefield. He drove a steel pipe several feet into the ground and could sniff the stench of rotting flesh when he pulled it from the ground. Some days later, at 6.00 a.m. on 16 September 1980, Captain Comilang knocked at Mayor Sola's door with a squad of troops and then marched into the middle of the canefield where he ordered the digging to begin. At one metre the stench was overpowering. At two metres they found the seven mangled bodies. As has become quite common in southern Negros, their Constabulary torturers had evidently taken time and pleasure in inflicting some horrific wounds. Together with the commander of the Long Range Patrol, Mayor Sola was indicted for multiple-murder eight days later.

Despite the Church's determination to bring the mayor to trial, it soon seemed likely that he was going to get away with mass murder. As soon as charges were filed, he was released on a P150,000 bail bond and voluntarily took leave from his duties as mayor. For the next six months Sola walked free while a host of specious procedural delays postponed a first hearing – could not find a lawyer, too busy to appear, more time to prepare.

Bishop Fortich's efforts to bring the killers to justice received strong support when Pope John Paul II gave his blessing to the widows of the two murdered layworkers, Alex Garsales and Herman Muleta, before a crowd of 750,000 people during his February 1981 visit to Negros. When Church lawyers won a Supreme Court order suspending his bail two months later, Sola finally made his first court appearance to enter a plea of not guilty. Significantly, the planters' association president Armando Gustilo, who had declared war on Bishop Fortich during the Pope's visit, appeared as attorney for Mayor Sola. For the next six months, Sola avoided the discomforts of Bacolod Prison as a guest of the commander in the Constabulary's compound. After the Bishop, trying to defuse rising tensions, agreed to a low bail of only P50,000, Sola resumed his duties as mayor in September and began procedural moves which could have delayed the trial for ten or fifteen years.

Mayor Sola was at first somewhat wary of returning to Kabankalan and spent most of his time socializing in Bacolod City. Gradually, the reticence wore off. On the afternoon of 10 March, 1982, nearly two years after the murders, he was driving out of the Kabankalan hills back to his hacienda in a truck with two police bodyguards.

'On the alert! Everyone in position!' The lookout gave the signal. Red pick-up truck! Ready. Slowly, slowly, then in quick succession, rattle and retort. With every click of the trigger, the soldiers of the Red Army imagined the victims killed by Sola. Then one comrade climbed on the truck. The chest and head of the former Mayor of Kabankalan had nearly disintegrated from bullets. "Yoohoo! Sola is dead! We have avenged his victims!"

So read the eye-witness account by Red Fighters from the 'scene of the ambush' as published in the 28 March 1982 issue of *Paghimakas* [Struggle], the NPA's Negros newspaper. The

Paghimakas

REBOLUSYONARYO NGA PAHAYAGAN
SA NEGROS

TUIG IV ISIP 2	PINASAHI NGA GWA	MARSO 28, 1982

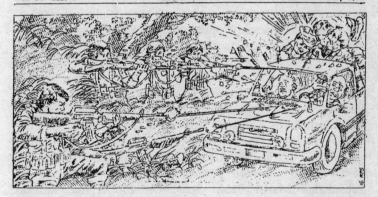

MAPINTAS NGA MAYOR SG KABANKALAN GINSILUTAN SG BHB SG KAMATAYON

guerilla army also issued a press release explaining that they had killed him because 'in spite of the enormous amount of evidence and eyewitness accounts against him there was no hope for Sola to get convicted in government controlled courts'. Despite pressure from the Church, Sola 'had connections with other corrupt officials like him. Roberto S. Benedicto, Marcos' most trusted dummy, intervened in Sola's behalf'.

Through threats, Sola had intimidated almost all state witnesses and had nearly won an acquittal. His death was then people's justice. 'As news about Sola's death spread, there was great rejoicing among the people. The masses are jubilant and take great pride that now they have an ever-growing people's army to count on'.

Two days before a crowd of 5,000 mourners laid him to rest in the Kabankalan Catholic Cemetery on 17 March, the Constabulary announced that it had cracked the Mayor Sola murder case. The Negros Provincial Commander, Colonel Rogelio Deinla, concluded from circumstantial evidence gathered at the scene of the crime that the communist NPA was responsible. Superior firepower, ambush tactics, and the size of the force, fifteen to seventeen men, all indicated an NPA operation. The theory was confirmed on 21 July when the Commander of the Constabulary's Task Force Kanlaon, Colonel Mario Hidalgo, told the *Visayan Daily Star*: 'Two members of an NPA hit squad captured last week following the firefight with elements of Task Force Kanlaon had admitted participating in the ambuscade of Kabankalan Mayor Pablo Sola'. On 24 August, Ricardo Oebanda Jr, an NPA guerilla captured by the Task Force, executed the following affidavit before the Judge Advocate: 'It was Buhawi and Habagat, the military armed [sic] of District I, while Buhawi is the first guerilla unit of Region, which executed the ambush of Mayor Sola'. The NPA had claimed responsibility for the killing and now the Constabulary's Task Force Kanlaon had gathered conclusive proof of their involvement. The case, it seemed, was closed.

Only two months later, however, the 4 November edition of the *Visayan Daily Star* hit the streets of Bacolod City with the banner headline – MURDER COMPLAINT POISED VS. FRS GORE,

O'BRIEN. In an exclusive interview, Task Force Kanlaon's commander Colonel Mario Hidalgo, the very same who had announced the NPA confessions only three months ago, 'revealed that at least seven witnesses have accomplished affidavits which could justify the filing of multiple murder charges against the two Catholic missionaries'. The Colonel allowed the reporter interviews with the witnesses and his chief investigator, Captain Galileo Mendoza. The latter said that 'his report and recommendations, together with sworn statements of the witnesses, tend to show that both Fr Gore and Fr O'Brien could be implicated in the case as "principals by inducement".'

The question is an obvious one. Why did Colonel Hidalgo's position on the Sola murder case change so dramatically, and so unconvincingly, in only three months? On 21 July he announced conclusive proof of NPA responsibility, and on 4 November he accused the two priests. It was not a question of new evidence. During sixteen months and nearly fifty court hearings into the accusations against the priests, his Task Force investigators introduced no physical evidence of any kind and offered only paid winesses telling lies so transparent that, in the end, charges had to be dismissed.Colonel Hidalgo was clearly the author of a frame-up of a rather crude construction. That is beyond dispute. The question is: why did he make the effort when he did?

Fr Gore's enemies were, of course, legion – the Kabankalan elite, sugar planters, senior Constabulary officers, and the Sola family. But that cannot account for the charges against Fr O'Brien, who was well liked by most of those who dislike Gore, or Fr Dangan, a newly ordained priest who had offended no one during his brief service in Kabankalan. If we move out of Negros for a moment and place these events in a broader, national context, then perhaps we can see the military factor in this complex equation. At each stage in its development, the case against the 'Negros Nine' follows a rising tempo of military attacks on the Church throughout the Philippines. In other regions, such as Samar or northern Luzon, the anti-Church attacks were a part of a sledge-hammer assault on the NPA's guerilla army. In Negros, by contrast, the Constabulary was intent on destroying an organization which seemed to them equally dangerous – the Basic Christian Community.

When the Nicaraguan revolution launched its final push for the capital Managua in early 1979 with the support of guerilla-priests and Christian Communities, warnings sounded in Washington and reverberated through the network of US military advisers to American allies in the Third World. The radical Church was now marked as a subversive threat. In the months following the Sandinista offensive, Philippine intelligence analysts prepared a series of reports on their own religious radicals.

The first in-depth analysis appeared in June when Colonel Galileo Kinantar published a report titled 'Contemporary Religious Radicalism in the Philippines' in the *National Security Review*. Allied with the exiled Movement for the Free Philippines in the United States, right-wing radicals advocated a Third Force line both anti-Marcos and anti-Communist, and were forming a secret army to overthrow the regime in a violent *coup d'etat*. A more serious danger came from the left-wing Christians for National Liberation, which the Colonel described as 'a threat to national security in so far as it is attached to the Communist Party of the Philippines and the New People's Army through the National Democratic Front'. Athough still small in numbers, left-wing religious 'now have the dynamism, influence and potential to exert pressure on the entire church hierarchy and undermine the stability of the State'.

'Considering the subversive thrust of the religious radicals', concluded Colonel Kinantar, 'the State cannot but act in a firm and determined manner. National security considerations demand that these religious radicals be identified and [made] the object of punitive measures'.

As the Marcos regime mounted a crackdown on Church activism throughout 1982, such intelligence findings began leaking out of classified files to explode in banner headlines across the front pages of the crony-controlled press. President Marcos' abolition of formal martial law controls in 1981 coincided with a major economic crisis, a combination of events that produced a sudden upsurge in mass opposition to the regime – strikes, protest demonstrations, and sharp public criticism. Instead of reverting to martial law, the government targeted individual social sectors for repression. In 1981 the labour movement suffered raids, black propaganda and summary arrests that left a number of top independent union leaders in prison. With labour temporarily whipped into quiescence, the military then turned on the Church with the same tactics throughout 1982. Evidently, 1983 was to be the year for an assault on moderate opposition politicians, but the unexpected strength of popular reaction to Senator Benigno Aquino's assassination threw the government on the defensive and derailed its plans.

'The economy was going down in 1982-1983 and people across the country started to protest the foreign control of our country', explained Fr Baby Gordoncillo, director of Church Social Action Centre in Bacolod and a leader in the defence of the Negros Nine. 'So when the popular movement intensified, the government cracked down – first on labour and then on the Church. The poor have turned to the Church in their sufferings, and the Church sided with the poor. To silence the people the State has tried to silence the Church'.

Defence Minister Juan Ponce Enrile fired the first shot in his war on the Church on 26 December 1981 with an allegation that Negros radical Fr Luis Jalandoni was now the Philippine delegate to 'the Moscow-based Communist International [Comintern]'. Interviewed on Manila's TV Channel 13, Enrile 'surmised Jalandoni now occupies a powerful position in the CPP [Communist Party of the Philippines] hierarchy', and further charged that there were six other Catholic priests 'having links with the illegal activities of the CPP and its military arm, the New People's Army'.

Six weeks later the *Bulletin Today*, owned by a close Marcos confidante, leaked the contents of another intelligence report under a page one headline – 2 BISHOPS, 19 PRIESTS LINKED TO DISSIDENTS. The military report broadened the definition of subversion to include not only support for the NPA but any Church criticism of the state. For example, Bishop Angel Hobayan of northern Samar 'ordered the closure of the Catholic churches in the diocese and suspended the celebration of masses during the Christmas season of 1979 to protest the arrest of Fr Restituto Cardenas for possession of subversive documents'. Reacting to Church protests, Deputy Defence Minister Carmelo Barbero denied that there was any intelligence that the two Bishops had 'joined or actively supported the NPA', but insisted that the military did have detailed documentation on links between radical clergy and the rebel army.

After a five month silence, the military's black propaganda campaign against the Church suddenly revived in July 1982 in response to a report by Australian journalist Peter Hastings in the *Sydney Morning Herald* of 29 June. The wave of military repression that culminated in the arrest of Australian priest Brian Gore on 2 September was, ironically, prompted by an inaccurate and inflammatory article in an Australian newspaper. Under the headline CHRIST'S GUERILLAS PLOT VIOLENT REVOLUTION, the *Herald's* foreign editor Peter Hastings wrote: 'If you think that the extreme radical clergy are merely those angry about social and political conditions in the Philippines and wish to change them through constitutional means you should think again'. Indicative of their 'uncompromising' Marxism and commitment to 'violent change as a part of Maoist-oriented New People's Army', radical priests in northern Samar Island were not wearing clerical collars and at least one radical nun was going about without a brassiere.

The controversial portion of Hasting's article was his interview with northern Samar Bishop Angel Hobayan, the prelate erroneously attacked in the Manila press in February as an NPA supporter. 'Of the twenty-seven priests in his diocese he said that he had "lost" eight', wrote Hastings. 'He saw my quizzical look and threw me a document across his desk. It was the agenda for the Calbayog meeting [of Samar's radical priests]. "Read that", he said, "and you will see what it is about".' The article also included pithy caricatures of Philippine liberation theology. 'There is no such thing as individual sin only societal sin'. 'Thus salvation lies in revolution'. 'The Church itself, being a part of society, needs to be destroyed'.

Ten days later Defence Minister Enrile ordered General

Fabian Ver to investigate the *Herald's* charges that Bishop Hobayan 'has lost eight of the twenty-seven priests in his diocese, apparently to the rebels'. In a national television interview two weeks later, Minister Enrile again cited Hasting's article as evidence that eight Samar priests had been 'lost' to dissidents and used it to attack Archbishop Sin for his failure to control Church radicals. The minister also referred to Hasting's evidence of collarless clerics and braless nun to demonstrate the extent of subversion in the Samar Church. 'The article', added Enrile, 'also quoted priests and nuns as saying that they want to destroy our society because it is an anti-Christ society'.

The Vicar-General of the northern Samar diocese wrote Hastings an angry letter on 18 August charging him with 'irresponsible reporting typical of that of a government-controlled newspaper' in Manila. 'No wonder Minister Enrile posed in the national dailies like a roaring lion ready to devour your innocent and defenceless prey – the clergy of northern Samar. As a whole, your article serves as black propaganda against the clergy in general and particularly that of northern Samar'. On the critical point of the eight 'lost' priests, the Vicar General charged that Hastings was 'grossly misinformed'. None of the diocese's twenty-seven priests were fighting with the NPA. The Vicar concluded by accusing Hastings of bias against the northern Samar clergy because of their vocal opposition to a local Australian aid project and dismissing him as 'a typical blend of propagandist through whom the Church of Samar has always been harrassed'.

It was a humbler Hastings that replied to the Vicar-General on 9 September. 'I appreciate your distress over the word "lost". I took the Bishop to mean... eight priests were lost, if only temporarily, to dialogue... and not as some have inferred including your Defence Minister, that the eight were "lost" in the sense of having gone over to the NPA. I regret that I did not make the statement clearer. I have written to Mr Enrile explaining the error'.

Unfortunately, Defence Minister Enrile had already used the *Herald's* report as pretext for action. On 1 September, a squad of thirty troops from the Army's Eastern Command raided the Paul

VI Social Action Center in the city of Catbalogan, western Samar. Led by the Command's intelligence chief, the troopers discovered a .22 calibre revolver, seized 'these jeeploads of subversive documents', and charged three including Sr Helena Gutierrez (Oblates of Notre Dame) with rebellion and illegal possession of firearms. In its press release, the Eastern Command claimed the Church offices 'doubled as the headquarters of the New People's Army' and stated that the one nun and two priests who 'eluded arrest' were wanted on charges of subversion. One of the elusive priests, Monsignor Norberto Hacbang, Ecclesiastical Governor of the western Samar diocese, issued a public statement several days later saying that he had not been underground at the time of the raid but was in Manila celebrating mass at a public fiesta. Most of the supposedly 'subversive' papers seized in the raid were, in fact, materials critical of the Australian aid project in northern Samar and documentation of military abuses throughout the island.

A week later on 8 September, the military made a midnight raid on the Social Action Offices in Iloilo City, leaving empty handed after ransacking the files and eating a birthday cake they uncovered in the refrigerator. The Constabulary's Provincial Commander later explained to the local Archbishop that the military suspected Church offices were being used as the 'communication and supply bureau of the underground movement'. As public justification for the raid, the Constabulary leaked a report to a local radio station that one employee at the Church centre was commander of the 'Iloilo underground'. Over the next few days, armed troopers patrolled Catholic buildings and raided Protestant church offices.

The Military's raid on its selected Negros target was delayed until Fr Gore returned from a six-month home leave on 22 September. The very next night, a squad of troopers from Task Force Kanlaon raided Oringao and, failing to gain entry to the parish house where the priest was sleeping, contented themselves with searching an unoccupied building nearby. The next day when Fr Gore went to Task Force headquarters to make inquiries, the officer in command of the raiding party claimed that he had seized a grenade and subversive documents from the parish house. By the time formal charges for illegal possession of explosives and ammunition were filed at the Kabankalan court on 28 September, the Task Force had added five bullets to its original seizure of one grenade. It is perhaps significant that the first charges filed against Fr Gore after the Oringao raid – illegal possession of weapons and subversive documents – were the same as those filed against Sr Gutierrez in the Samar raid only three weeks earlier. Evidently improvising from their script as they went along, the Task Force also indicted Fr Gore and the six lay leaders of Oringao's Christian Communities six days later on an implausible charge – plotting to overthrow the duly constituted government of Kabankalan.

Between the rebellion charge against Gore on 4 October and the murder allegations against the two priests on 4 November, national events again intruded into the Negros situation. During the intervening four weeks, there was a near breakdown in Church-State relations as the military went on battle-ready status against the Catholic Church. A brief examination of these events shows how the escalation of charges against Fr Gore – from rebellion to murder – followed a deepening of the military's nationwide attack on the Church.

As usual, Defence Minister Enrile fired the opening salvo in this new assault. Speaking before government officials in Samar on 6 October, he claimed that seventy-five priests and nuns in the island's three dioceses 'have joined or are helping the dissidents in the area', a marked inflation of his Ministry's figure of nineteen subversive priests for the whole country only eight months earlier. He further charged that a group of Samar 'rebel priests' were plotting to 'liquidate' Bishop Angel Hobayan, the hapless subject of earlier military allegations and Peter Hastings' interview.

Speaking on behalf of the Church's National Secretariat of Social Action, Bacolod's Bishop Fortich issued an immediate press release pointing out the obvious contradiction in the military's February claim that Bishop Hobayan was 'linked with the NPA' and Enrile's present charge that 'rebel priests' were now seeking to kill their supposed ally. Adding further to the improbability of the charges, the priest Enrile identified as leader of the rebel liquidation squad, Fr Josefino Gonzales, issued a press release from his northern Samar parish denying any involvement with the Communist Party and demanding 'that my good name be restored'.

A number of religious groups dismissed Enrile's allegations as vendetta for embarrassments he had suffered in past months from Samar clergy. The alleged hit-man, Fr Gonzales, had, in fact, been involved in exposing the recent massacre of 210 villagers in his parish by private security forces responsible to Minister Enrile. Indeed, the Samar Social Action Center raided in September had played a key role in mobilizing a national protest against the Constabulary sergeant who gunned down Dr Bobby de la Paz, a community health worker affiliated with the Center, only four months before. 'Apparently', said the concerned Priests and Religious of Samar, 'the military blames the Samar Church for the national reaction against the nefarious crime'. Undeterred by these protests, the military imprisoned the chairman of the Social Action Center, Fr Edgar Kangleon, only four days after Enrile's allegations of seventy-five subversive clergy in Samar.

On the day of Fr Kangleon's arrest, Minister Enrile had flown to northern Luzon where he again captured newspaper headlines by announcing a P260,000 reward for two rebel priests – Fr Balweg and Fr Agatep – dead or alive. The next day Fr Zacarias Agatep, carrying a P130,000 price tag on his head, was ambushed by Constabulary troops in the northern Luzon province of Ilocos Sur where, as a parish priest, he had once led peasant protests against the local provincial warlord. Fr Agatep was the first Filipino priest to die a revolutionary death. The manhunt for the surviving rebel priest Fr Balweg intensified as the video-cassette of his recent BBC-TV interview – mediagenic with an M-16 rifle in hand and eloquent in his talk of revolution as daily communion with the people – began circulating freely in the lounge rooms of upper-class Manila.

As the repression mounted, the ever-cautious Cardinal Sin began to speak out against the mounting attacks. 'It would seem', he said in a public address at the Manila Hilton on 21 October, 'from all the evidence at hand, that to believe that the series of moves against the priests and nuns is a coincidence would be to strain the bounds of credibility'. Aside from the well publicized cases in Samar and Negros, Fr Shay Cullen, a Columban missionary, had been strongly criticized by local officials for exposing a child prostitution racket in Olongapo, the leave town for the US Navy Base at Subic Bay. A Good Shepherd nun, Sr Pilar Verzosa, active in the church anti-abortion movement, was accused of murdering a government official with an Armalite. 'Sister Pilar', said Sin, 'is so frail that I doubt she can lift a pistol, let alone an Armalite'. Striking a note of cautious defiance, Cardinal Sin insisted that he would not withdraw his priests from NPA guerilla zones and would encourage them to continue their involvement in political activity for the good of the people.

TWENTY PRIESTS, NUNS HUNTED read the front page headline on the 5 November edition of the *Times-Journal*, a Manila daily owned by Mrs Marcos' family. Acting on orders from President Marcos to stop 'the pollution and contamination' being spread by rebel priests, the Armed Forces had, the day before, unleashed a national manhunt for twenty radical religious. In addition to these twenty believed operating openly with the NPA, another ninety-seven priests and nuns 'have been listed as secondary targets for aiding the New Peoples Army'. Demonstrating his determination to 'check the spread of subversive ideas among the people', President Marcos announced the crackdown personally in a public speech to officials in his home province Ilocos Norte where four rebel priests were fighting with the NPA.

On the same day Marcos ordered a national manhunt for 117 radical religious, the Negros Constabulary announced the pending murder charges against Gore and O'Brien under the *Daily Star* headline – MURDER COMPLAINT POISED VS FRS. GORE, O'BRIEN. There is then a very precise coincidence between each stage of the government's nationwide anti-Church campaign and the mounting charges against Fr Gore. In September it was minor charges of illegal weapons possession against Sr Gutierrez in Samar and Fr Gore in Negros. Two months later when President Marcos escalated his attack on the Church by accusing 117 religious of rebellion, a capital crime, the Negros Constabulary charged Fr Gore and Fr O'Brien with murder.

Although very much a part of a national pattern of repression, the Negros arrests had one unique feature – they were also an attack on the Basic Christian Communities. In framing its case against the clergy and laity of Negros, the military accused only those few actively involved in the Communities – from among dozens of Oringao layworkers, the six who headed the parish's six *centros*, the apex of the Community network; from among thirty-two Negros Columbans, the two who were pioneers of the Community movement; and from among a dozen Filipino priests in southern Negros, the one who was most active in organizing Communities. Why, then, this attack on the Christian Communities?

'What is now emerging as the most dangerous form of threat from the religious radicals is their creation of the so-called Basic Christian Communities [BCC] in both rural and urban areas', wrote Colonel Kinantar in his June 1979 intelligence survey of the Philippine Church. 'They are practically building an infrastructure of political power in the entire country. They are clear evidence and indication of a link-up between Left religious radicals and the CPP/NPA where the former gives the latter political, financial and communications support'.

As Marcos abolished the formal controls of martial law in 1981 and moved to a more open political system, the regime began to regard the Christian Community 'infrastructure of political power' as a potential threat. Throughout his decade of dictatorship, Marcos worked assiduously to either expropriate or neutralize *all* the institutions of power – economic, political, and social. He restored democracy only after that task was accomplished and all the hierarchies that could in any way challenge his move from dictatorship to dynasty were safely under control. To that end, the regime expropriated major corporations, stacked the courts, politicized the military, infiltrated the labour movement, muzzled the media, jailed the opposition, and intimidated the Church hierarchy. Just at the point when all these top-down structures had been subjugated, an 'infrastructure of political power in the entire country', the

Christian Communities, began rising up from the grass roots. This new infrastructure was so vast and leaderless that it could not be controlled by the same tactics that had worked so well with senators, bishops and corporate executives. The Christian Communities were a threat.

Inspired by Vatican II and the needs of the country's remote rural parishes, the Basic Christian Communities [BCC] started on an experimental basis in the early 1970s and by the end of the decade had spread across the archipelago. In 1982 when the military crackdown began, the Communities were operating in about one-third of all Philippines dioceses. Several southern islands had impressive networks; for example, the Diocese of Palo, Leyte Island, had 400 cells and the Prelature of Ipil, Mindanao about 3,000.

Depending on diocesan leadership and local conditions, there are three general types of BCC ranging from the other worldly to social activist. Emphasizing individual spirituality and preparation for the after life, the conservative type is little more than a prayer group and takes no stand on social issues. The other types of BCC generally integrate their Biblical faith with social activism in an effort to build God's kingdom of love and justice here on earth. In fulfilling their social mission, the BCC's have adopted a variety of tactics – from local development work to political protest or open alliance with the NPA. Within this spectrum, Fr Gore's communities would fall somewhere in the moderate middle – activist in pursuit of social justice and in opposition to government abuse, but somewhat critical to the NPA.

The wide range in political attitudes among Christian Communities has been most marked on the large southern island of Mindanao where the NPA is particularly active. Starting with a militant program in the mid 1970s that soon brought conflict with the Constabulary, the BCCs in the Diocese of Kidapawan on the island's west coast soon integrated with the NPA and became a mass base for the guerilla army. In the Diocese of Malaybalay on the island's central plateau, by contrast, Bishop Francisco Claver, SJ, has developed a comprehensive BCC network as a non-violent alternative to the NPA. Soon after the

Vatican created the Prelature of Ipil on Mindanao's northwest coast in 1980, its first Bishop, Federico Escaler, SJ, declared that Christian Communities would become the basis of a new kind of diocesan structure and encouraged the growth of a moderate type of BCC that combines spirituality with social work. As the military intensified its pacification operations on Mindanao, there has been enormous pressure on all BCC in the war zones, regardless of diocesan leadership, to either crumble or seek refuge with the NPA.

Ignoring the range of political opinion among the activist Communities, most local Constabulary commanders have made a crude equation: BCC=NPA. In many areas of the archipelago, the military itself is forcing these sums to add up. Whether by expropriating land for crony corporations in Mindanao or by harsh pacification campaigns against the NPA elsewhere, the military has forced peasants to protest, frequently through their Christian Communities. Equating protest with subversion, the military then attacks the BCCs or their leaders, leaving them a choice between abuse-torture-death or refuge with the NPA.

As the confrontation between planters and Constabulary versus Church and Christian Communities intensified in southern Negros during the early 1980s, many Columbans and Filipino clergy began to have doubts about the viability of the BCC as a non-violent alternative to the NPA. In the months after Gore and O'Brien were arrested, the NPA began operating in their parishes, pushing northward through Tabugon into Oringao and drawing the Constabulary death squads in their wake. As the violence escalated, some Columbans became quite vocal in their criticisms of the Christian Communities.

'I think Niall [O'Brien] and Brian [Gore] were overly optimistic about the capacity of non-violence and the Christian Community concept to change things', said Fr Michael Martin, the Columban Superior, weighing his words as our interview moved past midnight. 'Those communities challenged the power structure at that famous Church-Military meeting in Oringao. They lambasted the *barangays* [official village leadership], they lambasted the military. Now those people, Mayor [Sola] and the military, just won't take that sort of treatment.

Within a week of that meeting, the two layworkers [Alex and Herman] were savaged [torture-killed] and the seven were executed on Sola's farm. Brian did not think that would happen after such provocation. You have to have a means of fading away, of surviving, if you are going to provoke the powers'.

'Like Bishop Claver in Malaybalay [Mindanao] who once said the people didn't need the NPA because they had the BCC', Fr Martin continued, 'Brian may have tended to see the Communities as a substitute for violent revolution. He may have been wrong. In this kind of situation non-violence has its uses and its limits. Once the powers move against you with violence, then non-violence cannot work. You have to have some way of falling back and disappearing. Brian may understand the limits of his work now that he has time to think things over'.

When he started his Christian Communities in Oringao nearly ten years ago, Fr Gore did see them as a non-violent alternative to government indifference and revolutionary violence. Reflecting on his work with the Christian Communities in his prison cell, he was no longer sure. Having stood up for their rights, the people of Oringao now face a ruthless repression from the town's planter elite and its Constabulary allies. The military's violence offers the Christian Communities the choice between getting back down on their knees or allying with the NPA guerillas who can provide an armed defence.

On my last day with him in prison when I asked Fr Gore what he thought of his parishioners' chances, he focused on me with his engaging smile. 'The choice belongs to the people of Oringao. If our Christian Communities do decide to join the NPA, then the revolution will be better for it'.

Chapter Six:
Repression and Revenge

The most remarkable thing about the trial of the Negros Nine was that it actually happened. In some fifty court sessions over the space of sixteen months – from February 1983 to June 1984 – the majesty of the law and the might of the Philippine Republic were committed to the remarkable proposition that three Catholic priests of impeccable reputation were guilty of leading a conspiracy of murder and rebellion.

The charges must be understood in some detail before they can be appreciated. On the night of 28 February 1982, so goes the prosecution's story, two missionary priests called a meeting of a dozen Catholic conspirators in the Oringao parish church to formulate a plan for the murder of Kabankalan's Mayor Sola and the capture of the town. There before the altar and in the presence of the blessed host, Fr Brian Gore told his lay workers that Mayor Sola would be assassinated to avenge the murders of their seven comrades and to prevent him from killing again. There beneath the cross of Christ crucified, Fr Gore drew detailed sketches on a blackboard to explain his plan for the murder of the mayor. His second-in-command, Fr Niall O'Brien, ordered that all the mayor's companions would be killed and their weapons captured.

After another meeting before the same altar, the two priests assembled their Christian guerillas, fourteen layworkers led by a Filipino priest. It was just after midnight on 10 March. As Fr Gore drove them through the mountains in a blue Ford truck, Fr O'Brien distributed the weapons, M-16s and carbines, while reviewing details of the operation with his men. Arriving at the ambush site about 5:00 a.m., the two foreign priests dropped the 'blocking force' of five under the command of Fr O'Brien's parish cook at a mango tree. They then drove 100 metres further and left the 'strike force' of eleven under the command of Fr Vicente Dangan, who carried an M-16 rifle, at a camonsil tree. With the ambush in place, the two white priests drove off towards town, presumably to plan the later assault.

When the Mayor's red pick-up truck passed under the spreading boughs of the camonsil tree twelve hours later, the Catholic strike force opened up in a blaze of gunfire that left five dead and ninety-one shell casings on the ground. The coroner's examination later determined that several of the deceased had also been shot in the head at close range. The prosecution did not tell us whether Fr Dangan exercised a guerilla commander's prerogative of personally administering the coup de grace. Nor did it tell us why the planned attack on the town of Kabankalan never took place.

That a provincial prosecutor or municipal police chief would concoct such a fable in pursuit of some local vendetta is not remarkable. That colonels and generals should risk their reputations in its defence, the state should commit the law to its prosecution, and the regime should gamble its prestige on a conviction before a global television audience when it had absolutely no evidence – that is remarkable. Understanding this case, and accepting its reality, requires us to abandon a First World ideal of justice as an absolute and enter a Third World reality where truth is cut and stitched to suit an autocrat so absolute that his whims can and do dictate the pleadings in remote municipal courtrooms.

Following this case casually in the press and on television in Sydney for a year before I returned to Negros, I felt as if I were listening to a traveller's tale from a remote tropical island. The charges were interesting, even fascinating, but did not seem somehow serious. My week in the Bacolod City courtroom in June of 1984 came at the tail end of the year-long legal drama. The pyrotechnics of the prosecution's case were done and the defence was now dragging out the proceedings to buy time for President Marcos to crumble under international pressure and order a settlement. The gallery where a horde of cameramen from rival Australian networks had jostled and elbowed for a prime shot was now half-empty. The proceedings were said to be dull and I went along mainly as a courtesy to Gore and O'Brien who had given me so much time in prison interviews.

Sitting through a day-long court session I noticed a distinct change in my attitude. The defence was establishing Fr O'Brien's presence for six weeks in Manila, 300 kilometres away, at the time of the conspiracy and was presenting a string of witnesses, Catholic clergy and laity, whose testimony could not have been more boring – dinner parties, picnics, account ledgers, airplane tickets, luncheons and the like. As the evidence mounted through the day, the truth became so clear and Fr O'Brien was so clearly innocent. Pressed to deny the undeniable, the prosecutor, unrestrained by the judge or the rules of court, turned nasty with a bemused smile. Timid laity were intimidated by a bullying style that the prosecutor's position as an agent of dictatorship made convincing. Priests and nuns not so easily cowed were slandered with innuendos of sexuality. Priests were sexual predators, their luncheons with nuns flirtation, their friendships with Catholic laywomen fornication. This trial was not an impartial inquiry into who did what or when, but an assault on the fabric of civil society by a demoralized dictatorship using its unrestrained power to bend, break and twist truth beyond recognition.

So I bonded with the crowd of peasants, priests and nuns, losing my objectivity to applaud with them when a witness was defiant. During a break I tried to comfort a Church bookkeeper badly shaken by the prosecutor's badgering. I pressed my advice on another witness, who did not really need it, about how to resist the naked psychological aggression of the prosecution's cross-examination. I felt myself riding with the defence in some sort of crusade.

As I calmed in the hours after the close of court, I tried to draw insight from emotion. The trial itself, with all the weight and power of the law, gave reality to the fantasy of these fabulous charges. I was being plucked from the comfortable distance of the First World and plunged into a Third World reality where truth was no longer absolute but relative. In Sydney one could indulge in a dismissive chuckle about the absurdity of a Catholic conspiracy of three priests and fifteen parishioners murdering a mayor and rising up in rebellion against a municipality. Suppose these Christian guerillas had captured Kabankalan's town hall, how long could they hold it against the 500 crack troops of a nearby military task force – five minutes, ten? Ridiculous. No, to understand this case I would have to accept the prosecution's absurd logic – that such a Catholic conspiracy might, in fact, have murdered the mayor – and study the allegations, as defence lawyers were forced to do, fact by fact, witness by witness. Only then could I understand how and why a frame-up of such crude construction had been put together.

That is a point that must be understood at the outset – the case against the Negros Nine was a complete fabrication. There was never any actual evidence against any of the nine, and the prosecution's paid witnesses were, in the end, so unconvincing that even a biased judge had to dismiss all charges against all accused.

Not only did the trial establish the innocence of the alleged Catholic conspirators, it exposed, quite unintentionally, a very real government conspiracy to convict the accused on false charges. Initially concealed behind a legal facade of courts and prosecutors, each component of the government conspiracy exposed itself – whether through frustration, incompetence or inadvertence – as the prosecution's case began to collapse into transparent lies and contradictions. Through their advocacy of the Negros poor the Columbans and their Church had provoked an array of powerful antagonists who, in the end, combined to mount this case against them – a national military establishment determined to curb religious subversion, individual officers who harboured grudges against the two Columbans for their inter-ference, the Sola family who blamed Gore for the Mayor's death, and, most importantly, the sugar czar Roberto Benedicto who acted in defence of the Negros planters and in pursuit of personal vengeance.

'I am being framed by people in Kabankalan who have personal grudges against me', Fr Gore told the *Visayan Times* on 6 October 1982, two days after being charged with rebellion, 'and by the military of Task Force Kanlaon to destroy the effective work of the Church among the poor people'.

He was, as it turned out, only partially correct. When the case started that September, none of the Negros clergy understood the strength of the forces arrayed against them. At first they thought it was a purely parochial conflict between one controversial priest and one planter family backed by some local Constabulary. As the charges grew from rebellion to murder and the priests charged from one to three, the Negros Church began probing to discover the depth of the conspiracy against its clergy. In defending itself against a dictatorship, the Negros diocese was forced to mount a global protest movement that reached from the mountains of Negros to the streets of Melbourne and Dublin, and from there to the White House in Washington, DC. Beginning as a personal struggle between priest and planter on a remote Philippine island, the trial of the Negros Nine was ultimately resolved through American and Australian diplomatic intervention at the highest levels.

For a month following the military's midnight raid of 23 September on Fr Gore's parish, Church and Constabulary were locked into a tense stand-off that temporarily stayed the priest's arrest. 'The family of the mayor [Sola] feel Father Gore was in some way connected with the killing, which is completely wrong', insisted Fr Mark Kavanagh, the Columban parish priest of Kabankalan, commenting on reports that the murdered mayor's family and friends were planning additional charges against Fr Gore. The town's police chief, Major Juanito Yulo, insisted, however, that Fr Gore's Christian Communities encouraged communism 'because everything is owned by everybody'.

Finally, on 18 October Brigadier General Alfonso Trance, the Constabulary's regional commander, handed Bishop Fortich a warrant for the arrest of Fr Gore and his six layworkers on charges of rebellion. Accompanied by a crowd of 600 clergy and laity, the Bishop escorted the seven accused to the Kabankalan town jail where they were locked up. Next day in a heavy downpour, Bishop Fortich and ninety priests, almost the entire diocesan clergy, co-celebrated an umbrella mass for 6,000 people before the prison. The same day 500 members of the Oringao Christian Communities hiked down from the hills to take up a vigil outside the prison.

'After my arrest', Fr Gore reminisced in Sydney when it was all over, '500 villagers came down from Oringao and stood outside the jail, chanting, singing and chanting again. Standing between the people and the prison with their guns displayed, the soldiers found the quiet force of those songs making them neurotic. If their guns wouldn't intimidate people, what would? The soldiers only knew violence and were intimidated when they met the non-violence of the Christian Communities'.

After three days of unending demonstrations, the town judge finally cracked, reversed his earlier decision, and released the seven accused on a bail bond of P103,000. The Sunday following their release, Bishop Fortich proclaimed his unqualified support for Fr Gore in a circular letter read at all masses through the diocese.

'Fr Gore went from *sitio* to *sitio* [hamlet] even up to the mountains to meet and organize the people within the chaplaincy of Oringao', began the Bishop's *Circular Letter No. 358*. 'Through these BCCs [Basic Christian Communities], the people realized that they are the children of God, that the land is a gift from God to man and that man must make the land productive to help himself and to help others. Fr Gore then became a true father to these communities. His heart became truly imbued with the sentiments of the Filipino struggling to be identified as a people, aspiring to live as dignified children of God'.

'But as usual, the priest became the object of antipathy for *some* people. For they knew that these small, helpless people can always go to the priest who would always try to entertain their problems and help them. This is what Fr Gore tried to do in his humble capacity as a priest. He is not perfect, because no man is perfect in this life. But even with his imperfections, he won the hearts of his people'.

'Thus, to my dear people of God', concluded the Bishop after reviewing the criminal charges and arrests, 'I appeal that you continue to pray hard so that God's justice may triumph in the end. Let us bear in mind that the life of a priest and a bishop is to be a living reflection of the life of Christ. While He was on earth, Christ was also criticized, maligned, brought to court and ultimately nailed to the cross – not for any crime, but because He loved mankind'.

At the first substantive hearing in the rebellion case on 6 December, Church lawyers began to expose the shoddiness of the military's evidence. The voluminous 'subversive' documents seized from Fr Gore's parish turned out to be rather tame – parish circulars, the UN Declaration on Human Rights, a statement of the Catholic Bishops' Conference of the Philippines and some statistical data. Outside the court, some 2,000 parishioners from Oringao and Tabugon demonstrated with expressive placards – THE PRICE OF A WITNESS: P500 AND A SACK OF RICE, and WELCOME TO ALL REPORTERS WHO AREN'T LIARS.

For the next three months the prosecution made no move to pursue the charges. The Columbans found the calm unsettling. Then on 4 November, the *Visayan Daily Star* published an interview with Colonel Mario Hidalgo, commander of the Constabulary task force that had charged Fr Gore, under the headline MURDER COMPLAINT POISED VS FRS. GORE, O'BRIEN. Colonel Hidalgo and the chief investigator of Task Force Kanlaon, Captain Galileo Mendoza, claimed to have statements from seven witnesses implicating the priests in Mayor Sola's murder as principals by inducement. Despite those detailed and damning allegations, the Task Force did not file formal charges for three months. There is no satisfactory local explanation for the delay, and it appears that once again national politics was dictating developments on Negros.

After months of wild, unsubstantiated allegations about communist subversion in the Church, the military unexpectedly produced a convincing informer – Fr Edgardo Kangleon, the Social Action director of the western Samar diocese. Military raids, arbitrary arrests of religious and an incessant 'black propaganda' throughout September and October 1982 left the Samar Church demoralized and divided. Bishop Hobayan of the northern Samar diocese was attacked as an NPA ally in February and then identified a target of assassination by NPA sympathizers among his own priests in October. Defence Minister Juan Ponce Enrile denounced northern Samar's radical priests as communists in July, ordered a raid on the western Samar Social Action Center in September, and identified seventy-five Samar religious, a substantial percentage of the island's clergy, as NPA supporters in October. By the time the military detained Fr Kangleon on 10 October the Samar Church was on the point of collapse.

Although one of their priests had been handcuffed, imprisoned indefinitely without charges, and denied all visitors, the Samar hierarchy, broken and divided, made no protest. The contrast with Bishop Fortich's mass mobilization of clergy and laity in Negros after Fr Gore's arrest could not have been more striking. Indeed, while western Samar Bishop Filomeno Bactol remained silent after his priest was arrested, Bishop Fortich, in his capacity as director of the National Social Action Secretariat, issued a strong statement demanding 'the immediate release of Rev. Fr Edgar Kangleon'. Concerned about the crisis, the Catholic Bishop's Conference dispatched an attorney to investigate and he filed a confidential report on the western Samar diocese implicitly critical of its Bishop. 'I had a talk with Bishop Bactol and he seems *helpless* to do anything to avoid the arrests of Monsignor Hacbang and the rest. He was *speechless* when I told him that I was not allowed to confer with Fr Edgar [Kangleon]'. In a special report to the Bishop's Conference on the Samar situation in late October, a fact-finding team of three clergy and three attorneys concluded that the 'government is trying to destroy the religious institution by dividing its members' in order to 'render the whole institution ineffective, especially in the area of documenting military abuses'.

As these investigators had predicted, the western Samar Diocese of Catbalogan virtually collapsed on 27 November. In a letter to Bishop Bactol, twenty of the diocese's twenty-eight priests announced that they were taking indefinite pastoral leave as an 'ultimate protest against the systematic arrests, intimidations, vilifications and harassments of the local Church by the military'. As the Samar Church drifted rudderless to shipwreck, Fr Kangleon, with only three years in the priesthood behind him, was left for two months in solitary confinement and under constant military interrogation.

On 6 December, Fr Kangleon cracked. In a record of interview at Camp Lukban, Samar with Lieut. Colonel Romeo Padiernos, he named names:

Q: (Col. Padiernos): Will you please narrate the circumstances surrounding your involvement in the revolutionary movement?

A: (Fr Kangleon): ...This committee was to be composed of the [Communist Party's] National Democratic (ND) elements working in the [Catholic Social Action] Centre... I was the ND financial officer of the group. Again, our tasks were technical and financial – to utilize as propaganda materials church-related documents and magazines, to fit programs and activities under our influence into the National Democratic (ND) framework and orientation and to generate as much savings from these projects to be used as donations to the movement. Requests for office materials were facilitated and we reproduced some issues of the *An Larab* and *Ang Bayan* [NPA newspapers] ...

Q: (Col. Padiernos): Who were the different personalities involved in the revolutionary movement

A: (Fr Kangleon): Sister Thelma Lauron,... Fr Josefino Gonzales, Fr Pete Lucero, Fr Edgar Dones,... Fr Norberto Hacbang...

Q: (Col. Padiernos): Do you have something more to say, add or retract from your statement?

A: (Fr Kangleon): I am giving these informations with the ultimate purpose of applying for amnesty.

Significantly, two of the priests Fr Kangleon named were those the military had identified in earlier press statements as NPA supporters. Fr Hacbang had been charged with 'eluding' arrest during the Constabulary raid on the Social Action Center in September. A month later, Defence Minister Enrile accused Fr Josefino Gonzales of plotting to assassinate northern Samar Bishop Angel Hobayan for the NPA. Either military intelligence had been very good, or Fr Kangleon had learned his lines well.

A few hours after Fr Kangleon signed his confession, the attorney from the Catholic Bishop's Conference again arrived in Samar to interview his client. Typical of his performance in the case, Bishop Bactol expressed utter ignorance when the attorney asked for confirmation of reports about the priest's confession. At 10:00 a.m. on 7 December, two day's after the priest's declaration, his lawyer finally was allowed to see him. 'Fr Edgar

[Kangleon]', the attorney reported to the Bishops, 'denied having been physically tortured but he admitted that he has his own limits. I observed that Fr Edgar was pale, haggard, tense and he told me that he has lost ten pounds. His primary concern was his release and that he was asking for amnesty. He was being offered a chaplaincy in the armed forces with the rank of captain'.

As might be imagined, the military and media made Fr Kangleon an overnight sensation. In multi-media interviews he told his tale of life as an NPA agent with a convincing calm. The barrage continued for weeks, catapulting Fr Kangleon from solitary confinement in Samar onto the covers of weekly magazines, the front page of newspapers, and prime-time television. The military's media campaign continued through December into January, leaving the western Samar diocese in ruins and the Philippine Church on the defensive. If Church resistance to unrestrained military pacification could be so easily broken in Samar, then why not in Negros?

During the week of 21 February 1983, while the media memory of Fr Kangleon's revelations were still fresh, the military made its move against the Negros Nine. On Monday the Commission on Immigration served Fr Gore with a subpeona summoning him to Manila to appear at deportation hearings in ten days. In an interview with the local press, he charged the military with trying to 'short-cut' the court case since they are not confident that their witnesses 'can stand up to cross-examination in front of the world'. Since deportation requires a far lower standard of evidence than court conviction, the Constabulary evidently hoped to short circuit a long legal battle. On Friday, the long awaited murder charges were finally filed against the Negros Nine, a move evidently designed to reinforce the strength of the Constabulary's case at the deportation proceedings.

On Sunday, the day before his departure for Manila, Fr Gore preached a long sermon to his parish, perhaps his last, reflecting on their collective experience. In full command of the richness of the Ilongo language, he mixed self-mockery, mimicry and oratory to make a strong point.

'Maybe we should not have mobilized to defend our rights.

But what if there is land grabbing? It is only natural that we have to defend ourselves. But we also know that there are men who don't want the poor to get together to solve their problems and to defend themselves. They just want the poor to take whatever they dish out. But when we unified in defence of our rights as Christians, we saw that we must love and help each other in the way we live'.

'Now it is clear that it isn't just us right here in the parish of Oringao that the powerful are persecuting. This is a declaration of war on the Church. Some politicians have declared war to destroy the Church, particularly a Church which is standing up to defend the rights of the people. . .'

'It is very important that here in Oringao, with all these lying witnesses in our midst, that we must be strong even if the priest is called to Manila. That is their desire: "Gore is no more, so now let's see if the Community will collapse." Is that what you want, to be members of a false Community?'

'That is the truth of the matter. But there are old folks among you wailing, "Whatever will happen to us now that Father is gone?" It would be just as well if that kind of old folks were fed to the worms, so as useless as they are at least they can help the plants grow.'

'And there are many among the women in the frontlines of this struggle moaning, "Oh dear, Father is gone . . . " You women must stay in the frontlines. But there are times when you make cowards of your husbands, make them weak, and then you should be punished. For this is a time when you must stand straight because President Marcos doesn't like what he sees when he looks at the Communities in Negros. He gets very angry because our President believes what his trusted men are telling him in Manila although he really doesn't know what is going on. These are the cronies, those who are close to his soup ladle, his lap dogs. But if the people stand up and say "we won't take this . . .".'

The role of the national military establishment in framing the charges was gradually becoming clear. As Gore indicated in his Oringao sermon, neither he nor the Negros diocese was any longer convinced that the case was a purely parochial matter, a struggle between one priest and one politician for control of a few villages. That intimation would be amply confirmed at the deportation hearings.

Reflecting the sensationalism of Fr Kangleon's revelations, prosecutor Ariston Rubio opened the government's case by claiming that Fr Gore had used his position as priest to engage 'in activities undermining the social order by advocating principles inimical to the state'. Addressing an audience of some 300 Catholic clergy and laity, Rubio aroused a stir in the audience as he continued. 'He has advocated violent revolution by calling the people to take up arms to topple the government, blaming the plight of poor on military abuses'.

On 7 March, the second day of hearings, the military showed its hand. The courtroom crowd of priests and nuns booed and laughed as Lieutenant Mariano Gallo, commander of the patrol that raided the Oringao parish, testified that the Christian Communities were aiding the NPA and Gore was partly responsible. 'We have been monitoring Fr Gore for about ten years and have compiled a dossier on him', said Lieut. Colonel Orville Gabuna, regional chief of intelligence for Negros. He claimed that the 10,000 members of Oringao's Christian Communities 'look up at him like a God', a reverence Gore had exploited to lead them into subversion. 'These people are ignorant and poor. Many have fled their homes because of continuing conflict between government and communist rebels. They are easy prey to Fr Gore who teaches them how to earn a living and, in the process, gains their sympathy and obedience.'

As Colonel Gabuna began to list all the things that Gore had done to win the people's confidence – start a piggery, install irrigation, teach herbal medicine – Immigration Commissioner Edmundo Reyes interjected. 'So you mean to say that Fr Gore was implementing the government's KKK [village cooperative] program before President Marcos himself thought of it?' The audience roared with laughter.

Significantly, the military witnesses included the commander of Task Force Kanlaon, Colonel Mario Hidalgo – the same officer who only nine months before had announced the capture of NPA guerillas responsible for the mayor's murder. Ignoring his earlier statement, Colonel Hidalgo now charged that Fr Gore was the 'mastermind of the murder'. He also claimed that Gore had used his influence with the people to harass landlords and had ordered his parishioners to 'squat in public lands'.

Leaving the courtroom at the end of the day, Bishop Fortich attacked the military's equation between the Christian Communities and the NPA. 'The people know what the *Kristianong Katilingban* [Christian Community] is. It was organized by the Catholic hierarchy and the Catholic Bishops' Conference of the Philippines. If indeed it is the arm of the communists, then all bishops are communists. That's simple logic'.

That night President Marcos called Commissioner Reyes to Malacañang Palace to inquire about the slow pace of the deportation proceedings. Reyes explained that the case was weak because of poor military testimony. Marcos replied that he would do something. Next morning at the opening of the third session, the Judge Advocate General appeared to announce that the military would not proceed with the hearings. Within minutes, Commissioner Reyes dismissed the case and returned Fr Gore to the courts for trial.

The deportation hearings had exposed the role of Marcos and the military in framing the case against Fr Gore. Called as witnesses before the Commission of Immigration, Colonel Hidalgo and Lieutenant Gallo of Task Force Kanlaon no longer appeared impartial investigators searching for clues. They were the most biased of partisans. The ease with which Colonel Hidalgo could ignore his earlier evidence of the NPA's responsibility in the Sola murder is understandable. He was just an officer taking orders through the chain of command. At the apex of that command structure was, of course, President Ferdinand Marcos whose personal interest in the case surprised both Bishop Fortich and Fr Gore. Why was he concerned? If the first piece in the puzzle, the national military establishment, was now in place, there were obviously others still to come.

The unexpected collapse of the deportation hearings left the Constabulary with an improbable accusation backed by a handful of venal witnesses whose stupidity might well expose their perjury. Delayed by their unexpected need to fabricate a more convincing case, the Constabulary did not issue murder warrants for the arrest of the Negros Nine until two months after the Manila hearings collapsed.

The serving of the arrest warrant itself revealed a second piece in the conspiracy puzzle. On 5 May 1983, Colonel Francisco Agudon, Negros provincial commander, and Brigadier General Meliton Goyena, national commander of the Constabulary's Civil Security Units, called at the Bishop's palace to deliver the warrant. Colonel Agudon was there in pursuance of his command responsibilities, but General Goyena's presence was, to say the least, exceptional. Visiting Negros on an official mission with the Constabulary's overall Commandant, General Fidel Ramos, Goyena had evidently stayed behind when his party returned to Manila to keep an old promise. As Negros provincial commander ten years earlier, General Goyena, then just a colonel, had confronted an angry Fr Gore over a labour case and threatened to cut the priest's throat. There are times when paper can cut deeper than steel.

'I am sure he would have remembered me as that troublesome priest', said Fr Gore reflecting on the case after his release, 'and would probably have worked to confirm the field reports from Task Force Kanlaon about my supposed involvement in the murder. Goyena is on the personal staff of General Ramos and, among other things, is his special advisor for Negros'.

At twilight on Saturday, 7 May, a heavily armed military convoy descended from the hills of Kabankalan and discharged its cargo, three priests and six Catholic layworkers, into the town jail. Advised of the arrests earlier in the day, Bishop Fortich issued an order for all diocesan priests to cancel their Sunday masses and assemble their congregations in Kabankalan for a huge co-celebrated mass of protest. Soon after they were imprisoned, General Fabian Ver, Armed Forces Chief of Staff, called Bacolod at 6:00 p.m. to announce that President Marcos, responding to a plea from Cardinal Sin, had granted the three priests the privilege of house arrest. Since the order did not include the six layworkers, the priests refused to leave the prison and signed a formal waiver of their right to release.

Advised of their refusal, Bishop Fortich drove ninety

kilometres through the night and reached Kabankalan jail at
10.00 p.m. Meeting privately with his priests, the Bishop
explained that Roberto S. Benedicto was applying enormous
political pressure to keep them in prison and urged them to
accept house arrest. The priests resisted, arguing that leaving
layworkers in prison while priests walked free violated the
whole spirit of the Christian Communities. After much agonizing, the priests accepted the privilege and were released at 11:00
p.m.

'Fortich regarded winning house arrest as his first big victory
over Benedicto in our case so we had to take it', recalled Fr Gore.
'The Bishop explained that we just had to take it since it was defeat for RSB [Benedicto]. The Bishop had used his connections
with Cardinal Sin to go above Benedicto direct to Marcos.
Marcos had conceded the privilege because he was worried that
Fortich had cancelled all masses. That is about the most serious
thing a Bishop can do. Fortich explained that Sin did not know
about the six layworkers, so he did not include them. It was simply an oversight.

'So the three priests were out and the six layworkers were left
in Kabankalan jail', Fr Gore continued in a reflective tone. 'We
were released late Saturday night and Sunday morning the
Bishop held a huge mass in Kabankalan Church, no longer a
mass of protest but a mass of thanksgiving. But the people were
not happy with us or the Bishop. On Sunday morning when the
wives and relations of the six layworkers came down from
Oringao and saw me free in church that was one of the worst ex-
periences of my life. I felt I had betrayed my promise to them.
But Bishop Fortich had pressured us and convinced the six
layworkers with his smooth talking.'

Ten days later bail hearings began in Kabankalan with all the
drama that was to mark the next fourteen months of litigation.
In Bacolod's San Sebastian Cathedral, Bishop Fortich presided
over a vigil of 2,000 people broadcast live on radio throughout
the province. Outside the Kabankalan courtroom stood 2,000
members of the Christian Communities singing *Ave Maria*, their
banners of protest fluttering in the wind. Task Force Kanlaon
blockaded the road out of Oringao and prevented a thousand

demonstrators from leaving the village for town. That night the Constabulary troopers detained four Christian Community members outside the Oringao Church and tortured two, one an adult male and the other a sixty-three-year-old woman.

Running for seventeen sessions over the next seven weeks, the bail hearings were a full dress rehearsal for the trial which followed six months later. The judge who had granted Fr Gore and the Oringao layworkers bail in the original rebellion case, Rafael Gasataya, had been promoted in January and replaced by Judge Emilio Legaspi, a civil servant with no judicial experience. As members of Bacolod's tight-knit legal fraternity, the Church lawyers had been told that Judge Legaspi, like almost all of those appointed during a recent judicial revamp, was hand-picked by Benedicto. The judge's erratic, biased performance over the next fourteen months would give credence to those rumours.

The defence lawyers also had reservations about the prosecutor Lindy Diola. While almost every other government attorney in Bacolod City had refused to take the case, Diola, a protestant, had accepted without reservation. There were rumours that Benedicto had made him an attractive offer. Balding and pot-bellied, Diola, with considerable cunning and infinite aggression, would make a formidable antagonist. He was after all a success story in a ruthless system.

As a stalwart of the Bishop's free Legal-Aid Office for over a decade, defence attorney Frankie Cruz, a tall, thin man with a hawk-like face, was a crusader who had first met Fr Gore in 1971 when they had represented evicted farmers in the Bayhaw case. Before an unbiased judge Frankie Cruz might have neutralized Diola's combative style, but before Judge Legaspi he lacked that margin of skill or aggression to restrain the prosecutor. The two attorneys circled each other during the first sessions but by the end of the bail hearings they were flailing like flyweights. In one session toward the end of the hearings, prosecutor Diola exploded at the defence attorney's objection to his cross-examination, hit him in the stomach with a stack of documents and challenged Cruz to step outside.

The silent protagonist in the courtroom drama was the

Columban's private investigator, Fr Michael Martin. As the
Columban Superior on Negros, Fr Martin attended every court
session, allocated funds, briefed witnesses and coordinated
defence strategy. Once charges were filed, he made it his
business to get to the bottom of the conspiracy against his priests
by investigating every possible lead. Raised in an Irish village,
he had an intuitive feel for the intrigues and pressure points in
such small-scale societies. By assiduous interviewing in the
village of every peasant witness for the prosecution, Fr Martin
uncovered lies, bribes and inconsistencies that were ultimately
used to demolish them on the stand.

'Once just to let him know that I knew', Fr Martin recalled as a
the case was drawing to a close, 'I went into Judge Legaspi's
chambers and told him the names of those who had cooked the
evidence; the names of those who were pushing the case from
on high; and the names of the people who were giving him his
orders.'

Since there was absolutely no forensic or analytic evidence
against the priests, the prosecution's case rested on allegations
by three sorts of witnesses: Fr O'Brien's former parish cook, the
'star witness' in the case; alleged eyewitnesses from the ambush
area who claimed to have seen the priests there on the day of the
killing; and several villagers from Fr Gore's parish who claim to
have participated in the ambush. In every case the witness was
now on the Constabulary payroll and gave testimony riven with
obvious lies, contradictions or simple errors of fact.

Describing himself as a confidante of Fr O'Brien, former
parish cook Vicente Pancho Jr claimed that the priests had
driven from Fr Gore's parish to pick him up at 3:00 a.m. on the
morning of the murder. Although he had no prior experience
with firearms, the priests appointed him commander of the
blocking force and explained the ambush plans as they drove to
the site, dropping him and his team off at 5:00 a.m. After the
killing later that day, Pancho turned his gun over to another
assassin-in-Christ and fled down the road to his sister's home in
a nearby town where he hid for several days. In denying the
priests bail, Judge Legaspi accepted Pancho's testimony on his
close relationship with the priest and stated, falsely, that 'Fr

O'Brien himself even admitted that Vicente Pancho... had been in his employ for almost a year'.

The transcript shows, in fact, that Fr O'Brien testified that Pancho worked as his cook for only *six weeks* before the mayor's murder, hardly sufficient time to become a 'confidante' in a parish house with a staff of ten. Moreover, the parish diary of kitchen shopping expenses shows entries dated and written in Pancho's own hand for the very days that he claimed to be participating in the ambush and hiding in his sister's house in another town. The kitchen book also shows that it was signed by a relieving priest since Fr O'Brien was in Manila for the entire period of the alleged planning and execution of the ambush, a fact later confirmed in the trial by testimony from twenty priests and nuns who had met him in Manila.

Pancho's inclusion in the ambush scenario forced the prosecution to concoct a travel route that is improbable in the extreme. Instead of driving direct from Fr Gore's church at Oringao, where all but Pancho were supposedly meeting, to the ambush site five kilometres away, or even by a less direct thirty-five kilometre route, the priests allegedly drove fourteen heavily armed men eighty-five kilometres through seven military check points at such a suspicious hour to pick up a team leader who knew absolutely nothing of firearms. It is extremely unlikely that their truck could have cleared so many military check points in a guerilla combat zone with strict Constabulary security. (See map next page.) Finally, Pancho's supposed retreat would have taken him past the front gate of Mayor Sola's sugar hacienda, the locus of the very armed men his 'blocking force' was supposed to deflect. Pancho's motivation for testifying is understandable. Fr O'Brien had fired him as parish cook for stealing and the Constabulary put him on their payroll.

Despite its evident improbability, Pancho's testimony seems brilliant by comparison with that of the three witnesses from the village of Bayhaw near the ambush site who claimed to have seen the priests there at 5:00 a.m. dropping off their armed guerillas. When asked to identify Fr Gore, whom he claimed to know, Lucio Raboy turned away from the defendants and picked Fr Michael Martin, an Irish Columban priest with no

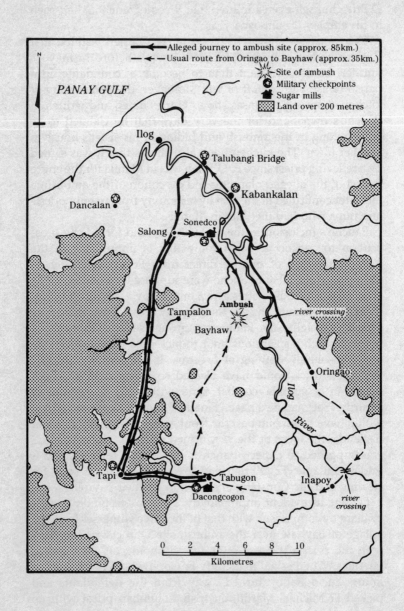

resemblance to Fr Gore. 'Foreign priests look so similar', he explained to a jeering audience of 100, including ten nuns and fifteen priests. 'This is not a popularity contest or a market day', commented Judge Legaspi as he gavelled the spectators to silence.

His confidence shattered, Raboy broke down under cross-examination. When defence attorney Cruz asked if the investigator from Task Force Kanlaon, Captain Galileo Mendoza, had pressured him to testify, the witness answered: 'He [Medoza] threatened to implicate me in the case of the mayor'. As the audience stirred, Cruz pressed his advantage:

Cruz: Captain Mendoza told you to say that the Ford Fiera [truck] was driven by Gore and O'Brien with armed men at the back?

Witness: Yes.

Cruz: He also told you to say that you saw Fr O'Brien that morning?

Witness: Yes.

Cruz: You protested against all these things that Captain Mendoza wanted you to say?

Witness: Yes.

Like the other witnesses from Bayhaw village, Raboy had been living in the Constabulary headquarters compound for several months. All three are impoverished peasants who were allowed to enroll in the Constabulary's civilian militia after signing their affidavits – positions that carry a comfortable salary and rice ration.

To check the truth of their testimony, I spent a day in Bayhaw village asking if the three could have been near the ambush site on the day. My fluency in the local Ilongo language allowed a ready rapport and the village spoke with one voice – none of the witnesses were anywhere near the ambush site that day. One witness was working his potato field on a distant hill and the other two were plowing a cane field near the river bank far below the road. Although most of the villagers are now protestants, eighteen of them have risked military torture and harrassment to sign affidavits for these Catholic priests. They also told of another villager who had been arrested and forced

226 • *Priests on Trial*

to sign a false statement by the Constabulary alleging to have seen the priests. Upon his release, he abandoned his farm and fled into the mountains with his family rather than perjure himself.

As I closed my notebook to conclude my interview with an old peasant whose straw hat, bare feet and tattered shirt proclaimed his poverty, he said: 'Excuse me, but you did not get my name. Write it in that notebook so you can tell everyone who made these statements. We are not afraid'. And as I walked away, he called me back to ask my address so 'we here in Bayhaw can keep you people in Australia informed about this case'.

To establish the details of the conspiracy, the Constabulary presented the first of several witnesses who claimed to have paticipated with the priests in the planning and execution of the ambush. The most elaborate evidence was given by Sofronio Manila, who claimed to be a president of one of Fr Gore's fifty-two Christian Communities and said he knew Fr O'Brien as well by the black spots on his face. Asked to examine Fr O'Brien closely in court, the witness could find no such spots. During a one-hour direct examination by prosecutor Diola, Manila described in detail the meetings before the altar at Oringao Church on 28 February and 8 March to plan the ambush. According to the witness, Fr O'Brien had said: 'If ever we ambush Sola, we will kill all his companions and get all their arms'.

'Do you want to impress upon the court', asked defence attorney Juan Hagad in his cross examination, 'that the details of this cold blooded plan were made by the two priests who consider the Church a Holy Sanctuary as every Catholic does?'

Before the witness could answer, the court interpreter bowed his head and burst into tears. Some of the women spectators began weeping audibly. Defence attorney Frankie Cruz rose to protest the 'apparent blasphemy of the witness'. The judge immediately declared a five day recess.

The last witness, Fr Niall O'Brien, gave detailed testimony to establish that he had been in Manila from 8 February to 22 March and had alibis for the dates of all the alleged meetings and the ambush. In his later bail decision, Judge Legaspi, for reasons he did not explain, gave no credence to Fr O'Brien's uncontroverted evidence. Moreover, O'Brien's testimony on his close friendship with the late mayor cast doubt on the alleged motive for the crime. 'I was profoundly shocked and appalled', said Fr O'Brien, recalling his reaction when news of the mayor's death reached him on holidays. 'I knew the late mayor very well'. At the actual trial the mayor's widow corroborated the priest's story, saying that O'Brien was a close friend and family counsellor. While other Columbans had attended Mayor Sola's mass-murder trial as silent witnesses for a speedy prosecution, O'Brien had preserved his relations with the family by staying away.

As this apparent contradiction indicates, the state failed to establish a motive for the crime. The prosecution argued that the priests' 'purpose was to avenge the killing of seven members of their organization and... to stop him [Mayor Sola] from causing more harm and sufferings to the members of the Christian Communities'. In fact, these seven victims, for whose murder Mayor Sola had been indicted, were not members of the Christian Communities and did not even live in either Gore or O'Brien's parish.

On the last day of the bail hearings, the Sola family finally showed its hand and appointed a private prosecutor to assist the state in its case against the Negros Nine. For the next year the Sola family's attorney would be Lindy Diola's shadow at every hearing, rising when the prosecutor had finished to continue cross-examination and harass defence witnesses in a way that even Diola would not. More importantly, his presence was an accusing finger reminding the court of a widow's right to revenge. Another piece in the conspiracy puzzle was now firmly in place.

'I have no doubt that the Sola family blames Brian [Gore] for the mayor's death', explained Fr Michael Martin, the Columban Superior, while the trial was still in progress. 'Not directly. They don't believe that he was involved in the ambush. But they feel that if Sola had not gotten so angry with what Gore did in Oringao, he would somehow be alive today. Sola was a very emotional man who was very threatened by what happened at

Oringao – the loss of his power and authority to the Christian Communities. So he went out of control and initiated the events that led to the killing of the seven and his own murder. And for that the Solas blame Brian'.

Judge Legaspi closed the bail hearings on 6 July and started seven months of stalling which left the three priests under house arrest and the six lay workers in prison. In its petition for bail at the close of sessions, the defence detailed the myriad inconsistencies in the testimony of prosecution witnesses and charged that 'the whole case is a frame-up and the evidence against the accused a fabrication'. Warning that any delay 'will only alienate the people from the government at this moment of crisis', the defence asked not for bail but for 'the verdict of acquittal'.

A month after the bail hearings closed, the final piece in the conspiracy puzzle fixed itself securely in place. In a televised speech before Constabulary troopers at the Bacolod City sports stadium in August 1983, Roberto Benedicto – uncrowned king of Negros and the closest of Marcos cronies – passed judgment on Gore and O'Brien by implying strongly that they had murdered the mayor. Speaking in an angry shout only a decibel below a scream, he said, according to Fr O'Brien's transcription: 'Priests who talk of violence – we must see that they are under guard. The fact that they wear the garb of religious orders does not put them above the law. If they kill, if they kill a mayor, they must pay for it. We condemn them for the death of that mayor'.

The pro-government *Visayan Daily Star* carried an article on Benedicto's speech on page one of its 16 August edition: 'Benedicto also lashed out at "people who talk of violence", referring to anybody "regardless of whether they are opposition leaders or priests", adding that they should be considered as "enemies", because they endanger the safety of the country. "If they kill a mayor of this country, we condemn them because he is an official of this country" '.

An enormously powerful man, Benedicto had ample reason to dislike the Church in general and the Columbans in particular. Like Marcos himself, Benedicto was raised in the Aglipayan Church, a nationalist schism whose existence is predicated on an historic image of the Catholic Church as an agent of colonial oppression. Significantly, two of his key agents in framing this case against the priests – prosecutor Lindy Diola and Task Force Kanlaon's investigator Captain Galileo Mendoza – were both non-Catholics.

As the sugar industry's czar, Benedicto had reason to be dismayed with the Church's support for the militant sugar workers' union, the NFSW. When the union struck La Carlota Sugar Mill in central Negros in February 1982, priests and nuns had joined picket lines and the diocese threw its resources behind the union action. As a man with a deep family pride, Benedicto had good reason to detest the Columban missionaries. Only a few months before the Constabulary filed its first charges against Fr Gore, the Major Religious Superiors had commissioned the Columbans to publish the photo-essay on the Negros sugar industry titled *Social Volcano*. The Columbans had concluded the essay by attacking Benedicto's management of Philsucom's pricing policy and claiming his farm mechanization program had displaced one-third of Negros' sugar workers.

Not only did he have motive, Benedicto also had the material and intellectual means to execute such a Machiavellian revenge. As Philsucom chairman, Marcos' confidante, and one of the ten wealthiest people in the Philippines, he had the money and the men to manufacture such a case and keep it before the courts. Moreover, through his experience as the top Allied espionage agent in the Philippines during World War II Benedicto was well schooled in the arts of intrigue.

Commissioned a reserve officer upon graduation from the University of the Philippines in the late 1930s, Benedicto fought with the US Army against the Japanese at the outset of the war and later escaped from a Japanese concentration camp to return to Negros. When the famous Filipino air ace, Lieut. Colonel Jesus Villamor, landed by submarine from Australia in December 1942 on a mission from General MacArthur to organize an intelligence net, he chose Benedicto as his commander and gave him a crash course in the clandestine arts. Explaining his choice of an inexperienced law graduate, Villamor said Benedicto 'impressed me with his coolness, his energy and vitality and his logical, analytical and cuttingly sharp mind'.

From 1943 to 1945, Major Benedicto survived Japanese raids

on his headquarters in the mountains of Negros to maintain an espionage network that covered the archipelago. At the close of the war, the Philippine government awarded him the Legion of Honor for his role in providing the intelligence that led to the destruction of the Japanese fleet in the Battle of Leyte Gulf.

Task Force Kanlaon, the Constabulary unit that gathered all the allegations against the priests, is Benedicto's personal contribution to the battle against the NPA guerillas in southern Negros. Benedicto's Philsucom purchased the Task Force combat trucks and tithed the sugar mills to pay for their gasoline and expenses. The dashboard of each truck bears a photo of Mr and Mrs Benedicto in the place where most Filipinos have a saint's image. According to a number of Negros lawyers with whom I spoke, Benedicto did indeed control the Negros appointments in the 1983 judicial reorganization, Judge Legaspi's included.

Bishop Antonio Fortich, who has a detailed knowledge of the case, is convinced that Benedicto is the architect of the charges against his priests. Benedicto disliked Gore for 'getting the workers to stand up for their rights', and in 1980 had petitioned the Vatican to transfer the missionary priest out of the Philippines. 'Benedicto has the men in this province to make up this case', said the Bishop, pausing to pour me a cognac. 'He controls just about everyone here in Negros. The Constabulary commander, Colonel Agudon, was Benedicto's man from the start. The judge, Legaspi, is also his man.'

Bishop Fortich also feels that Benedicto used his influence with President Marcos to block a negotiated settlement of the case and keep it in the courts. 'In June 1983 I was in Tacloban [Leyte] for a sort of religious ceremony with the President and Cardinal Sin. While the First Lady was down front handing out *Santo Niño* statues, the President was alone and I saw a chance to talk with him. So I motioned to Sin and we approached the president to discuss the Gore case. He said: "Those two priests are irritants disturbing our country." You see somebody was feeding Marcos a line. How else would he have known? And that somebody was Benedicto'.

'After some discussion, Cardinal Sin suggested that the two missionaries would leave the country and the charges would be cleared: "After all, Mr President, they cannot leave in disgrace since they will go to other countries". Marcos answered: "All right, at your instance, your eminence". So it was clear that Marcos was willing to arrange things.'

'Then a month or so later I was in Manila and had a chance to speak with Commissioner Reyes of Immigration. He said he would be willing to deport the two missionaries, but the seven Filipino layworkers would have to stand trial. Now what happened to the President's offer?'

Like Bishop Fortich, the priests now fully understood the forces arrayed against them. After Benedicto had publicly declared his anger, they realized that their exoneration was no longer a simple matter of presenting the truth in open court.

'There was a build-up of planter opposition to the Church and the Columbans over the years', Fr Gore explained in a prison interview. 'The planters saw the whole Church as responsible for the formation of the NFSW, the only uncontrolled, non-company union in Negros. Anything the planters can't control bothers them – the NFSW, the Christian Communities, or the new Church. Once control of the sugar industry was centralized under one man, Benedicto, then he had the power he needed to deal with us – the courts, Task Force Kanlaon and the provincial Commander, Colonel Agudon'.

By the time murder charges were filed against the priests in February 1983, the array of Constabulary commanders was decidedly stacked in favor of Benedicto and against the Church. Indeed, paralleling the struggle between Church and State in Negros was a murky, violent conflict for control of the local Constabulary. The victory of Benedicto's proxy in this struggle, Colonel Francico Agudon, was instrumental in the sugar czar's campaign against the Church. As the former commander of General Douglas MacArthur's Allied Intelligence Bureau on Negros during World War II, Benedicto had learned the skills he would later use to play a deft and distant hand in this subterranean war for military control of Negros.

The battle began in April 1980, the month of the mass murders in Kabankalan, when Colonel Paterno Lomongo was summarily transferred shortly after being decorated as the best provincial commander in the country. The colonel had good relations with the Negros diocese and Bishop Fortich gave him a public farewell banquet 'as a token of our gratitude, love and affection to a military leader whose sincerity and understanding created a harmonious relationship with us'. Although relations with Lomongo's successor Colonel Agudon were cool from the outset, the Bishop was still close to his subordinate, the local commander for southern Negros Captain Robelito Comilang.

By all accounts an officer of exceptional courage and guile, Comilang played all sides in the chaos of southern Negros – Church, Salvatorres and NPA – to win glory and promotion. Apparently sympathetic to the Church, Captain Comilang had excellent relations with the Columbans and travelled the mountain villages with Bishop Fortich to participate in dialogues with the people. Opposed to Comilang's closeness to the Church and jealous of his success, Colonel Agudon tried to cripple the Captain's authority by cutting the funds for his network of civilian militia units in the south. Instead of disbanding his followers, Captain Comilang went into business with the NPA guerillas.

'Captain Comilang was doing illegal logging deals with the NPA in Magballo not far from Tabugon', Fr O'Brien explained on a muggy morning in Bacolod prison. 'As a result of factional intrigues, Colonel Agudon cut off the money for Comilang's CHDF [Civilian Home Defence Forces]. So Comilang went into the logging business with the NPA. And he was an ambitious man as well who wanted to rise fast by seeming to have the NPA under control. So they had an understanding – no PC [Philippine Constabulary] patrols in southern Negros and no NPA raids. Several months before the [Mayor] Sola killing, Comilang and the NPA mounted joint operations in the mountains of Himamaylan [near Kabankalan] to wipe out some Salvatorres that were giving the PC a hard time and the NPA a bad name'.

Although it was ravaging the island's watershed, the illegal logging was vital to the operations of the Negros sugar industry. With the exception of Dacongcogon and some of the smaller mills, all of the island's sugar factories relied on their own light rail systems to haul the cane from surrounding haciendas. For example, Central La Carlota, the second largest mill in Negros, had 225 kilometres of rails that required replacement of some 30,000 rotting hardwood ties every year. According to mill executives, Captain Comilang's logging operations with the NPA provided over 100,000 ties at bargain prices to mills in southern Negros, particularly the Binalbagan-Isabela factory near his command post.

Throughout 1982 Captain Comilang played the hero in the Negros press and provoked his superior's determined opposition. In July Comilang arranged the surrender of 5,000 Salvatorre cult followers in dramatic ceremonies throughout southern Negros – 300 in Fr Gore's Oringao parish, 700 elsewhere in Kabankalan, and 1,300 in the mountains of Isabela, together with 300 NPA supporters. A week after this blaze of headlines, Colonel Agudon ordered Captain Comilang to detail all his southern militia units to Bacolod for re-training. Two months later, however, Captain Comilang captured headlines in the Manila press with his greatest triumph. Working closely with the clergy, to the point of interrogating witnesses inside a Bacolod church, he uncovered the seven mangled bodies of tortured peasants in Sola's hacienda and arrested the mayor on charges of mass-murder. Benedicto was reportedly angered at the disgrace of his close political supporter, and Colonel Agudon ordered Comilang to his Bacolod headquarters for staff duties.

Fearing for his life, Captain Comilang won a transfer out of Negros to regional Constabulary headquarters where he was able to maintain contact with his loyal militia. In July 1981, about the time Mayor Sola's mass murder trial was getting underway, Colonel Agudon moved against Captain Comilang's crack militia unit in the town of Isabela by ordering its fifty members to disband and report to nearby sugar mills as security guards. Convinced their lives were at risk, the militia seized the Isabela town hall and ruled the municipality at gunpoint for three days. Among the fifty were fourteen desperately loyal followers of Sergeant Nick Roca, a death squad commander gunned down in the Isabela market only four weeks earlier. The sixty hour seige ended when Colonel Agudon promised the men that they would be integrated into Task Force Kanlaon, a unit outside his direct operational control. To sweeten the deal, Negros Governor Montelibano loaned his Toyota Landcruiser to the militia commander, Sergeant Numeriano Ortega, who had just married an Isabela policewoman and wanted to take her on a honeymoon to his hometown on neighbouring Panay Island.

Returning three weeks later on 13 August, Sergeant Ortega, his bride Rosemarie and four militia bodyguards were driving off the long wooden pier from the Panay ferry when they were stopped at a military checkpoint just north of Bacolod. As the Landcruiser went into reverse, Colonel Agudon gave the order to shoot and his Constabulary troopers, backed by a Coastguard contingent, cut down the militia men in a barrage of grenades and automatic weapons fire. Only the bride survived. Shortly before he was suspended pending investigation, Colonel Agudon struck another blow at his rival on 21 August when he announced that he was about to 'name names' of Constabulary officers behind the illegal logging racket. Transferred to Constabulary headquarters in Manila, Agudon kept his word by filing formal charges against Captain Comilang for cutting railway ties in the mountains of Sipalay, an NPA area, and selling them to Binalbagan-Isabela sugar mill. On 3 September, the Constabulary's Commandant ordered Captain Comilang's arrest for violations of the forestry code.

Like Lazarus, Colonel Agudon survived examination by two separate teams of military investigators to rise again in Negros. Exonerated in November, he was given a prestigious defence post in Manila for several months before being re-assigned to Negros. 'When Agudon murdered that CHDF [militia] commander at Banago [pier] and was called up to Manila for investigation', explained Bishop Fortich, 'it was Benedicto who saved him and sent him back to Negros. He owes RSB [Benedicto] more than ever now'. Thus, by the time murder charges were filed against the priests in February 1983, Benedicto had all his assets in place – Judge Legaspi in the Kabankalan court, Task Force Kanlaon in southern Negros, and Colonel Agudon in command of the Negros Constabulary.

After six months of prayer, petition and fasting, the patience of the three priests was at an end. With the consent of their Bishop and Superior, they surrendered themselves to Colonel Agudon on 5 January 1984 and asked to join the six Oringao layworkers in Bacolod prison. 'We are separated from our co-workers', the priests explained in a letter to their supporters, 'at the very moment when solidarity with them meant so much to us and was a necessary witness that all we preached about Christian brotherhood were not just empty words to be abandoned when the crunch comes'. After protracted negotiations, the colonel refused them admission to the prison but accepted them as his personal 'guests' at the Constabulary compound in the sugarcane suburbs of Bacolod City. That same day, Judge Legaspi was quoted in the Negros press as saying that he had taken indefinite leave from his judicial duties due to 'circumstances beyond his control'.

Once the priests were in the stockade, Judge Legaspi suddenly ended his indefinite leave and handed down the bail decision in only nineteen days. It is a document that defies both logic and legal precedent. Fr O'Brien's alibi was 'indubitably self-serving and unauthenticated'. Referring to testimony riddled with contradictions major and minor by a witness who failed to identify Fr O'Brien, the judge said that there was a 'pre-arranged and pre-concerted design to commit the crime with the details methodically laid down as vividly narrated by witness Sofronio Manila who, as a co-conspirator, was in a position to supply the details otherwise unknown to non-particpants'.

The judge granted bail for Fr Dangan, but closed his order with a chilling warning for the other eight accused. The prosecution's case provides such a 'strong evidence of guilt' that 'unless overcome by competent evidence, of which at the moment there is none, ...the imposition of capital punishment may well be justified'. The Bishop told the local press that he was appalled by the shoddiness of the decision. 'I can't understand why one was granted bail while the eight others were not. The group was supposed to be charged with conspiracy, so the act of one was the act of others'.

After handing down the bail decision, Judge Legaspi took

another long holiday which again provoked the priests to action. Conditions inside the Constabulary compound were physically comfortable but emotionally intolerable. At midnight Colonel Agudon liked to fire bursts from his M-16 rifle just outside the priest's sleeping quarters to unsettle them a bit. The compound was filled with prosecution witnesses working as servants for Constabulary officers. Colonel Agudon's washer-woman, Gloria Indiape, was the wife of one of the supposed eye witnesses from Bayhaw village. Although Gore had bailed her out of jail and worked with her for several years on the Bayhaw Iand grabbing case in his early days as a labour leader, they now passed each other in silence. A poor relative of Mrs Sola, she had balanced blood and money against gratitude and pushed her husband into testifying against Fr Gore. Most importantly, the priests could not justify their comforts when their co-accused lived in far less tolerable conditions.

'At 4:00 p.m. on 26 January', recounted Fr Gore at an interview inside cell number seven, 'we made our escape from the PC headquarters in the Columban Hi-Ace van. An Austra-lian reporter just happened to be talking to the gate guard as the vehicle went through. Looking behind for pursuit and pissing in our pants, we drove across the city and broke into prison. Our lawyers were teed up and came into jail with a commitment order, admittedly a bit out of date. It was two hours before Agudon noticed we were gone. A week later Marcos accepted our return from house arrest. We were finger-printed, given our numbers – 30855, 30856, 30857 – and put on a ration of P3.00 per day.'

Bacolod prison is a kingdom of the damned. Built a century ago by the Spanish regime to house mountain bandits and insurgent peasants, the main building is a hollow square of windowless cells whose cast iron gates face a cement courtyard with a single trickling tap to provide water for 250 inmates. The other 250 to 300 prisoners live beside a garbage heap and open-pit toilet in a long, low thatch and bamboo hut. There is no med-ical clinic, communal kitchen or work program. Prisoners live on rations of three small cups of rice and three finger-sized fish a day.

Court delays are so long that most prisoners are released before standing trial since they have already served the maximum sentence for the crime. I met one prisoner who had been inside for three years on charges of petty theft filed by an ex-girlfriend after he broke off the relationship. One epileptic who had a fit in court was told by the judge not to come back until he was cured. Public defenders urge confessions on their clients to win an early release. Fr O'Brien showed me an infant girl abandoned when one parent died and the other escaped.

Bored and desperate, the prisoners form gangs and knife fights are frequent. The prison's 200 guards administer a very rough justice. Two years before I came here to visit Gore and O'Brien, I interviewed Jerry de la Cruz, accused of murdering the manager of Hacienda Esperanza, in the warden's office. Just a few feet away from the table where I sat taking notes, the guards were beating a slight prisoner about the naked torso and legs with a heavy table leg. The wood made disconcerting hollow sounds as it struck his chest and the prisoner's screams rose to such a pitch that it was difficult to hear. When it was over, the warden apologized, saying that he was sure I could understand how difficult it was to maintain order among such a rough lot. Of course, I could. He rewarded my tolerance by promising Jerry a good position in the guards' kitchen.

'There is so much work to be done in this misery', Fr Gore said to his Superior on his first days inside. 'What an opportunity!' The three priests set up a medical dispensary, using paramedical skills learned in the mountains to treat the prisoners. They counselled the desperate, comforted the distraught, and mediated disputes before they became fights.

The high point in the priests' prison mission came in mid-May when Fr Gore defused a dangerous confrontation between prisoners and guards. As tensions mounted on the eve of parliamentary elections, several guards with grudges against some prisoners provoked a fight as pretext to call in the tense, trigger-happy Bacolod City riot police. The prisoners inside the old Spanish quadrangle barricaded the iron cell gates and broke up their beds for clubs. Armed with M-16s and tear gas, forty riot police electrified the cell doors and prepared to open fire. 'It would have been a blood bath', said Fr Gore recalling the incident a few weeks later. As smoke from prisoners' fires began filling the air, Fr Gore emerged from his cell and crossed the quadrangle to speak with Colonel Geolingo. The police chief agreed to call off his troops while the priest restored order. After a few words to the men in each of the cells, the fires were put out and the barricades taken down. The riot police withdrew and a massacre was avoided.

As the trial resumed and photographs of the three priests behind the cast-iron bars spread round the globe, Gore and O'Brien became absorbed in giving international telephone interviews or entertaining the daily delegations of reporters, diplomats and clergy. Over 5,000 students from the city's Catholic high schools and colleges visited the jail to hear lectures from the priests. Seeking to supplement a wretched diet, a dozen or so prisoners did a lively trade in bamboo mosaic souvenirs with a 'Free the Negros Nine' motif. 'The scene in the jail is its own drama', commented Fr Martin in a weary moment. 'The two prima donnas, their cast of six supporting actors, and chorus of miserable prisoners'. As the accelerating pace of the global protest campaign focused the priests' attention on phone calls and interviews, the Columbans strained, successfully, to maintain close contact with the Filipino clergy and the local protest movement.

Once the priests were inside prison, Judge Legaspi again cancelled his holiday to open the trial on 24 February. Reminding the court that it took seven weeks to hear only eight witnesses in the bail hearings, Attorney Juan Hagad argued that the trial now had 127 witnesses and could run for years unless steps were taken to accelerate proceedings. 'You cannot find any other criminal case in this country being tried [once] weekly', objected Judge Legaspi while pointing out a host of problems – insufficient stenographers, no scheduled courtroom, and inadequate prosecutor staff. After hearing just four of 127 witnesses on the trial's first day, the judge ordered a week's recess until the next hearing.

Two days later, Australian Foreign Minister Bill Hayden visited Manila and the delays suddenly ended. Although his

Prime Minister, Bob Hawke, had given assurances that they would not threaten an aid cut over the Gore case, Hayden did everything else possible to communicate his concern over the case to Marcos. At a meeting on 24 February, he assured the Philippine president that Australia would not interfere in the case but simultaneously urged him to ensure a speedy trial. As Hayden later told Gore in a long distance phone call to Bacolod prison, Marcos agreed to order a courtroom and sufficient stenographers for daily hearings.

'It is only through you that the people outside can get proper information and let the whole world know that this is an open and public trial', said Judge Legaspi on the trial's first day as he opened his courtroom to unrestricted media coverage. While the prosecution presented its case over the next six weeks, the courtroom filled to overflowing with spectators and pressmen jostling for prime position. The klieg lights added to the muggy tropical heat and witnesses dripped sweat when the battery of Australian television cameras turned on them. After decades of obscurity in the civil service, Judge Legaspi revelled in his role as ringmaster of Bacolod's media circus and took delight in introducing distinguished foreign lawyers and reporters to the gallery. He often called a press conference at the end of the day's hearings to explain the case or protest against allegations of 'bias and being pressured by certain quarters'. Miffed at allegations in a *Newsweek* article that the government was trying the priests for a murder committed by the NPA, the judge opened one session by demanding that the magazine's reporter come forward and warning that 'the court will ban *Newsweek* if it continues to distort the case'.

The dynamics of power within the courtroom suddenly changed in early March when ex-Senator Jose Diokno – former Secretary of Justice, opposition leader and outstanding trial lawyer – flew down from Manila to join the defence team. On his first day in court, Diokno demolished prosecution star witness Juanito Bulano Jr, a twenty-seven-year-old Oringao resident who claimed to have participated in the ambush with the Negros Nine. Local defence lawyer Juan Hagad had prepared the ground by extracting an admission that Bulano –

and indeed all the prosecution's alleged ambush participants – had been members of the Salvatorre cult. Like the earlier eyewitness Sofronio Manila, Bulano had been wanted on charges of rebellion and murder in connection with the cult's uprising at the time he signed his affidavit implicating the priests. Moreover, he was now on the Constabulary payroll.

Through seven full days of cross-examination, Diokno probed Bulano's story in every detail to expose telling contradictions that cast serious doubt on his credibility. When Bulano admitted that he neither knew the priests nor had any experience with weapons before he joined the conspiracy, Diokno told the court that 'it's incredible' the priests would have recruited such a man. A week later Bulano reversed himself and claimed that he had considerable experience in handling firearms. On the sixth day of cross-examination, Bulano, obviously cracking under the pressure, admitted he was not sure if Fr O'Brien had handed out the firearms in the Ford truck en route to the ambush. In earlier testimony he had said: 'I saw him taking out the firearms from a sack and then give them to Vicente Pancho'. On the final day, Bulano stated that there was a bright moon on the night they drove to the ambush, an obvious contradiction to his testimony two weeks earlier that it had been a moonless night.

Diokno showed his skills in the deft, decisive way he discredited Captain Galileo Mendoza, the chief Constabulary investigator. Although it was his direct superior who had announced the two NPA confessions to the mayor's murder, Captain Mendoza expressed an absolute ignorance of his commander's statement, as he did of the NPA publications claiming responsibility for the ambush. Constabulary investigators had collected ninety-one shell casings from the ambush site, but Captain Mendoza was unable to present any forensic evidence, fingerprints or ballistics testing, that positively linked the priests to the ambush. Pressed to produce the notes of his investigation, Captain Mendoza claimed that they had been 'lost'. In a remarkable coincidence, the officer who had preceded him as chief investigator of the case, a Captain Malvas, also claimed that all his notes and photographs had been 'lost'.

Diokno finished his cross-examination of Captain Mendoza with a series of questions that established an obvious bias in the way the witness had investigated the charges against the three priests. Diokno began by challenging Captain Mendoza's decision to prepare narrative summaries of his interrogations of eyewitnesses such as Bolano instead of the verbatim question-and-answer procedure required by the Constabulary Investigator's Manual:

> *Diokno:* So you did not follow the basic rule of every investigator to put down into the affidavit all the facts that the witness recall or under question made in his sworn statement, you did not follow that?
>
> *Witness:* About investigations, that is only my guidance, not a law.
>
> *Diokno:* Why don't you follow the guidance of your superiors?
>
> *Witness:* We are following that, sir.
>
> *Diokno:* But in this particular case you did not follow it although you followed it in general?
>
> *Witness:* Yes, sir.
>
> *Diokno:* I suggest to you sir, that the reason why you only reduced into writing affidavits that inculpate the accused, ...you did not verify independently of the affidavits the truth of the affidavits, you did not look for any evidence that exculpated any of the defendants, you did not investigate from March until September 1982..., and in the conduct of your investigations you departed several times from the guidelines of Investigator's Manual... is because you were under orders to get the accused... and not really conduct full investigation into all facts of the case... Is that correct?'
>
> *Fiscal Diola:* Misleading!
>
> *Diokno:* ...The reason you conducted such investigation is because from the beginnng you have a closed mind, a set theory that the accused is guilty and you could not find any evidence at all to disprove that theory?
>
> *Fiscal Diola:* Objection!
>
> *Court:* Let the witness answer.
>
> *Witness:* I did not have a set theory, sir.
>
> *Diokno:* If you have no theory that the accused were guilty, if

you had no set mind, no intention of framing the accused, will you please explain to me why you never took any step to verify any of these statements or even to determine the whereabouts of Fr O'Brien and Fr Dangan...?

Witness: ...Not exactly, sir, on that very date. What I made mention, Your Honour, only was my presumption that he [Fr Dangan] was in La Castellana.

Diokno: Having that presumption, why did you not find out... whether Fr Dangan was innocent or not?

Witness: I was not able to contact any witnesses.

Diokno: You did not try to find any witness.

Fiscal Diola: If Your Honour please the question is misleading...

Court: Sustained.

Diokno: The answer is very plain anyway. I have more than disposed of this witness.

The crowd burst into a long ovation when Diokno sat down. The judge banged his gavel and prosecutor Diola rose to insist that the spectators be disciplined. After attorney Frankie Cruz failed to draw out Captain Mendoza on Mayor Sola's conflicts with Constabulary officers involved in illegal logging, the defence ended its cross-examination of the witness.

The last prosecution witness gave strong evidence for the defence. As Kabankalan's police chief at the time of the murder in March 1982, Captain Rosendo Malvas was in charge of the ambush inquiry until dismissed from his post through what he called 'political harassment' in July. Arriving at Bayhaw village about three hours after the shooting, Malvas interviewed eyewitnesses who claimed to have seen seventeen men leaving the area. But none were close enough to describe anything more than the colour of their pants. Significantly, the villagers said that the armed men had fled towards Matama village, in the opposite direction to Fr Gore's parish at Oringao. Concluding his cross-examination, Diokno asked Malvas if he had found 'a single bit of evidence tying the defendants to the ambush of Mayor Sola?' The former police chief answered: 'As regards the accused, I have no evidence against them'. The spectators applauded loud and long.

After Captain Malvas, the prosecution's fifteenth and last

witness, stepped down on 5 April, Judge Legaspi called a recess to allow both sides time to prepare motions before the defence began its evidence. Four days later the Church launched 'Exodus '84', the largest of its protests against the trial of the Negros Nine. Starting as a trickle of small groups from the hill villages at the extreme north and south of the island, the marched swelled as it moved through the foothills to become a flood tide of 10,000 moving towards the capital from the north and 15,000 from the south. Marching for up to four days in rain and tropical sun, they rallied before the Cathedral with the banners of NFSW union chapters and Christian Communities. The people of Oringao and Tabugon came en masse, as did a large delegation from Bayhaw village near the ambush site, a penance for the perjury of their fellows and a protest against an unpopular government.

Filed with the court on 27 April, the defence 'motion to dismiss' made telling points against the prosecution's case – the NPA admitted the killing, Fr O'Brien had an uncontrovertible alibi, star witness Vicente Pancho was cooking dinner for a parish priest not leading a 'blocking force' of Christian guerillas, and the military's performance was so 'irregular' that it can only be explained by 'hostility towards Fr Gore, Fr O'Brien and the very concept of Christian Communities'. In his reply of 11 May, prosecutor Lindy Diola claimed that the inconsistencies in the testimony of state witnesses were 'only minor' and argued that the prosecution needed a chance to test the defence alibis in court.

In a triumph of legal illogic that responded to neither defence nor prosecution memorandum, Judge Legaspi dismissed all charges against Fr Dangan while continuing the case against the other accused. On 22 May the provincial warden discharged the Filipino priest and the Negros Nine became the Negros Eight. As leader of the 'strike force', Fr Dangan would seem, in the prosecution's version, to be the most culpable of the nine. Since this is a conspiracy case based on witnesses who have given evidence of similar weight against all nine accused, legal observers felt that grounds for dismissal against one key protagonist, Fr Dangan, should have been grounds for dismissal against all.

The answer to this riddle lies not in law but locale. Judge Legaspi and Fr Dangan trace their origins to Antique Province on neighbouring Panay Island where their families are still neighbours. With his understanding of local politics and an active network of informants, Bishop Fortich offers a convincing explanation. 'Fr Dangan's family is strong and they told Legaspi – "Watch out if you find our son guilty. We know he is innocent". And that is a powerful family which must be taken seriously. So the Judge found Fr Dangan innocent and freed him.' After the priest's release, the Bishop said to Fr O'Brien, 'Niall, don't you have any friends in the IRA?'

In the end it was power, not truth, that won justice for the Negros Nine. As the Dangan decision indicated, Judge Legaspi was immune to legal argument, no matter how brilliant or persuasive, but highly sensitive to the power that had placed him in office and would determine his advancement. When the Dangan family could communicate power in a meaningful way to Judge Legaspi, their son went free. In May the power equations suddenly changed and the Judge began to respond.

The May 1984 elections for the Philippine parliament were the downfall of Roberto S. Benedicto. In the 1978 elections for an interim session of the regime's new legislature, all fifteen of Benedicto's candidates in Panay and Negros won by wide majorities. No other crony did so well and there was widespread speculation that Benedicto would become Marcos' running-mate in the 1987 presidential elections.

Determined to repeat his performance in the 14 May parliamentary elections, Benedicto fielded strong candidates in all seventeen Panay and Negros districts. As national treasurer of the ruling KBL Party and Philsucom chairman, Benedicto could provide his slate with ample funds to outbid the opposition for votes. As they did elsewhere in the archipelago, however, Negros priests counselled their parishioners to take the money up front and then vote according to their conscience. Benedicto's control over the Constabulary and the ruling party machine facilitated massive vote counting frauds in much of Negros. In the new municipality of Don Salvador Benedicto, named recently like so many things in Negros after Benedicto's father, the number of votes exceeded the town's total population. The frauds were so massive that an angry crowd of 45,000 rallied at Bacolod plaza to protest and burned Benedicto in effigy a week after the election.

When the ballots were finally counted, Benedicto had suffered an humiliating defeat. Despite massive fraud, not one of his seventeen candidates was elected. In Iloilo City the man whom Benedicto had declared a personal enemy, Fermin Caram Jr, won more votes than any other candidate in his province. In Negros his cousin Teodoro Benedicto, a namesake of the family's pioneering landgrabber, did so poorly that not even an intensive voter-buying cum ballot-box-stuffing operation could make the loss look respectable. In short, Benedicto's defeat was so bad that he had embarrassed his old and dear friend, the President. Compounding his political ineptness, Benedicto's management of the sugar industry was an economic debacle of the first magnitude. As the sugar czar fell in favor and took an extended foreign holiday, the coconut king Eduardo Cojuangco moved closer to the first family and captured Benedicto's place at the President's side.

'In the elections Benedicto has been repudiated badly', said a softly-smiling Bishop Fortich when I interviewed him a month later. 'His candidates in Negros were soundly beaten and in Iloilo his entire machine lost. He has been buried publicly in the press. The sugar planters hate him and claim that they are oppressed by NASUTRA [Benedicto's sugar trading agency]. Now that Benedicto's power is on the decline, we might be able to settle this case. If he had won the election, I am sure that all these mysterious delays we have encountered would continue.'

A simultaneous change in the international politics of the case complemented the new balance of power in Negros. Over the past year, the Columbans had been relying primarily upon Australian diplomatic pressure on President Marcos to neutralize Benedicto's influence. As a large and wealthy nation on the southern fringe of Southeast Asia, Australia has considerable economic and diplomatic influence in the region. Australia's closeness to the Philippine government seemed, however, to impede not enhance the influence it would exert on Marcos to order a dismissal of the case. Although Foreign Minister Bill Hayden wrote Fr Gore a nice note in March 1983 soon after taking office to express his 'very deep and personal interest in your situation' and promise his staff were 'doing everything that they can and using all of their skills', in the end Australia's efforts accomplished little of substance. By publicly renouncing any threat of an aid cut-off in December when the negotiations with Marcos began in earnest, Hayden discarded the only weapon that could in any way impress Marcos. His personal meeting with Marcos in February 1984 thus accomplished little. The speedy trial Hayden pressed for would, had Benedicto maintained his power, have simply meant a quicker conviction and deportation for Fr Gore.

In the end, it was tiny Ireland on the other side of the globe that, more than any other player in the complex drama, won justice for the Negros Nine. During the weeks before President Ronald Reagan's state visit to Ireland on 1 June 1984, the Irish Church mounted an impressive public protest that threatened a shadow over the president's triumphal return to his ancestral home. On 28 May, the leader of the opposition Fianna Fail party, Mr Haughey, received Mrs Olivia O'Brien, the priest's mother, at Leinster House and promised to discuss the case with Reagan during the visit. Evidently seeking to defuse the protest before his departure, President Reagan made a public promise in a television broadcast to do whatever he could for the jailed Irish priest. After a long distance call to a White House aide, Mrs O'Brien told the Irish press: 'If the president can do anything, it will assure him a great welcome here'.

Acting on the president's instructions, the US Ambassador to the UN, Jean Kirkpatrick, raised the matter with Marcos when she stopped in Manila at the end of May. Pressed by the Ambassador's characteristically blunt remarks and intimidating style, Marcos ordered his Minister of Justice to open negotiations for a final settlement. With his economy plunging deeper into depression and an application for a large bail-out loan pending with the World Bank, Marcos had become exceptionally sensitive to diplomatic pressure. A week later on 8 June, prosecutor Lindy Diola returned from a meeting with his superiors in Manila to announce a full pardon in open court, an offer the defence summarily rejected since it implied an admission of guilt. Marcos, in fact, had made the same offer a year earlier after the arrests and they had rejected it then.

Diola was playing a double-handed game. Still carrying a confidential brief from Benedicto, he delivered the Marcos offer in a manner calculated to offend the defence team and sabotage future negotiations. Returning from Manila on the night of 7 June, he took his opponents out drinking at a Bacolod beer house – Sydney television reporters, Australian legal observer Robin O'Regan, and some foreign correspondents. Hinting at a major development in the case, Diola said he would say nothing until the fresh bottle of scotch on the table was done. Then at 1.00 a.m. when it was 'too late to file a story to Australia', he described the offer with just enough dissimulation to make it seem the breakthrough they had all been waiting for. The entire party rushed across town to the prison where there was cheering and drinking in cell number seven half-way to dawn. The next morning the bleary-eyed defence team could barely conceal their rage when Diola unveiled the same pardon they had rejected a year ago. And when he told them that it was the President's final offer, they believed him and severed negotiations.

Discussions reopened four days later when Marcos made an unexpected announcement at a press conference with foreign correspondents. When Bob Wurth of the Australian Broadcasting Commission asked if negotiations were still open, the president replied that he was still ready to honor his 30 June agreement with Cardinal Sin, a reference to the conversation he had with Bishop Fortich and the Cardinal at Tacloban nearly a year ago.

When shuttle bargaining between Bacolod and Manila began in earnest, thus avoiding Lindy Diola, the defence team refined the Bishop's Tacloban offer – all charges would be dropped against all defendants and the two Columban priests would leave the country in fifteen days. 'We are concerned', said one of the Bishop's aides the day after negotiations began, 'that Marcos will free the three priests and then pursue the criminal charges against the six lay workers. Marcos could use the six to control the Church in Negros'.

While negotiations proceeded, the defence lawyers began

slowing the pace of their evidence to keep the trial running for months if necessary 'The difficulty', explained attorney Juan Hagad, between flights to Manila, 'is that the government cannot be embarrassed since it might damage their chances for foreign financial aid. So we have to be very cautious in allowing the government a way out – a way to make it look as if they are simply following correct court procedures.'

As the case headed towards resolution through June, the courtroom atmosphere changed. No longer serious in his prosecution, Diola took a boyish pleasure in taunting priests with hints of sexual dalliance. As the audience burst into jeers and clapping at every point for the defence, Judge Legaspi looked up from his pad smiling and blinking meekly instead of gavelling them into silence as he had in better days.

By late June the deal was done quietly in Manila. The government countered the defense proposal of fifteen days departure time for the priests with a generous offer of thirty. All charges would be dropped against the six layworkers. But Roberto Benedicto still had to ratify the terms of his surrender. 'At the final conference in Manila when Justice Minister Puno received our letter', recounted Fr Gore from the safety of Sydney, 'he asked Diola: "Have [Armando] Gustilo and Benedicto agreed to the release?" Diola said yes. So they had final approval.'

On 3 July, 1984, twenty-two months after the first charges were filed against the priests, Judge Legaspi called the Negros Nine into court and ordered them to stand while he read his decision. Referring to his orders of January and May, the Judge said it would have been premature for him to have granted bail or dismissal before the defendants' alibis had been corroborated by court testimony. Now that twenty-nine defence witnesses had been heard, the Court felt that 'the evidence adduced by the defence tended to weaken, *to some extent*, the evidence for the prosecution, relegating the same to a mere preponderance of evidence which, in criminal proceedings, is insufficient to warrant conviction.' The judge then blamed the defence for failing to present their witnesses at the bail hearings a year ago, a decision that left him no choice but to proceed with the trial.

'Perhaps the defence counsel purposely did it . . . to avoid any possible harassment or threat to their witnesses by the prosecution. It is a matter of one's choice of strategy for effective trial technique.' Refusing to exonerate the defendants, Judge Legaspi dismissed the charges on a legal technicality. After nearly two years before the courts, the Negros Nine were free.

On 5 July the three priests made a triumphal tour of their Oringao and Tabugon parishes where thousands turned out to greet them. At Oringao, Bishop Fortich celebrated an open air mass for the whole parish as a farewell gesture for Fr Gore. Even before his departure, life in Oringao was changing. A Filipino priest has taken over the parish to continue the Christian Communities, but three military detachments are now based in the village and sweep the hills for NPA guerillas. The military's night patrols, according to Fr Dangan, have been 'sowing fear and intimidating the people'.

Long overdue for home leave, Fr O'Brien left almost immediately on a flight for Dublin to be home in time for his parent's fiftieth wedding anniversary. Two weeks later Australia's consul walked Fr Gore to the door of the aircraft for the connecting flight to Australia. Fr Dangan resumed his parish duties in La Castellana with a promise to build more Christian Communities. 'We will double our efforts, even triple them', he promised the people of Negros. The six layworkers have returned to Oringao but have been advised to stay away from Church work until tempers cool. An American priest donated his inheritance to provide the six with funds to build a new life. Some have bought small farms, others are studying. Unlike the western Samar diocese which was broken by the military's assault, the Negros Church, by all accounts, has emerged from its trial stronger than ever.

At the close of the bail hearings at Kabankalan's municipal court in July 1983, Fr O'Brien was asked to comment on the significance of the case. There are many answers to that question, but his seems somehow appropriate here.

'For the last five weeks I've been sitting on the witness' chair, and as I sit there I look out on all the people of Kabankalan lined up in the court before me, people whom I've known from my first day here, twenty years ago. I can also see out over the balcony down to people praying on the Plaza below and I can see over the town which is the first town that I ever worked in. I have a great feeling of joy because I know that while I'm on trial, what's really on trial is what we have stood for – our understanding that God is a God of the living, and when He sees people deprived of life, He is attracted like a magnet to wherever they are. If we stay where the people are suffering and struggling for life, no matter how depressing and how sad it may be at times, we will be close to God and the passion which is in all of us and which sometimes gets dimmed and lost during life. Suddenly you realize that without knowing it, you are at the place where you really want to be.'

SOURCES

CHAPTER 1: The Church on Trial

Despite the longevity of the Marcos regime, the literature is surprisingly sparse. The journals *Asia Week, Far Eastern Economic Review* and *Asian Survey* have carried regular articles on the Marcos regime that are often quite informative. The best early work on the New Society was done by University of Hawaii political scientist Robert Stauffer, and more recently David Wurfel of the University of Windsor has produced a number of insightful analyses about the regime's future.

Walden Bello & Severina Rivera, *The Logistics of Repression* (Washington, D.C.: Friends of the Filipino People, 1977).

Reuben R. Canoy, *The Counterfeit Revolution: Martial Law in the Philippines* (Manila: Philippine Editions, 1980).

Robert Stauffer, 'Philippine Corporatism: A Note on the New Society', *Asian Survey* 17, no. 4 (April 1977), pp. 393-407.

Robert Stauffer, 'The Political Economy of Refeudalization', in, David A. Rosenberg, ed., *Marcos and Martial Law in the Philippines* (Ithaca, N.Y.: Cornell University Press, 1979), pp. 180-218.

Robert Stauffer, 'Philippine Authoritarianism: Framework for Peripheral 'Development' ', *Pacific Affairs* 50, no. 3 (Fall 1977), pp. 380-84.

David Wurfel, 'The Succession Struggle in Philippine Politics and Its Impact on Regime Continuity' (paper, Philippines After Marcos Conference, Australian National University, November 1983).

David Wurfel, 'Dilemmas of Normalization in Philippine Politics' (paper, Australian National University, 19 April 1983).

Filipino historian Reynaldo C. Ileto has done pioneering work on the continuity in Philippine religious movements from the eighteenth to the twentieth centuries which serves as much of the basis of these statements about the role of religion in politics.

Australian historian Dennis Shoesmith has written several informative articles on political conflicts between the Marcos regime and the Catholic Church. Much of his work appears in research bulletins published by Asian Bureau Australia in Melbourne. A good account of the role of the Church in the Nicaraguan revolution is found in George Black's book on recent events in that country.

George Black, *Triumph of the People: The Sandinista Revolution in Nicaragua* (London: Zed Press, 1981).

Gustavo Gutierrez, 'Notes for a Theology of Liberation', *Theological Studies* 31, no. 2 (June 1970), pp. 243-61.

Reynaldo C. Ileto, *Pasyon and Revolution: Popular Movements in the Philippines, 1840-1910* (Manila: Ateneo de Manila University Press, 1979).

Reynaldo C. Ileto, 'Ancient History in the Present Crisis' (paper, Philippines After Marcos Conference, Australian National University, November 1983).

Reynaldo C. Ileto, 'Rizal and the Underside of Philippine History', in, Alexander Woodside & David K. Wyatt, *Moral Order and the Question of Change: Essays on Southeast Asia Thought* (New Haven: Yale University, Southeast Asian Studies, 1982), pp. 274-337.

Dennis Shoesmith, 'Church and Martial Law in the Philippines: The Continuing Debate', in, *Southeast Asian Affairs 1979* (Singapore: Institute of Southeast Asian Studies, 1979), pp. 246-57.

Dennis Shoesmith, 'Church and State after Marcos' (paper, Philippines After Marcos Conference, Australian National University, November 1983).

Robert Youngblood, 'Church-Military Relations in the Philippines', *Australian Outlook* 35, no. 3 (December 1981), pp. 250-61.

CHAPTER 2: Tropical Island

The available literature on Negros plantation society and the mechanization of sugar cane cultivation on the island is slender indeed. Rosanne Rutten, a Dutch anthropologist, has done the only detailed study of life on a Negros hacienda and her book is well worth reading for anyone who wishes to pursue the subject in detail. Although a useful source of data about the extent of mechanization, Dr Violeta Lopez Gonzaga's study suffers from its rush to publication and lacks both the careful empirical analysis and descriptive passages of the Rutten book.

Nanette Garcia-Dungo, *A Southern Industrial Complex* (Quezon City: Community Development Research Council, University of the Philippines, 1969).

Violeta Lopez Gonzaga, *Mechanization and Labor Employment: A Study of the Sugarcane Workers' Responses to Technological Change in Sugar Farming in Negros* (Bacolod City: La Salle Bacolod, 1983).

Alfred W. McCoy, ' "In Extreme Unction": The Philippine Sugar Industry', in, Randolf S. David, ed., *Political Economy of Philippine Commodities* (Quezon City: Third World Studies Program, University of the Philippines, 1983), pp. 135-80.

Rosanne Rutten, *Women Workers of Hacienda Milagros: Wage Labor and Household Subsistence on a Philippine Sugarcane Plantation* (Amsterdam: Anthropology-Sociology Center, University of Amsterdam, 1982).

CHAPTER 3: Social Volcano
With the exception of some elegant histories published by gentleman scholars in Spanish before World War II, there is very little written on the social history of Panay and Negros. Aside from hagiographic accounts, there is also little available on the history of the Philippines sugar industry.

Ma. Fe Heranez Romero, *Negros Occidental Between Two Foreign Powers, 1888-1909* (Bacolod City: Negros Occidental Historical Commission, 1974).

Alfred W. McCoy, '*Baylan*: Animist Religion and Philippine Peasant Ideology', *Philippine Quarterly of Society and Culture* 10, no. 3 (1982), pp. 141-94.

Alfred W. McCoy, 'Culture and Consciousness in a Philippine City', *Philippine Studies* 30, no. 2 (1982), pp. 157-203.

Alfred W. McCoy, 'The Iloilo General Strike: Defeat of the Proletariat in a Philippine Colonial City', *Journal of Southeast Asian Studies* (1984, forthcoming).

Alfred W. McCoy, 'A Queen Dies Slowly: The Rise and Decline of Iloilo City', in, Alfred W. McCoy & Ed. C. de Jesus,

eds., *Philippine Social History: Global Trade and Local Transformations* (Sydney: George Allen & Unwin, 1982), pp. 297-358.

Carlos Quirino, *History of the Philippine Sugar Industry*
(Manila; Kalayaan Publishing Co., 1974).

CHAPTER 4: Priests to the Poor

There is almost no published material available in English on
the Negros labour movement in the postwar period. I have
relied largely on interviews, Church publications listed below
and articles appearing in the local Negros press – *El Civismo*
(1952-72), *Visayan Times* (1980-84), and the *Visayan Daily Star*
(1983-84). Most of the Negros religious publications are available at Asian Bureau Australia in Melbourne.

Association of Major Religious Superiors in the Philippines,
The Sugar Workers of Negros (Manila, 1975).

Association of Major Religious Superiors in the Philippines,
Social Volcano (Manila, 1982).

Antonio Ledesma, SJ, et al., eds., *Liberation in Sugarland:
Readings on Social Problems in the Sugar Industry* (Manila:
Kilusan ng Bayang Filipino, 1971).

Elias T. Ramos, *Philippine Labor Movement in Transition*
(Quezon City: New Day Publishers, 1976).

Task Force on Detainees, *Itum: Bitter Times in the Land of Sugar*
(Bacolod City: Task Force on Detainees, 1979).

Task Force on Detainees, *Pumipiglas: Political Detention and
Military Atrocities in the Philippines* (Manila: Task Force on
Detainees, 1981).

CHAPTER 5: Mountain Mission

Most of the material for this chapter came from interviews and
from an examination of unpublished material on the Basic
Christian Communities gathered by the Asian Institute of
Management in Manila. Published sources are readily available
only for peripheral matters – Australia's Samar development
project, the Houtart seminars, and early primers for rural
Christian social work.

Concerned Citizens for Human Rights (Samar), *Samar Island
and the Northern Samar Integrated Rural Development Project*
(Sydney: Catholic Commission for Justice and Peace, 1982).